ATTITUDE

ATTITUDE

DEVELOP A WINNING MINDSET
ON AND OFF THE COURT

JAY WRIGHT

WITH **MICHAEL SHERIDAN** AND **MARK DAGOSTINO**

FOREWORD BY
CHARLES BARKLEY

BALLANTINE BOOKS
New York

Published in the United States by Ballantine Books, an imprint of Random House, a division of Penguin Random House LLC, New York.

BALLANTINE and the HOUSE colophon are registered trademarks of Penguin Random House LLC.

Hardback ISBN 978-0-399-18085-9
Ebook ISBN 978-0-399-18086-6

Printed in the United States of America on acid-free paper

randomhousebooks.com

2 4 6 8 9 7 5 3 1

FIRST EDITION

Book design by Simon M. Sullivan

To Patty, whose amazing attitude inspires me every day,
and to Taylor, Collin, and Reilly for their
unconditional love

Contents

Foreword

WHEN I WAS drafted by the Philadelphia 76ers in 1984, I found myself a place to live. It wasn't far from Villanova.

In that era, we were a group of young men fresh out of college who loved basketball. I played with and became friends with the guys who won the national championship in 1985: Ed Pinckney, Dwayne McClain, Harold Pressley, and all of the rest. I got to know the coaches too. We spent a lot of time with one another in the summer months playing ball and then having fun hanging out at our favorite spots, Alligators and the Yorkshire.

One of the young coaches I met was Jay.

I honestly don't remember if Jay had the style then that you see now. I just remember a good young guy who loved basketball. We spent a lot of time together, and as it turned out, we both left Philadelphia in 1992. I was traded from the Sixers to Phoenix, and Jay left for the University of Nevada, Las Vegas, with Rollie Massimino.

In this business, though, you always keep tabs on your friends. So I kept track of Jay's career. I followed him during his time at UNLV (1992–1994), and when he got the head coaching job at Hofstra (1994–2001).

The thing I liked most about Jay was that he went away and made a name for himself on his own. A lot of assistant coaches move up to the top spot. They may not even deserve it. But Jay went away and made his own name, getting to the NCAA Tournament twice at Hofstra. He wasn't just handed the Villanova job in 2001—he earned the job.

I would have loved to have played for Jay Wright, and I'm going to tell you why: The guy has not changed in thirty years. That same guy I hung out with at Alligators is the same guy I went to dinner with recently. Even with the success he has had, culminating in a national championship, he's the exact same guy.

The best way I can describe Jay is that he is successful in life, not just as a basketball coach. For a lot of players, their success in life is dictated by how great they are at basketball. For a lot of coaches, it's measured by how many games they win. To me, you don't define Jay that way.

Understanding the responsibility of Villanova is, in my mind, Jay's greatest leadership quality. If you go to Villanova, you aren't going to a place where basketball is the most important thing. You are going there for an education. Jay is a great caretaker of the Villanova culture.

I know that for a fact: My daughter is a Villanova graduate, and Jay is the reason she went there. Before she attended Villanova, I didn't really appreciate the full significance of the place. The quality education she received and the family atmosphere made it special for her.

Hardly anyone picked Villanova to win the national championship in 2016. It was incredible that they won—and even more incredible *how* they won. A lot of you may have seen my celebration dance on our TNT set when Kris Jenkins' shot sealed that game at the buzzer.

Here's why I was so excited: It's a terrible thing when people tell you that you haven't won the big one. I'm on that list of people who didn't win a championship. It's something you have to live with. I tell people all the time that I root for the guys who haven't won the big one.

When that shot dropped I was thrilled for Jay. He was off the list.

But to me, Jay has always been about a lot more than any list. He's a great leader. As you read through this book, I think you'll see why.

—CHARLES BARKLEY, November 2016

Introduction

Game On

AS WE GATHERED into our huddle, the sound of nearly 75,000 fans shook every seat in Houston's massive NRG Stadium.

The NCAA Championship game. Tied at 74. With 4.7 seconds left on the clock.

It was difficult to hear anything over the roar, but I had absolute confidence in our team. Within our basketball family at Villanova we liken every season to a journey, and this one had been our longest and most thrilling ride yet. Marcus Paige's miraculous off-balance leap of a three-pointer to tie the game was an incredible shot, the kind you come to expect from an opponent the caliber of North Carolina. The Tar Heels had erased our 10-point lead in the span of a few minutes, thanks mostly to their skill, precision, and composure.

But when I looked into the eyes of our players and coaches, I saw no anger or regret. No one bemoaned Paige's "lucky shot," or that any of our guys had failed to stop him from grabbing the pass that led to that shot, or anything else. When you're playing against the best of the best, huge plays happen. You can't allow yourself to be consumed by them. You move on to what you can control—the next possession.

With so much on the line, we'd executed well. Even in the final two minutes in this pressure-packed setting, we hadn't flinched. I was proud of our team—and I let them know it.

The play we tend to call with 4 to 7 seconds remaining on the clock is called "Nova." As we stepped into the huddle, each of the players understood the responsibility that they would have on this possession. Executing that play in 4.7 seconds against the Tar Heels defense, though, would not be easy. The ball would be inbounded from under the North Carolina basket. We'd have to advance nearly the length of the court in order to score.

We broke the huddle with a familiar shout: "ATTITUDE!" That's the word we use to break every huddle, in every game—championship or not.

As the crowd grew even louder, co-captain Ryan "Arch" Arcidiacono walked past the midcourt line and gestured to one of the officials, pointing to a spot on the floor. This was the same area in front of the UNC bench where our other co-captain, Daniel Ochefu, had lunged and fallen to the court in his attempt to deflect the pass to Paige seconds earlier. Arch noticed there was still moisture on the floor, and he asked the official to have a ball boy mop it up.

Daniel was standing nearby as the young man began mopping. When he finished, Daniel asked to borrow the mop. For the next twenty seconds, the 6'11" Ochefu painstakingly made sure every drop of sweat was dried from that floor. Some people chuckled as the scene unfolded. Even I began to grow impatient at Daniel's thoroughness. But we knew there was a good reason he wanted that area dry: It was exactly where he planned to set a screen to spring Arch loose from his defender.

When Daniel finally returned the mop, junior Kris Jenkins accepted the basketball from the baseline official and inbounded it to Arch in the backcourt as the clock started. Arch began dribbling. Daniel set a crisp screen on the now-dry court, giving Arch just enough daylight to slice through the defense and race up the left side of the floor. Knowing his history of making huge baskets, North Carolina's defense rightfully stepped up on him as he neared the three-point arc.

In a final-possession situation like this one, diagrammed plays offer a nice blueprint. But in the frenetic pace of live action, Xs and Os take a backseat to execution and the split-second decision-making by the players who have trained for just this sort of moment.

I wasn't entirely sure what Arch would do against Carolina's swarming defense, but I was sure he would make the right choice. And he did.

Somehow, even in the din of that immense stadium, Arch heard a lone voice calling his name. "Arch!"

It was Kris Jenkins. He was right behind him.

Trailing the play, in a wrinkle we'd practiced but never used before in a game, Kris had sprinted down the floor and, with all of the attention on Arch, managed to get himself a clear look at the basket. Arch reacted and adapted instantaneously, dribbling to his right and feeding an underhanded pass to Kris. The soft pass hit Jenkins in perfect rhythm. With the entire crowd on its feet and barely half a second left in regulation, Kris raised up in his textbook form and released the ball. . . .

Kris Jenkins takes The Shot.

In the months since that night in Houston, I have listened to so many accounts of where people were when Kris took that shot and what was going through their minds as the ball left his fingers. Many of those people have also asked me: What were *you* thinking?

As a coach, you're always trying to be prepared for whatever comes next. For me, in that moment, considering the ramifications of the shot falling wasn't really an option. If Kris' shot had bounced off the rim, we would have been looking at five minutes of overtime with the power-house Tar Heels riding a wave of momentum thanks to their surge to tie the game.

Yet even as I processed all the potential scenarios, I was certain of this: I was proud of our guys, and that pride would endure whether we won the national championship or finished as the runners-up. These were humble and dedicated athletes who had come to embody the tenets of our program as well as any group we have ever coached. No matter the outcome, I would always consider these young men champions.

The attitude of this group—its commitment to our core values— had taken us to the precipice. Whichever way the ball fell, I would be able to remind our players that their ability to focus in those final minutes was an accomplishment that would follow them through their lives. At no point had they let mistakes or an opponent's skill detract from their approach. They had retained a sturdy attitude of optimism, and *that* was what they would carry with them for the re-mainder of their days on earth.

In that sense, I knew we had already won.

Which also meant I knew we could handle whatever came next. Win or lose, every one of our players would know in their heart that it was just one game, one moment, one second, in something much, much bigger.

Our attitude sustains us and is the foundation for all that we do— off and on the court.

This year marked my fifteenth season as head coach at Villanova. All of us in the basketball program benefit from a tradition that dates to the first Final Four in 1939—in which the Wildcats, under coach Al Severance, earned a spot. We are part of a wonderful university that takes pride in caring for one another in the spirit of the Augustin-ian fathers who founded Villanova.

That's something we try to never lose sight of.

We believe that a great attitude is a prerequisite for success—and that any success we achieve on the court is less about strategy and technique than it is about a team-first, can-do spirit. We work extra hard to ensure that everyone in our program—from the head coach through a freshman student office worker—understands that their contributions are valued. We even have a phrase for it, one of many we invoke often to remind ourselves of the core values that drive us: "Everyone's role is different but their status is the same."

These ideas transcend basketball. They can be applied to any kind of organization.

Many great leaders have passed through the Villanova Basketball program. You'll read more about some of them here. But you'll also learn about other leaders with names even the most ardent Villanova fan may not recognize.

I believe there is a leader in every one of us.

I have been approached about writing a leadership book several times in recent years. I have declined those opportunities because I don't view myself as an authority on the subject. However, I am proud of the men and women who have worked with us to build upon Villanova Basketball's success that culminated with our school's second NCAA national championship in April 2016. (You probably remember the first one too—the 1985 "perfect game" coached by my mentor, Rollie Massimino.) Their stories offer lessons that can be applied by CEOs, schoolteachers, coaches, and anyone else whose job description includes getting the very best out of themselves and others.

The fundamentals of the culture that helped us build this successful program, and which propelled us through this remarkably successful season, are powerful. So that is what I'm going to share here: the story of one remarkable year, highlighting some of the bedrock principles and values that we believe made it all possible, peppered with stories from Villanova's history and moments from my own life and career that helped make me who I am today.

The fact is, none of us control what happens to us in life—but we do control our responses to those circumstances. Here at Villanova, we believe it's important to remain positive no matter how tough it gets, or how many points you give up, or how much of a challenge you face in the final 4.7 seconds of a game. That is exactly why "Attitude" is the most important of our Villanova values, and the very last word we say to one another before taking the court. Attitude was most definitely a factor in our response during those final ticks in Houston, and it's a key part of everything every one of us carries forward, not only in our memories of that momentous day, but in everything we do in our lives.

If that doesn't make a whole lot of sense to you right now, I sure hope it will by the time you finish reading this book. After all, if you've read this far, chances are that you already know what happened when Kris put that ball in the air with less than a second remaining on the clock. But this story goes much deeper than that, and what I want to share in these pages is something more than strategy, something more than a recap of our game play and victories (although you're going to get plenty of that). What I aim to do here is to step back, sometimes way back, to take you on the journey that led up to that glorious moment in Houston—so that you, like all of us who wear the Blue and White, can fully appreciate, understand, and bask in the true spirit of the Nova Nation celebration that followed.

It's the same thing I do with our guys when we gather in my living room to watch an NBA game, or when I walk them into the Pavilion, our on-campus arena, to look at the storied jerseys that are now raised in the rafters. By taking the time to look back at the memorable moments and remarkable history that ultimately made our winning season possible, I hope that each of us might learn a thing or two about ourselves—and that through this process of digging a little deeper, we can all walk away like champions.

ATTITUDE

1

It's Not About the Championship

IN MANY WAYS, the story of our 2016 Championship win began the season before, in what seemed like another "storybook season"—right up until the moment we suffered the agony of a crushing defeat.

For fans and the media and most people looking in from the outside, it seems a season can only be called "storybook" if it comes complete with a storybook ending. In our basketball family, we don't see it that way. Not at all.

This may come as a surprise, but our big goal each year isn't to win the Championship. Our goal is something much simpler: We want to be the best team we can be by the end of the season. That's it. And at the end of the 2014–2015 season, we were one heck of a good team.

Not to say that we don't want to win, or that a loss to a No. 8 seed in the second round of March Madness was what we were looking for. No one wants to lose. It's just that while the press and some fans described the end of our 2014–2015 season like some sort of tragedy, it was my job to keep everyone in our program focused on how well we'd played all year—and to think about the lessons we could learn from our mistakes.

The World Evaluates on Its Own Terms.
We Evaluate on Our Own.

Looking back on it, we really were having a storybook season.

Despite the graduation of James Bell and Tony Chennault, two pillars of our success during a 29–5 campaign in 2013–2014, we had made great strides on this 2014–2015 journey. Darrun Hilliard and JayVaughn Pinkston had become true leaders as seniors in our program. Ryan Arcidiacono, Dylan Ennis, and Daniel Ochefu comprised our junior class. We started those five and relied on sophomores Josh Hart and Kris Jenkins, along with freshman Phil Booth, as key pieces for us off the bench. We had sophomore Darryl Reynolds ready on those nights when we needed help at the forward position too.

This was a deep team.

The group also displayed a toughness that I loved. Everyone on the roster was dialed into the tiny details that can spell the difference between victory and defeat. From the start of the season in November and on through February, these young men established Villanova as a Top 10 team in both major polls. By March, we were in the Top 5 and considered a favorite to land a No. 1 seed in the NCAA Tournament.

Still, we hadn't taken home a Big East Tournament Championship since 1995. There are a lot of folks who downplay postseason conference tournaments because they aren't the NCAA Tournament, but I've never felt that way. I came of age coaching in the 1980s and '90s, and I cherish being a part of the Big East Tournament. I knew how much that win would mean to our Villanova community.

On the final day of the regular season, we honored our last Big East Tournament champions during halftime of our game against Georgetown at the Wells Fargo Center, where both the 76ers and the Flyers play their home games. Many of the key people who had lifted Villanova to the top of the conference twenty years earlier—head coach Steve Lappas, All-American Kerry Kittles, Jonathan Haynes, Jason Lawson, Alvin Williams, Eric Eberz, and Chuck Kornegay—were there that day. To have those guys in the stands during our final game of the regular season was magic. We take pride in playing hard always, but I think the presence of that team gave us an extra boost of determination. And when the game ended, and we won, we invited all of those guys to join us on the court as we took hold of the Big East regular season championship trophy. What a special moment that was, to see our players mingling with those Wildcat heroes.

Tradition means everything at Villanova, and we honor it every chance we get. Our fans love to see the legends from years past, and we want our current players to appreciate that we are all part of something much larger than any one of us. Our performance that whole season was a continuation of the work those guys had put into their big win in '95. Two decades after the fact, you could still see the rewards of that title written all over their smiling faces.

A week later, we walked into what has to be one of the greatest settings in all of sports, and certainly one of my personal favorites: Madison Square Garden on a Saturday night, playing for the Big East Championship. With the fire and spirit of the 1995 team fresh in our memories, we put an end to our long Big East Tournament Championship drought with a 69–52 win over Xavier.

That win was our fourteenth in a row and our thirty-second in thirty-four games. Like I said, it was a storybook season.

After the postgame press conference, as I walked into the spacious locker room that usually belongs to the New York Knicks, the team cheered and sprayed me with water. (They're too young for champagne!) I emphasized the pride we as a staff took in the willingness of these young men to give wholly of themselves to our values. They in turn reveled in the simple pleasure of messing up their coach's hair.

The next day—after a quick stop at the CBS studio to tape a segment with Greg Gumbel, Clark Kellogg, Doug Gottlieb, and Seth Davis—we met up with our charter bus to make the two-plus-hour drive back to the Main Line. (That's a common nickname for the area outside Philadelphia where Villanova is located.) Most college teams spend a whole lot of time on buses, and it's natural to develop a rapport with the driver. At Villanova, there has been a long line of good people in that role, most notably the late "Doc" Dougherty, who skillfully steered us throughout legendary Coach Rollie Massimino's tenure (1973–1992). Our current steward of the roads is John Mills, a genial, deep-voiced man who has the perfect temperament for long hours at the wheel. As much as we as a coaching staff appreciate John, that is nothing compared to how the players view him. They absolutely love the guy, and you see it in their interactions with him every time they board the bus. On this day, John was as pumped up as any of our players, and he clearly wanted everything he did to reflect the winning feeling our team was carrying.

Somehow, while we were up in the CBS studio, John had navigated Manhattan's crowded streets to find a primo parking space just a few steps from the front door at CBS. A bunch of us high-fived him as we climbed aboard, and in a matter of minutes we were through the Lincoln Tunnel and on our way. Unfortunately, after all of that, the bus broke down on the New Jersey Turnpike, but we barely minded. If you're going to have engine trouble, there is no better time for it than in the afterglow of a Big East Championship. Help arrived in no time, and we made it back to campus just in time for our NCAA Tournament Selection Sunday Watch Party.

The Selection Show event is something we all look forward to. We invite about five hundred people to join us in the Villanova Room, a large ballroom located in the Connelly Center, the main student center on campus. Included are the players' and coaches' families, Villanova staff, alumni, and students. There is a buffet dinner and then we all turn our attention to the giant television screens in each corner to watch the show. The media is there to chronicle our reactions, and in the wake of our Big East win, the excitement was even more palpable than usual. When the announcers started unveiling the bracket, one region at a time, the room fell silent and everyone stared at those TVs. When they got to the East Region, and announced that we'd been seeded No. 1, you can imagine the scene: The cheers echoed off the walls, flew straight through the windows, and joined the chorus of cheers erupting from other buildings all over campus.

This was our tenth NCAA bid in eleven seasons, and as I stepped up to the lectern, I reminded everyone—myself included—that it should never be taken for granted. There are 351 Division I teams that aspire to that goal at the start of every season, and earning one of those sixty-eight invitations means something. That was especially true for our seniors, including one young man in particular, JayVaughn Pinkston, or J.P. as we called him. I'll use JayVaughn as a way to examine something we value more than winning at Villanova: our players, and how they develop as people during their time with us.

JayVaughn Pinkston had come to Villanova as a McDonald's All-American from Bishop Loughlin Memorial High School in Brooklyn, New York. At 6'7" and a rock-solid 240 pounds, his frame hearkens back to the tough power forwards of yesteryear. In fact, if you were constructing an ideal forward, you might start with the kind of chiseled frame J.P. sports today.

Yet that physical snapshot is only part of who he is.

During his four years at Bishop Loughlin, JayVaughn wound up playing for four different head coaches, a fluke of timing and circumstance. That's very tough on a player. There's no continuity. It's a new system to learn every year. After each of those coaching changes, there were Amateur Athletic Union (AAU) teams and other high schools urging him to switch programs. Each time he refused.

JayVaughn was a tough city kid, and you could see that on the court. Like a lot of city kids, I think, he was comfortable being a man of few words. What struck me was that even though he didn't come across as a gregarious individual, the people at Bishop Loughlin loved him. I think that had a lot to do with the loyalty he showed to his school and the people who cared about him.

As a freshman at Villanova, JayVaughn had his career sidetracked after an incident at an off-campus fraternity party in November 2010. He got into a fight with another student, and the mistake cost him dearly. The university deemed it a violation of student conduct and suspended him for the remainder of that school year.

JayVaughn could have left Villanova, and it was an option I presented him with during a series of long discussions we held in the weeks after the incident. If he had wanted a fresh start somewhere else, we would have supported that. But he and his mom, Kerry, who had raised him by herself in the gritty Brownsville section of Brooklyn, were determined to see him through this. They resolved that he wouldn't leave Villanova without a degree.

Rather than simply return to Brooklyn for six months of idle time, JayVaughn chose to remain in the area. (The terms of his suspension prevented him from living on campus.) To pay the bills, he found a job in a warehouse. He paid rent to a local family to live in their home. J.P. was on his own from a basketball standpoint, unable to work out with our team. We stayed in touch via text and phone calls, but we saw him infrequently, usually at our weekly radio show after he finished work. When the show ended at 8 p.m., we would sometimes have dinner together.

For a guy who loves basketball the way J.P. does, it wasn't an easy time.

He was reinstated as a student in time to rejoin us for the first summer session in June 2011, but he was not in top basketball condition. He had to spend extra time in our weight room, working under the supervision of our excellent strength and conditioning coach, John Shackleton. Every day he got a little bit better, but there was a long road ahead. Still a freshman in 2011–2012, he moved into the starting lineup and, over the next few seasons, became one of the most respected players in the Big East.

J.P.'s rise mirrored that of our team. As he became one of our top defenders, we became a better defensive team. Over time he learned how to lead, and as he did we became a more confident unit. By the time he became a senior he was our rock, never caring what his point total looked like, concerned only with the team's success.

That is why, as far as we're concerned, JayVaughn is a model of success for a Villanova Basketball player.

Coming in, he wasn't a great student, but he wanted to become one. He arrived as a highly skilled individual player who wanted to become part of something larger than himself. He faced some tough challenges and overcame them with dignity. In the end, he left Villanova as a beloved figure with his degree in hand, and leadership traits he might have never known he possessed. He played a vital role on some of the best teams Villanova has ever had. In every way possible, JayVaughn helped prepare our guys for their next journey—the one that would end with us on top.

And in his own final college game, he played with focus, together with his teammates, to the very last second.

A few days after Villanova's campus erupted in joy at our top seeding in the East, we traveled west across the commonwealth of Pennsylvania to face our first-round opponent, Lafayette. The Leopards' coach, Fran O'Hanlon, is a 1970 Villanova graduate and one of the great Wildcat point guards in program history. The tone he set running things on the court for Coach Jack Kraft probably hasn't received the kind of credit it deserves, due to the fact he graduated a year before that team made its run to the NCAA Finals. Yet every one of the '71 crew, to a man, will tell you the enormous impact Fran had on his development. And when Coach Kraft passed away a few years ago, the former players decided Fran should speak for them at Kraft's memorial mass at the St. Thomas of Villanova Chapel.

Fran is a superstar coach, universally respected, and the idea that he'd had four days to prepare for us, a team he'd followed closely as an invested alumnus, worried me to no end. I was also concerned about the possibility of a letdown on our part. That happens sometimes after a big win, and to us, the Big East Championship was about as big as big gets. As coaches, we can never forget that we are coaching eighteen- to twenty-two-year-olds, and our staff knew that there was a possibility—maybe a good one—that we would come out flat in our NCAA Tournament opener.

Our guys never let it happen. Darrun Hilliard, our senior co-captain along with JayVaughn, dropped in a three-pointer on our opening possession, and we ended up making sixty-three percent of our shots that night. We were terrific for forty minutes and rolled to a 93–52 win. Our focus demonstrated a maturity that is so special in the development of a championship-caliber unit. We had played our best game of the season a mere five days after celebrating a Big East Championship. From where I stood on the sideline, it was an impressive win.

Naturally, Fran was gracious in defeat. He stopped outside our locker room to talk with our guys and wish us luck. His words in his press conference were very complimentary, and I think that meant something extra to our guys because they knew his history with our program.

After we wrapped up the postgame news conference, we hustled back to our hotel to watch the second half of the game between North Carolina State and Louisiana State University. We would face the winner in the Round of 32 for the right to advance to the Sweet 16, which we hadn't reached since our run to the 2009 NCAA Final Four in Detroit.

LSU led the entire way. It seemed almost inevitable that we would face the Tigers on Saturday night.

Only we didn't.

LSU struggled at the free-throw line in the final minutes, and NC State found a way to grab a 66–65 win. It's the kind of ending you've come to expect in the NCAA Tournament, where there are so many good teams. But we knew we needed to know a whole lot more about how NC State did it.

For every game we play, we assign one of our outstanding assistant coaches—associate head coach Baker Dunleavy, Ashley Howard, or Kyle Neptune—to handle the "scout" for that game. That means taking the lead on reviewing video and working with me to form the foundation of our game plan. The second game in a tournament is trickier than the first because you have less than 48 hours to deliver the scouting plan to the players so they can absorb and implement it.

We stressed to our guys on Friday that NC State, an Atlantic Coast Conference school that plays great teams all year long, wouldn't be intimidated facing a top seed. In January the Wolfpack had downed No. 2 Duke; the next month, they'd beaten No. 9 Louisville on the Cardinals' home floor in Kentucky. This was a team that knew what it took to knock off an accomplished opponent.

NC State smacked us in the mouth from the start. They got into us physically and sank some shots. For our part, we missed dunks and layups. Right away you felt like this was different. We weren't playing at our highest level, and NC State was playing as it had against Louisville and Duke. We'd found ourselves in a steel cage–style basketball match, with bruising defense that kept either team from opening up a lead.

As the clock ticked below thirty seconds in the first half, we trailed 29–28 with possession of the ball. If we could score here, we'd somehow walk into the locker room with a lead in spite of our struggles.

The opposite happened. The Wolfpack's BeeJay Anya blocked our shot, grabbed the rebound, and fired the ball to Trevor Lacey, who launched a prayer from well beyond the three-point arc that splashed through the net with one second left. Instead of a slim lead, we wound up staring at a 32–28 deficit.

Everyone remained calm in the locker room, and our guys were gutsy and willful as we emerged for the second half. But NC State had an answer for everything we tossed at them, building a 66–59 lead with 1:45 remaining in the game. We kept battling. Darrun heated up from the perimeter. We got some defensive stops. When Darrun made a three-pointer with forty seconds left, we pulled to 67–65. Then we forced a turnover at the other end.

With thirty-seven seconds left, we had a chance to take the lead.

Our execution was excellent on this critical possession. As we anticipated, NC State did everything in its power to keep the basketball out of the hands of Darrun, who would end the night with twenty-seven points. So we rotated the ball to the open man, who in this case was Dylan Ennis.

Dylan, a recruit from Toronto, was as well-rounded a young man as we have ever had at Villanova. He understood the business of basketball at all levels—AAU, high school, college, and NBA. In the classroom he was an excellent student. His emotional intelligence was off the charts, his ability to connect with strangers a preternatural gift. On the court he had been an integral part of our success and was the leading scorer in our win over Lafayette, so we knew he had the confidence to take a big shot. With fifteen seconds on the clock, that's what he did.

Dylan's shot at that moment was a prime example of a phrase we often use: "Shoot 'em up, sleep in the streets." Roughly translated, that means to be a great player you have to be strong enough to live with the consequences when the shots don't drop. It's part of living a basketball player's life.

In this case, Dylan's shot didn't drop. The shot was long, bouncing off the back of the rim. When Lennard Freeman (whom we had tried to recruit a few years earlier) grabbed the rebound for NC State, we sensed that we would all soon be sleeping on the street of public opinion.

The final score was 71–68. There would be no trip to the Sweet 16.

The image that summed it up for the national audience was when the television cameras caught a member of the Villanova band, Roxanne Chalifoux, playing her piccolo through tears after the horn sounded. Roxanne was invited to appear on *The Tonight Show* with Jimmy Fallon a few days later, and that would be the only national television appearance for any Wildcat that week.

Our emotions were a swirl of contradictions. There was the heavy sense of loss, sadness, and even shame. It's embarrassing when a No. 8 seed beats a No. 1 seed. We knew what it meant to our fans, and we understood how people would view it. But there was something else on our minds too, something that may seem curious to those outside our Villanova family.

As a coaching staff, we were incredibly proud of how JayVaughn and Darrun had kept their composure in that game, especially since both knew it could be their last college game ever. But the poise and commitment demonstrated by our entire team at a time when most teams would begin to panic was incredible. To get that game back to the point where we had a chance to win it at the end was something none of us will ever forget. We really value that kind of dedication when it shows up in the most stressful competitive situations a college athlete can face.

There is a movie we like to reference from time to time in our program: *The Last Samurai,* released in 2003. Tom Cruise plays a retired United States Cavalry officer whose travels bring him into conflict with samurai warriors in late-nineteenth-century Japan. I love the portrait of the proud samurai warriors whom the American at first confronts and later aligns with. The willingness of the samurai to battle to the end, regardless of the cost, is an inspiration. In this case, Darrun and JayVaughn were our warriors. They kept us together, and both are legends in our program to this day. Only those of us inside would understand the value of that.

BEYOND BASKETBALL

Failure Isn't Forever

Never fear failure. Think of it as an opportunity to learn. If you can approach every challenge without a fear of failure, knowing that you'll learn from any setback, you will find it easier to work with a free and uncluttered mind.

But I'll admit that I'm saying all that with the benefit of hindsight. In those moments after the final whistle, it isn't easy to think in those terms, especially for the young men who've just played the last game of their season or, for the seniors, their college careers.

As a coach in the moments after an NCAA Tournament loss, your role changes. You aren't so much a coach anymore. You're a first responder. You have young men who are broken down, crying. Ten minutes after the buzzer sounds, the NCAA rules state that the doors to the locker room must open to allow the media in to do its job. We only had a few minutes to remind our players that handling this situation is important too. How they stood up in the face of defeat and despair was, at that point, all they could control.

These moments are, for our program, about humility. We quickly reminded the team that in thirty-three prior occasions that season, we were on the happy side of an outcome, feeling good about ourselves. We reminded them that no one would feel sorry for them and that they shouldn't feel sorry for themselves either. When the reporters flood in and start asking their probing questions, we have to answer them knowing that we are part of something larger than ourselves: We represent Villanova University. "There are a lot of positives that come with that," I said, "and you can't enjoy those without accepting that there are times when this isn't necessarily pleasant."

And so the press came in. A lot of them were sympathetic. We recognized that it wasn't easy for members of the Philadelphia media, many of whom had followed us throughout the season and gotten to know and like our guys. So overall the questions were respectful and mindful of the fact that we were all hurting. The guys kept their composure throughout. I was just glad when it was over.

As the jubilant sound of NC State's celebration echoed through the halls, we packed up our things and boarded the bus for a short, quiet ride back to the hotel.

When we walked into the lobby of the Renaissance Pittsburgh, we were greeted by an overflowing group of fans that had cleared a pathway surrounding the regal staircase to the second level in the lobby. You could see in their eyes that they had been crying too, and for me, that experience was far more emotional than what had transpired at the arena.

That got to me. I was glad that our guys got to soak in that moment of love—because I knew the blowback that was ahead.

We set up a postgame meal for the team in a conference room, where all of us tried to process what had happened. Most players barely nibbled on their food. Instead they began drifting out to go to their rooms or greet their families. When the room was all but emptied, I wound up in a conversation with then-junior Ryan Arcidiacono and a couple of his teammates. I wasn't planning to discuss strategy. I was thinking my only role would be to console them. But they wanted to dig into it all, so we examined intellectually what had happened.

Maybe watching the LSU versus NC State game had lulled us into a false sense of security. It was a disjointed and uneven game. Was our intensity and fire a tick below what it should have been? How was it that those qualities had been so strong against Lafayette only two nights before? Did we let that slip?

We acknowledged that we hadn't played our best game. NC State was well prepared and fired up. On our side, everything that could have gone wrong did. We missed easy shots. "And yet no one abandoned our values," we kept noting.

With that in mind, we discussed what was ahead. Knowing there was heat to come from beyond the walls of the Davis Center, our practice center back on campus, the message I delivered to them was all about how much we had accomplished: A school record for victories. A Big East regular season championship. The conference tournament title. "We slipped up but we didn't give up," I told them.

I wanted them to appreciate that as much as I did.

I never thought I was talking to the guys who would end up doing it better than anyone ever has at Villanova.

The next morning, the sun shined as we made our way back to the second-floor conference room. It was Sunday, and it was time to break out one of our secret weapons. Actually, anything having to do with the word "weapon" is the complete wrong way to describe him. Let me put it another way: It was time to console ourselves with the words of a man who has proven himself again and again as one of our team's greatest assets.

According to his résumé, the Reverend Rob Hagan is Villanova's Associate Athletics Director in charge of Sports Medicine and Strength and Conditioning. To us, he is simply "Father Rob."

Father Rob is our team chaplain—our go-to spiritual adviser—and as such he plays a key role in our pre- and postgame rituals. He is an integral, indispensable, and undeniable part of any success we have as a team.

He may wear a white collar, but Father Rob is a guy's guy—able to move effortlessly in any circle without drawing attention to himself. He graduated from Villanova and went on to become an attorney, working in a prosecutor's office before becoming a man of the cloth. He radiates a quiet strength. On a spiritual level, Father Rob is as insightful and compassionate as anyone you could ever meet, a skilled listener whose blue-eyed gaze locks on you and never, ever wavers in conversation. Also, having been in sports as long as I have, you can kind of tell from a person's movements if they were ever an athlete, and Father Rob moves with the grace of someone who competed.

On that particular Sunday, Father Rob was scheduled to say Mass for our travel party of players, coaches, and staff before we flew back to Philadelphia. And boy, did we need it.

The truth is—and we talk about this as a team—those of us involved in this are a little wacky. To care this much about a game is not normal. If other people question it, they're right to do so. We are fanatical about basketball. We love it and can make it too important in our lives.

The night after the NC State loss I couldn't sleep. I replayed every tough decision that I'd made and second-guessed a lot of them. It was all I could think about. I'm sure it was that way for every player and every member of the coaching staff too. But that next morning we came together as a basketball family, and Father Rob reminded us again of what truly matters. We weren't over the loss by any stretch, but, as Father Rob pointed out, the sun had risen.

"One of the many kernels of wisdom we hear in scripture is 'Do not be a stiff-necked people,'" he said, "When you have a stiff neck you are kind of stuck, fixated in one direction. When we allow ourselves to move that neck and look around a bit, we can see the larger picture."

The hours after the loss to NC State were painful because we were fixated on what had happened, he explained. It was the kind of upset—a No. 1 seed getting knocked out early—that makes so many people love March Madness (unless you're the team walking off the court knowing that your season is over).

"If all we did was come to Villanova to win a national champion-ship," he said, "then I guess you would consider the 2014–2015 season a failure. However, if we remember that we came to this university to grow in mind and spirit, to build relationships and life-lasting friend-ships, we will see the larger picture."

It struck me just how deeply that message had seeped into our players' hearts over the course of that season and their years at Villa-nova. In our postgame press conference the night before, Darrun was asked by a reporter, "How does it feel knowing that you won't get a chance to be with your teammates again?"

"I haven't lost my brothers," Darrun said. "We are going to be to-gether for life."

The fact that our players view their teammates as "brothers" says a lot, and I thought of that as I listened to Father Rob minister to us.

"Saint Augustine speaks of the difference between those who have gone and those who have simply gone ahead of us. There is a distinct difference between 'goodbye' and 'I'll see you later—and I will take you, this experience, and the spirit we have shared with me in my heart wherever I go.'"

When I looked around at that team, I could clearly see that their way was one of sacrifice for one another, their truth was loving their teammates, and their life was about becoming part of something big-ger than themselves.

"When we give more than we receive," Father Rob said, "we may not win every game, but we *will* see a sunrise after every sunset and always see light through the darkness."

As Father Rob finished, we all understood that we were going to have to deal with our performance, and we would likely have to an-swer questions about that game straight through to the 2016 NCAA Tournament—if we were able to get back there. Yet his message also offered us the freedom to understand there is so much more to our lives than the games we play.

It was perfect.

The sense I had was that everyone on our team walked out of the hotel that morning feeling like, *Hey, this is not fun. But we can handle it. We're going to be all right.*

Shaking that loss wouldn't be as easy as listening to one Mass, though. There was a lot of hard work ahead, and for me that defeat stung. After all, I'd been a part of this university for nineteen years. Growing up outside of Philadelphia, I'd been a Villanova fan for most of my life. Everything in me wanted to live up to the legacy of this school, and of Coach Massimino, and to deliver a championship win that reflected just how far this team had come.

I kept asking myself, *How could we come so close and not make it, especially with a team that was playing this strong at the end of the year, which is what we always strive for? And what will it take to get back here next year and play even better?*

Sometimes the best way to answer tough questions in life is to look backward—to think about who you are and how you got here, and to apply the lessons of the past to attain a future you want.

It was time to do exactly that.

No one in basketball has meant more to me than my mentor and guiding spirit, Coach Rollie Massimino. Before I'd ever met him, I was fortunate enough to be in the stands at Rupp Arena in Lexington, Kentucky, when the 1985 Wildcats defeated Memphis State to earn the right to face—and beat—Georgetown two nights later for the title.

2

Where I Come From

As we grow in life, we learn a few things: A loss isn't always really a loss. An ending is sometimes just a beginning. There's something about Father Rob's "sunrise after every sunset" lesson that can be applied to life as much as it can to sports. Even if you can't see them right now, the lessons are often there. They were there for me, right in front of me, almost glaringly so, even when I was much younger.

As a kid growing up just outside Philadelphia—in suburban Bucks County, in the 1970s—it was almost impossible *not* to revere the city's Big Five of college basketball: La Salle, Penn, Saint Joseph's, Temple, and Villanova.

My parents, Jerry and Judy Wright, are two of the smartest people I know, but they didn't have the opportunity to go to college. So, like a lot of Philadelphians, I didn't associate myself with one particular team. I loved all the teams equally. That's kind of what you did as a kid. Whichever team was the best that year was the one I paid the most attention to.

It just so happened that in 1970–1971, when I was a very impressionable ten-year-old, Penn and Villanova were not only the top teams in Philly, but among the best teams in the country. Both were nationally ranked, and there was a lot of hype surrounding their only meeting of the regular season. That game was played on January 23, 1971, at the Palestra, the "Cathedral of College Basketball" on the Penn campus. For Philadelphia-area sports fans in those days, the Palestra was our mecca. Though I only knew it through our old black-and-white television set with the rabbit ears, I was drawn to every ounce of passion and energy that poured out of the players on that arena

With my parents, Judy and Jerry. My dad gave me my first lessons
in coaching as the skipper of my Little League team, the Larks.

floor. When the Quakers walked away with a 78–70 victory that night,
I began favoring Penn over Villanova.

Everything changed in the NCAA Tournament, when the two stal-
warts of the Big Five collided in the East Regional Final, played that
year in Raleigh, North Carolina. We all thought it would be a great
game. It didn't work out that way. The Wildcats of Howard Porter,
Clarence Smith, Hank Siemiontkowski, Chris Ford, and Tom Ingelsby rolled to a 90–47 win. (To this day, if you say "90–47" to Villanova fans of a certain age, they will immediately know what you're
talking about.)

That game seemed surreal to me. I had assumed that Penn would
win the national championship. They'd looked better all season. I
couldn't comprehend how this sort of shocker could happen. In my
mind, it felt like an awful fluke, as if Philadelphia's shot at a national
title had been pulled out from underneath us.

So I switched over to Villanova largely because it was the last Philly
team standing. But then something changed again: I started reading. I was old enough to peruse the sports pages of the *Philadelphia
Inquirer, Daily News,* and *Bulletin,* and I delved into their previews of
the Final Four. The more I read about the Wildcats' legacy and
coaches and players, the more I reconsidered my feelings. When Vil-

lanova's next game arrived the following Thursday night, I was firmly planted on the Nova bandwagon.

I gathered with my mom and dad and two sisters (my brother Derek wasn't born yet) in our family room to watch Villanova play Western Kentucky in a semifinal at the Houston Astrodome. Despite being played in a giant domed stadium, just as Final Fours are now, the '71 Final Four didn't look anything like one of today's mega-spectacles. First, it was held on a Thursday night (the move to the Saturday/Monday format was made in 1973), and second, the brackets we see these days on everything from billboards to the Internet were usually not more than a few lines of agate type in your newspaper.

However, this was one of those games that we treasure as fans. It went back and forth, with both teams battling for control. I still recall vividly the moment when Siemiontkowski was whistled for his fifth foul, disqualifying him at a critical moment late in the game. It seemed like my new favorite team was dead in the water.

It's a hard feeling to cope with, even as an adult. When you're ten, it feels like everything is collapsing around you. I couldn't hold back the tears.

Much to my delight, those tears dried up soon enough, thanks in part to the work of sixth man Joe McDowell. The Wildcats escaped the Hilltoppers and their All-American center, Jim McDaniels, and found a way to win in double overtime. The pro-Nova crowd in the Astrodome exploded, and so did I. You never forget a night like that. You never forget the wild ride from tears of sorrow to shouts of pure elation.

(Years later I was with a group that included most of the guys from that team—all active supporters of our program now—at the home of Chris Ford on the Jersey Shore. During a dinner on the deck behind Chris' home, I relayed that story about how I burst into tears when Hank fouled out, and it drew a roar of laughter. The sentiment expressed by one of the '71 crew was that they wanted to cry too, because that foul meant McDowell, who was right there with us on that dock, had to step in on a team that didn't rely on a deep bench.)

That miraculous win set up a championship game with the University of California, Los Angeles. I really believed that Villanova was going to beat the Bruins.

I didn't have a lot of company in that opinion.

At the time, UCLA was the unquestioned dynasty in college basketball. Under coach John Wooden, the Bruins were one year removed from the end of the Lew Alcindor (later known as Kareem Abdul-Jabbar) era and not yet ready to unveil a young center from San Diego named Bill Walton.

As just about everyone but me expected, UCLA hung on to defeat Villanova at the Astrodome, 68–62, and I was, of course, devastated. Across the country, people were astonished for a different reason: The fact that Coach Wooden had his team hold the ball in the final minutes (the shot clock would not arrive in the college game until 1985–1986) was a pretty big deal at the time. Most people viewed it as a tactic used by underdogs—not the mighty Bruins—to narrow the talent gap.

As for me, the loss didn't deflate my appreciation of my new team of choice. I was hooked on this whole Villanova Basketball deal.

It was around that time that my family was struck by a bit of good fortune. A relative on my dad's side, Jeannie Long, was the ticket manager at Villanova. We would see her at family functions, and as soon as she learned I liked college hoops she began offering us tickets to see the Wildcats.

I'll never forget the first time I walked up to the Palestra.

A little history here, to clarify: In the early 1950s, Villanova and other local schools began moving big games off campus. Rather than playing at the 2,500-seat Cat House (today known as the Jake Nevin Field House), there was enough interest to warrant shifting these games to the 9,200-seat Palestra. That pattern helped lead to the birth of the Big Five in 1955–1956 and lived on into the 1980s. Rare was the significant college game in Philadelphia that wasn't played at the Palestra.

That changed in the 1980s and '90s as each school invested in an on-campus venue. (Penn still calls the Palestra home.) Now Villanova may play once or twice a year at the Palestra, or not at all. (We did not play there in 2015–2016.)

I know some people lament that fact, but I choose to look at it this way: On any given Saturday you can have Villanova hosting a game at the Wells Fargo Center in front of 20,000 fans, Temple at the Liacouras Center with a crowd of 10,000, and a packed Hagan Arena with better than 4,000 fans at Saint Joseph's. I'm not sure there's any city in the country that can boast a one-day total of 34,000 people watching college basketball.

Anyway, the first time my dad brought me to a game at the Palestra, we arrived after the first game of a doubleheader was already under way—an Ivy League clash with Penn hosting. As the ticket taker tore our tickets, I could already detect a huge roar bubbling up from inside the center of the building.

I was transfixed by the Palestra before I even took my seat along one of the long bleacher rows that lined the building. And while there have been enhancements to the arena in the decades since—the concourse has been updated with images of Big Five stars of the past, and the lower level now includes chair-back seating—it has never lost its essential charm. The smell of popcorn wafting up from the concession stands tucked along those narrow concourses is usually all it takes to catapult me right back to those early visits in the 1970s. The place was my Xanadu.

Even now, when I'm privileged enough to walk our team into the Palestra to face Penn, we enter the same way generations of teams have before us, and I love every second of it. The bus drops us off at the curb on 33rd Street and we come in via the concourse. As we descend the ramps from the concourse to the playing floor, most of the players have to be careful not to bump their heads against the low concrete beams. The locker rooms are tiny by today's standards, and there is no separate room for the coaching staff to meet. The temperature outside may be in the single digits, but inside, under the banks of bright lights, it's always warm, inviting, and the purist's idea of college hoops perfection.

A Lesson from My First Coach

Like most kids in the 1970s, I played a seasonal schedule of the Big Three team sports with my friends: Baseball, in the spring. Football in the fall. Basketball in the winter. And even though I felt the deepest connection to basketball, it was baseball that taught me an important lesson I would come back to again and again.

My dad loves baseball, and he coached my Little League team, the Larks, from the time I was six until I was fifteen. During that time I watched and learned a lot about coaching and being a leader from my dad, but those lessons didn't only come during games. I'd sit with him at our well-worn kitchen table as he wrote out the team lineups, always curious to see what he would come up with.

When I was in eighth grade, we had a new kid on the team. I'll call him Eddie. Eddie was a nice kid, but he was one of the less skilled players on our team. Dad always started the lineup by placing me at shortstop (not because of nepotism, but because it was my best position), and then his next placement would be Eddie, starting in right field.

In Little League, the game can be harshly affected when the ball is hit to a player lacking in confidence. Yet every game, my dad put Eddie out in right field, and there were times when it hurt us. I was baffled.

One day I worked up the nerve to question Dad's decision. "Why are you starting Eddie?" I asked. "Why don't you use someone else?"

Dad looked up at me with curiosity, clearly surprised by my question. He took his glasses off and cleaned them on his polo shirt as he spoke to me. "If he's the weakest guy and we get him to improve, then our team becomes stronger," he said. "We want Eddie to feel good about himself. If he does, we'll all feel better for him and the Larks will wind up becoming a better team."

My middle school mind couldn't grasp the concept. I couldn't see past Eddie's early struggles. I just wanted to win games.

My dad looked at me with a stern look on his face. "We all have a role to play, son. You play yours. Eddie will play his. Now, why don't you let me play mine?"

With that, he put his glasses on and went back to his lineup.

I remember feeling like a jerk for calling out Eddie like that. Who was I to say who had the right to start on our team and who didn't?

Throughout the season, Dad would find ways to get Eddie involved in the game and make him feel important. I could go 4-for-4 at the

BEYOND BASKETBALL

Find a Role for Everyone

In any organization a leader's job is to make sure everyone feels confident in their role and that the role is valued. This gives everyone their best chance to compete at the highest level.

plate, and Eddie could go 0-for-3 with a walk, and Dad would whoop and holler about Eddie's walk. He'd spend extra time with him before and after practice, and he scheduled time for Eddie to come by our house and practice with me. "You have to help your teammates, on and off the field," Dad would say.

By the end of the year, Eddie was much better, and you could tell he was my dad's favorite player. I wasn't jealous. I remember feeling proud of Dad for his dedication to this kid who needed the extra attention to thrive. The takeaway is that it wasn't just about winning games—it was about teaching us the importance of being a team. Eddie became an example to all of us that everyone is important.

During one late-season game, it was the bottom of the ninth, two outs, the other team at bat with runners in scoring position, the whole game riding on the next play, and lo and behold, the batter launched a fly ball to right field. As if drawn by a beacon, that ball homed in on Eddie. I remember watching the play develop in slow motion and thinking, *We're screwed. No way Eddie's catching that ball.* The ball came down, Eddie's glove went up—and he made the catch. Game over. We won. *The Larks won!* The entire team ran out and crowded around Eddie, who started crying from disbelief. If it were a movie, this would've been the sappy ending everyone was waiting for.

The Larks made the playoffs that year, and that win was a big part of the reason why.

I was proud of Eddie. I was proud of our team. But I was especially proud of my dad. He made that happen.

We all have a role to play, Dad told me.

It's a lesson I would carry with me when I started coaching myself.

There are strengths in each one of us. Recognizing those and allowing them to flourish within an organizational structure sets the stage for success.

Of course, back then I never really imagined I would wind up coaching professionally. I thought I would be a pro basketball player, and so that's what I went after.

At the end of high school, I accepted a grant-in-aid to play basketball for Coach Charlie Woollum at Bucknell University. These were offered in lieu of scholarships by some schools back then, as they are now in the Ivy League. I thought I was a lot better than I was, and when my senior year of college ended after our 1982–1983 season, my hoops prospects were dim. The only nibble I had on the professional front was from a low-level team in France. I was way too much of a Philly homebody to enjoy living abroad, even in a place like France. But I knew that I loved sports, so I made the decision to pursue a career that would keep me close to the action.

I was thrilled to land a position in the marketing department of the Philadelphia Stars, a team at the center of the newly formed United States Football League, right after they'd played their first season in the summer of '83.

I couldn't have fallen into a better situation.

The original business model for the USFL was smart. Even back then, the National Football League was a powerhouse. Trying to take on the NFL in the fall, when the league had deals with all three of the major television networks, would have been a monumental task. So the USFL played its games in the spring and summer, partnering with another start-up—a fledgling cable network named ESPN—and tried to make football a year-round sport.

It felt to me like it was working.

As a recent college graduate, I was part of a marketing team whose job was to sell tickets and promote our players to boost attendance at Stars games in Veterans Stadium, the 65,000-seat venue where the Eagles played too. Our team president, Carl Peterson, also asked me to represent the Stars organization at certain functions. (Carl would later become the president of the Kansas City Chiefs.) We had a small staff, so a lot of us wore many hats.

One of those trips took me for a drive up the New Jersey Turnpike to attend a news conference in the Meadowlands. One of our rivals, the New Jersey Generals, was set to make a major announcement. So

I was seated in the front row—alongside legendary broadcaster Howard Cosell—as the Generals' owner, Donald Trump, introduced Heisman Trophy winner Herschel Walker as the newest General.

On those Monday nights during the football season when I wasn't standing in for ownership, I organized weekly outings that would take us to bars and restaurants around Philadelphia. Our group would include a cheerleader, a player, a coach, and me. I would usually be the guy to get up on the microphone and urge everyone in the place to buy season tickets. These outings helped me get to know some of the Stars' best players, guys like quarterback Chuck Fusina and wide receiver Scott Fitzkee.

The best part of it all, though, was that I met a beautiful cheerleader/marketing rep named Patty Reilly, who would later become my wife. Patty was a 1983 Villanova graduate. She had been a cheerleader when the 'Cats made their run to the NCAA Elite Eight in 1983. Patty was on the sidelines cheering for the Stars when we defeated the Arizona Wranglers—coached by George Allen—to bring Philadelphia its first football championship since the Eagles had captured the NFL title over Green Bay at Franklin Field in 1960.

I was there for that USFL championship, delivering stat sheets from the press box to Donald Trump in one of the suites. (I certainly never would have imagined the Generals' owner being elected President of the United States back then. I guess you really never can tell where life is going to lead someone, can you?)

I treasure that whole time period. I met my wife, I learned a ton, and I developed friendships that I maintain to this day. I was in my marketing-man mode and living a dream. Fate, though, was about to step in.

Keep a Bounce in Your Step

One of my former teammates at Bucknell, Pat Flannery, was an assistant coach at Drexel University. His salary was paltry, even by 1984 standards. Pat, who was a role model to me during our one season as teammates, was married and beginning a family when he received an offer from a Division III school, the University of Rochester. The head coach, Mike Neer, was in the market for an assistant coach, and the lure was that it paid more than the Drexel spot. So Pat decided to take a look and went to an interview with Mike.

It was very clear that the Rochester job was Pat's if he wanted it.

After mulling it over, Pat decided that he couldn't make the move from Division I to Division III, regardless of the money, but I could tell from our conversations that Pat felt badly about turning down the offer. So he told Coach Neer that he had a former Bucknell teammate who would be a great candidate: me.

When Pat came to me with the idea of getting into coaching, I was hesitant. I liked what I was doing with the Stars. I liked the people I was working with. The thought of a Division III coaching job in upstate New York . . . well, it didn't sound that enticing. But I decided to at least listen to what Mike Neer had to say.

The position at Rochester was actually three jobs: assistant varsity basketball coach, head junior varsity basketball coach, and assistant intramural director. It paid $10,000 over ten months. The off months came in July and August, allowing whoever took the post to earn additional money and make contacts by working as an instructor at the summer basketball camps that are held all over the country.

I had zero coaching experience. I also wasn't sure I wanted the job. That's not the best way to walk into an interview. Especially since I would be interviewing with Mike Neer and the school's athletic director, John Reeves, as he had oversight of the intramural staff. But as I left the interview, I felt a rush of energy I hadn't anticipated. Until then, I hadn't realized how much I missed the vitality of a college campus.

I was blown away when Rochester offered me the job. I couldn't understand what I had done to get over my lack of experience, but I later found out one of the reasons: When John Reeves walked behind me during my visit, he observed what he described as a "bounce in my step."

I guess the lesson there is, *Better to have a bounce in your step than not.*

So I reluctantly left behind the life I loved in Philly to see how I'd feel about coaching—and after only three days in Rochester, I knew that this was my heaven on earth. I quickly realized that spending extended hours at a desk, as I had done during business hours with the Stars, wasn't for me.

When I began work for Mike Neer, I started working out with the returning players. In most cases I was their age, and I was even younger than a few of them. Each day, I couldn't wait to get up and get in to work. And when my day was supposed to be over, I didn't want to leave. The idea of being around basketball guys who were learning life lessons all day long was incredibly appealing to me.

Just like that, by taking a chance on a job I didn't think I was qualified for and wasn't sure I wanted, I had found what I was most passionate about.

One of the coolest things about my two years in Rochester was the fact that I was in charge of my own team with the junior varsity. The first time I ever served as a head coach was a JV scrimmage against Genesee Community College, located in Batavia, New York. Its head coach was Bill Van Gundy, the father of famed NBA coaches Jeff and Stan Van Gundy. This was designed as a four-quarter scrimmage, meaning we would keep score with a winner declared at the conclusion of each period.

At the end of the first quarter, Genesee had the lead and they elected to hold the basketball while the clock ran down so they would win the quarter. This shocked me—I thought we'd play out each quarter. It was a scrimmage!

Mike Neer watched this unfold from the stands. When it was over, I was puzzled about Coach Van Gundy's strategy and even a little miffed. Mike just smiled at me. I don't think he called me "Kid," but he might as well have.

"Welcome to coaching," he said.

Lesson learned: *A coach is going to take every opportunity to get his team a win.*

During my first season, I absorbed everything I could from Coach Neer, whose program was a perennial in the Division III NCAA Tournament: His style of offense. His approach to defense. How he addressed the team.

As our season came to an end, I began to prepare for my first National Association of Basketball Coaches (NABC) convention, an annual event held in conjunction with the Final Four played that year in Lexington, Kentucky. This was 1985, and Villanova was making an unexpected run through the NCAA Tournament after an uneven regular season that left it in danger of missing the tournament altogether. Coach Rollie Massimino's Wildcats were a No. 8 seed whose first-round "reward" was a trip to Dayton to meet a Flyers squad that had advanced to the Elite Eight a season before on its home court (which is no longer permitted by the NCAA). Yet Coach Mass and his guys took full advantage of their new life. Villanova advanced to the Southeast Regional Final in Birmingham, Alabama, where the 'Cats outlasted North Carolina 46–43.

My first Final Four visit was shaping up perfectly. I had begun dating Patty, and she had plans to go to Lexington with her family as a Villanova alumnus. Not only would I get to cheer on the Wildcats, but I would get to spend time with my girlfriend.

The NABC convention itself just blew my mind. It was inconceivable to me that you would walk around a corner and be a few feet from Bob Knight, Dean Smith, or Denny Crum.

I was inside Rupp Arena, one row from the top of the 23,000-seat building, for the first semifinal game that Saturday afternoon. The Wildcats were one of three Big East teams in the Final Four, and they were the underdog against the only non–Big East representative, Memphis State. But Coach Mass was at the top of his game, and Ed Pinckney, Dwayne McClain, Gary McLain, Harold Pressley, Dwight Wilbur, Harold Jensen, and friends were too much for the Tigers, winning 52–45.

Now I had a dilemma.

My duties as the assistant intramural director meant that I had to be back in Rochester on Monday. I had a floor hockey tournament to run, and I was sick to my stomach at the thought of boarding the flight home on Sunday. Yet I also knew that I had a responsibility to live up to the duties of my job, even if I wished the circumstances would have allowed me to stay for Monday night's final. I flew back as scheduled.

You probably know the rest.

Coach Mass and the Wildcats staged one of the great upsets in the history of the NCAA Tournament, defeating No. 1 Georgetown 66–64. I caught as much of the game as I could that night, after we got done with the floor hockey. I watched at the house of our women's soccer coach, Terry Gurnett, and his wife. It was just the three of us, and I was the only one with tears in my eyes when it was over.

As a kid from Philly, it seemed like the greatest game of all-time. Watching the magic and family atmosphere that Coach Mass had created that night, I knew once and for all that coaching was the career for me. I wanted to do exactly what Coach Mass was doing. I was drawn to the energy and values his program espoused.

Not to mention, I'd been a fan since I was ten!

Now that I was certain about coaching as a career, I tried to line up as many chances as I could to work at summer basketball camps. Naturally, I hoped that two of those summer weeks would be spent working the Villanova camp. However, with the Wildcats being only two months removed from a national championship, that camp was huge. It was so big, and Coach Mass had such a machine, that my application to serve as an instructor was denied.

I was feeling pretty dejected. I was young and wanted everything to happen instantaneously.

Here's where one of those sunset/sunrise lessons comes in.

Just a few weeks later, I was on the road, recruiting for Rochester at Comsewogue High School on Long Island, when I ran into its coach, Frank Romeo. Frank was a good friend of Coach Mass and brought his team to the Villanova camp every summer. He asked me if I would be working there. I told him that they were fully staffed, so I would not. Frank then suggested that he could add me to *his* staff for the week to work with his team.

That sounded like a great idea to me, and I appreciated Frank's willingness to include me. Basically, I was a tagalong guy who somebody at Villanova had to wedge into the lineup of camp coaches. Another way to put it: I snuck into my first-ever coaching assignment at Villanova.

Every night during camp, individual instruction was doled out on the outdoor tennis courts, which had been temporarily converted to basketball courts. We weren't required to attend these sessions, but I took advantage every night I was there. Why? Because Coach Mass himself would walk around and observe us.

It's not every day that you get to meet an idol, and I've never forgotten the day I met one of mine. The Villanova Basketball camp welcomed in the vicinity of 850 campers and perhaps another 150 counselors. When I began working as a counselor, it felt to me like there were people everywhere. But from the distance of three decades, I can still recall exactly what Coach Mass was wearing when I first spoke to him: a white Villanova polo shirt, a pair of boldly flowered shorts—colored yellow, blue, and red—and a pair of loafers with no socks. He was seated on a golf cart, making the rounds, and it was apparent that he knew everyone. Fresh from a national championship, he was larger than life.

I was with some of the camp coaches when Coach Mass came in to address the group. Immediately you could feel his fire, enthusiasm, and passion. To me, it felt like he had a glow around him. As the session neared its end, I introduced myself to him and he replied, "Welcome." I feel pretty confident that he had no idea who I was. Yet he made me feel like a member of the family. I was part of his staff.

One of the best things about that camp was the friends I made. In addition to the members of the coaching staff—John Olive, Marty Marbach, and Steve Lappas—I really got to know the graduate assistants and Villanova players.

Later in the evening, after the official camp day had ended, we would often play pickup basketball games. I played with and against Harold Pressley, Harold Jensen, Chuck Everson, Wyatt Maker, and Brian Harrington, all of whom had played on the 1985 national championship team. Having watched them on television, I looked up to them and was glad to find that each was approachable and easygoing. They were all nice guys, and I sometimes reference that with our players today: "Even if you consider yourself a college kid, people look at you as something much more. Don't forget it."

On a couple of occasions, I noticed Coach Mass approach a member of his staff to find out who I was. And at the end of one particular night, Coach Mass approached *me*.

"You're going to be a good coach," he said.

Wow.

There aren't words to describe how proud I was in that moment. To me, Coach Mass was the greatest coach on the planet. From everything I'd read about him, and everything I'd picked up listening to the players and assistant coaches who worked with him, Coach Rollie Massimino represented everything I wanted to be: A family man. A leader who cared about his team beyond just basketball. And, yes, a national champion.

In that instant, my goals were set. And my goals were, I have to admit, *ambitious*.

I might not have known it at the time, especially since I was in my impatient twenties, but in order to accomplish those Coach Mass–sized goals, life would require me to learn what it's like to take the long view.

3

Creating a Culture of Success

ONCE THE VILLANOVA crew knew me and saw what I could do, I was in a much better position to get hired for their camp the following summer—and that's exactly what happened. Steve Lappas hired me. Steve was one of Coach Mass' assistants and later the head coach at Villanova, where he led the Wildcats to the 1994 National Invitation Tournament Championship and 1995 Big East Tournament Championship.

Steve would sometimes ask for my assistance in doing extra things during camp, and I always, *always* said, "Sure!" My willingness to help wasn't just because I was a nice guy. I wanted to land a Division I coaching job, ideally at Villanova. Showing up, lending a hand, being genuinely helpful to the guys in charge, even playing pickup games with those guys after hours—all of it made a difference. Some people call that networking. But to dismiss or look down on that sort of enthusiasm completely misses the point. I wanted to be a part of the Villanova team, and by volunteering, helping out, and having fun with the assistants and coaching staff, I was proving that I could be a team player.

That mattered.

In 1986 I moved from Rochester back home to Philadelphia to take an assistant coaching job at Drexel. Shortly thereafter, Marty Marbach departed the Villanova staff to become the head coach at Canisius College. That left a hole. Guess who spoke to Coach Mass and recommended me to fill it? Steve Lappas. My hard work at those camps paid off, and I got the job.

I could hardly believe it: I was in the Big East coaching alongside one of the game's icons at Villanova. I would look down the sideline during our games and see John Thompson, Lou Carnesecca, Jim Boeheim—some of the biggest names in our sport. As a fan, I couldn't imagine anything better. As a coach, all I wanted was to learn everything I could from Coach Mass on what it takes to perform at the highest level of college basketball. But he showed me something more: He brought me inside Villanova, a place that had seemed magical to me from afar and was even more mesmerizing as I was welcomed into its culture.

Villanova was founded in 1842 by the Order of Saint Augustine. For those who don't know the history or aren't affiliated with the Catholic faith, the educational method and tradition that Saint Augustine preached was one in which students learn to think critically, act compassionately, and succeed, all while serving others. Villanova's mission statement sums it up well, stating that the university is a community that "seeks to reflect the spirit of Saint Augustine by the cultivation of knowledge, by respect for individual differences, and by adherence to the principle that mutual love and respect should animate every aspect of University life."

That's not the kind of language that fills every university mission statement, and it's certainly not the sort of language one normally attaches to a competitive athletics program. But it is exactly these principles of love and respect, of compassion and of serving others, that give Villanova a certain special something that sets it apart.

The biggest lesson I picked up on right away? Coach Mass viewed his basketball program as a family. His approach fit perfectly into the culture of Villanova. But he was hardly the only father figure in the Wildcat family. In those days, there was one remarkable person who embodied the bond between the university and our program—our team chaplain, Father Bernard Lazor, O.S.A.

Father Lazor was from the coal-country region of Pennsylvania, and he was one of the toughest people, both mentally and physically, I have ever met. I recall once watching in panic as a loose ball and a pair of hard-charging players went directly for Father, seated in a chair near the end of our bench. He was in his late seventies at the time. One of the two players couldn't stop his momentum and bowled directly into Father. Everyone in the arena froze. Not to worry, though.

Here I am in 1990 with Coach Massimino and the rest of his staff: John Olive (back), Tommy Massimino, and Steve Pinone (right). You can see Coach Mass taught me how to dress as well as coach.

He stoically stood right back up, put the chair back in place, and assured anyone who would listen that he was perfectly fine.

It was amazing—and yes, surprising—to see such qualities in a priest. He was competitive too and had been a great baseball player in his day.

I was astonished to see what a strong role the team chaplain played in Coach Mass' program. He was at the games. He was with us on the road. He was there for everything and everyone. He seemed to hold both a leadership position and a support position, and that was remarkable to me. This wasn't someone who came in, gave a perfunctory prayer to get it out of the way, and then went about his day. The coaching staff and players all looked to him as one of their own and sought guidance from him, sometimes on a very personal level. Coach Mass would often have new altar vestments made as a gift, one small but significant show of appreciation for how much Father Lazor meant to the program.

Father Lazor held us to a very high standard while showing us he had a caring side too. He had compassion for the assistant coaches when we were struggling to balance the demands of our jobs. He gave us the quiet strength to keep going, but he also made it clear that working at Villanova was a privilege, so maybe we ought to stop complaining. (Tough love.) During games, Father Lazor was as fiery as any player or coach—maybe more so. When he thought an official got a call wrong, this normally reserved, white-haired gentleman in a Roman collar didn't hesitate to bring it to the referee's attention from his seat near the end of our bench.

As a team, one of the points of connection we had with Father Lazor was through the words he offered at pregame meals. It is common practice in college athletics to eat a team meal four hours prior to game time. At Villanova, during the Coach Mass era, the tradition included a Mass conducted by Father Lazor, with a homily included. (In the 1990s, this was condensed to a Gospel reading followed by a homily, usually lasting no longer than ten minutes, and we have maintained that tradition during my time as head coach.) His lessons were simple, direct, and from "the old country." He praised hard work, being a good person, selflessness, and putting God first. He also loved acronyms as a way to engage his audience, and his favorite was TOP: Talent. Opportunity. Perseverance. Those were the three ingredients needed to make any team a success. He came up with countless other acronyms, but TOP was the big one, and I've never forgotten it.

Over the course of the next four years, as I grew to become a part of the Villanova family, I felt that Father Lazor became a member of my extended family as well. And when Patty and I were married in 1991, Father Lazor was one of the celebrants.

Villanova felt like more than a family to me after those four years. It felt like my home. I could see myself staying there forever.

But, as Father Lazor may have said during one of his tough-love homilies, "forever" doesn't always turn out the way we think. Life was about to throw me a curve I never saw coming. Figuring out how to deal with the changes would take some serious digging into my own TOP.

In March 1992, our season came to an end with an 83–80 loss to Virginia in an NIT game at the Pavilion. Later that week, Coach called me into his office and told me he was thinking about accepting an offer to become the head coach at the University of Nevada, Las Vegas.

"And," he added, "I want you to come with me."

I was speechless. To me, Coach Massimino *was* Villanova. I was twenty-nine years old and couldn't comprehend him making such a move, especially to UNLV, which had won a national championship in 1990 and had been upset in the Final Four by Duke in '91. The Runnin' Rebels were at the top of the college basketball world, but the program seemed so different from our own. The UNLV home court was located just off the Las Vegas strip. On game night, the seats nearest the floor were nicknamed "Gucci Row" for the number of prominent and wealthy fans who occupied them. In a city without a pro sports team, the Runnin' Rebels were *the* sports show in Vegas. It was a scene that existed in what seemed like a distant galaxy.

My heart raced as I blindly replied, "Yeah, Coach. I'll go."

At that point, I would have followed Coach Mass anywhere, and apparently that included the desert.

Coach asked me to keep this all to myself, but of course I called Patty as soon as I left his office. I wasn't sure how she would feel about moving out west, but to my surprise, her response was, "Let's go!"

Not long after that, Coach Mass summoned me to his home near Villanova. When I arrived, along with the other assistant coaches, he was seated at his dining room table with UNLV's athletic director and an attorney for the school.

Coach turned to me and asked: "Would $75,000 be good for you?"

At the time, I was making $35,000 a year.

I responded, as coolly as I could, "Sure. That salary would be great."

Inside I was leaping for joy.

I was also struck when he went so far as to ask for a scholarship for our student manager, Brett Gunning. Brett was a sophomore at Villanova at the time, and Coach Mass loved the kid. Apparently Coach was trying to bring his *entire* basketball family out west, not just his paid staff.

Within days we were told to report to Philadelphia International

Airport, where we'd depart for Las Vegas on a private jet. I had never been on a private plane before. Frankly, I didn't even know that private air travel existed, so imagine my shock as we drove onto the airfield and I spied a sparkling gold jet waiting for us. Turns out it was the property of the Golden Nugget casino and its owner, Steve Wynn. We boarded the flight and flew in luxury to a private airfield in Vegas.

The UNLV vacancy was big news, and at that point no one in the media had linked it to Coach Mass.

Once we deplaned, we were hustled into black cars and driven to the rear entrance of the Mirage Hotel. We came to learn that the Mirage had a private area of bungalows that catered to some very exclusive clientele, including Michael Jackson. Among the guests during our stay was General H. Norman Schwarzkopf, of Desert Storm fame. The whole experience was surreal.

Each of us had our own bungalow with a butler and access to the pool. They supplied us with great food. It was all happening so fast. We couldn't really call friends or family at home for fear the news would leak. We did, however, start quietly reaching out to recruiting contacts to let them know. That's something you would not be able to do today, in the age of social media, but back then word traveled slowly.

The move to UNLV came during a push in the city to make Las Vegas a family town. Steve Wynn and the school's leadership were convinced that the city could transform its image and expand. In hiring Coach Mass they were bringing in someone who graduated all his players and projected the image they were trying to create.

All I could think was, *What exactly have I gotten myself into? And is this even the right place for us?*

As we settled into our new office space in the Thomas & Mack Center, it began to sink in that this was a much more challenging situation than any of us could have envisioned. Not only were we two thousand miles from the Northeast recruiting base we knew so well, but we were outsiders in a city that was still fiercely loyal to Jerry Tarkanian, the coach who had built the Runnin' Rebels program into a national powerhouse before he was forced to resign after the school was put on probation for NCAA violations. The legend of "Tark the Shark" was enormous—and it would eventually swallow us all.

We had no idea what we were getting into. As far as we knew, Coach Tark was headed off to San Antonio to take over the Spurs, and we would simply move on from there with everyone supporting us.

It wasn't anything like that.

During our first year, we spent some time in the Top 20. We had taken over a talented team. We were trying to learn the culture of the community and build the basketball program at the same time. But the reality was we weren't a united program. Those who remained loyal to Tark—and there were a lot of them, even in our own building— seemed to think that any success we had detracted from what he had accomplished. It was as disjointed and challenging a time as I have ever been through.

By the spring of 1994, I decided it was time to try something new.

Those twenty-four months were a learning experience like none other, and one of the biggest lessons for me was the realization that I am an East Coast guy. I never thought of myself that way before moving west, but I really missed life in the Northeast. I missed running into people I knew and being around the major cities I knew. In Vegas everything happened three hours later. It bothered me. I felt like I was missing everything and everyone—my family above all.

I had a much harder time with the transition than Patty. But when I sought her counsel over what to do, she agreed that I should follow my heart. My heart was telling me it was time to go out on my own.

I let Coach Mass know, and he gave me his full support.

I started paying close attention to the job market for head coaches in the East and spotted an opening at Hofstra. When I was in college at Bucknell, Hofstra was an East Coast Conference rival. I recalled the Pride having a good basketball team and a nice campus. So when

I saw that Butch van Breda Kolff had departed as Hofstra's head coach, I decided to apply. In response, I received a perfunctory letter that thanked me for applying but informed me that I would not be a candidate.

I mentioned that letter—and my disappointment—to Coach Mass.

The athletic director at Hofstra was Jim Garvey, a former Big East referee whom Coach knew well. On the eve of the 1994 Final Four in Charlotte, Coach placed a call to Jim. I was seated in Coach's office at the time, and what he said was: "Just do yourself a favor and interview this kid. I guarantee you that you won't be sorry."

From my vantage point, it seemed clear that Jim had already completed his interviews and had settled on another candidate, but like the great recruiter he is, Coach Mass kept hammering his point home to Jim. Finally, Jim relented and agreed to meet with me in Charlotte during the annual coaches convention.

Jim and I instantly hit it off, and shortly after my flight home from the conference landed in Las Vegas, my phone rang. It was Jim calling to offer me the job. I accepted without having visited the campus since my college days. I came in a day ahead of the press conference, they gave me a tour, and Patty—nine months pregnant with our second son, Collin—joined me for the news conference in Hempstead, New York, the following day.

Just like that, I was the head coach at a Division I program, albeit one without a prominent basketball profile. In the months after I was hired, *Eastern Basketball* magazine, a well-respected industry source at the time, listed all of the New York–area Division I schools—and Hofstra wasn't even included. They simply left it out. That's how far off the grid we were.

At the time I left for Long Island, UNLV had a great recruiting class due to arrive in the fall. Prior to my leaving, I called those recruits and told them they were in a great spot coming to play for Coach Mass. One of the internal debates I had before accepting the Hofstra job was whether it was wise to leave at that point. Even though we had faced difficulties, I was convinced we were building something special that could one day bring another national champi-

In my early days at Hofstra with assistant coaches (from left to right) Joe Jones, Tom Pecora, and Brett Gunning.

onship to UNLV. We were starting to get people behind us again, and it felt like we were about to turn a corner.

Little did I know, six months later, everything would be over. Coach Mass was forced out. In the end, taking the UNLV job after Jerry Tarkanian was a no-win proposition for anyone who followed him. It was the most unique sense of loyalty I have ever seen to a former coach.

In some ways, it took moving to Las Vegas for me to fully appreciate a lot of what we had at Villanova. So I wouldn't trade those two years for the world. They provided me with a firsthand glimpse of part of the college basketball experience that was very different from the one I had grown up with.

That would help me later on.

We arrived at Hofstra at a wonderful moment. It's a dynamic university, and it was ready to take off in the mid-90s. The president, Dr. James Shuart, was a former football player at the school and a great guy. Stuart Rabinowitz directed the law school then and today is Hofstra's president. These were energetic leaders interested in growing the university.

Basketball fit into that model.

Every idea I brought to the administration was at least considered. They weren't always implemented overnight, but they gave us the tools we needed to get Hofstra Basketball moving. For instance, as we got ready to host our first Midnight Madness, the event that tips off the season, we knew there was no way we could fill our gym for it. But there was a bar/restaurant on campus, so we had the idea to hold the party there. The administration agreed to it. We turned it into a "New Year's Eve party," counting down to the start of the basketball season on October 15, 1994. Our MC was Dr. Dre, and it actually attracted a good-sized crowd—and earned us some street cred in New York City with players we were hoping to recruit. It became an anticipated annual event, and within a couple of years we were turning people away at the door with a crowd of one thousand already inside.

Thankfully a patient administration and a steady stream of outstanding players from the metropolitan area, including Speedy Claxton and Norman Richardson, were willing to take a chance on our young staff. That allowed us to put plans in motion to build a new facility and eventually win a pair of America East Conference Championships.

It was harder to change the academic culture at Hofstra than it was the basketball culture. The university's rule was that if your grade point average fell below 2.0, you retained your eligibility to compete but sacrificed your scholarship (at that point, you had to pay your own tuition). When I came aboard, we had a player who had lost his scholarship but was still on the team while living in Queens and holding down a job.

The whole thing seemed upside down to me. Having come from Villanova, and UNLV, it was the exact reverse of how we preferred to do things. Our concept was if you fell below the minimum GPA, you could retain your scholarship but would lose the chance to compete in games.

Hofstra's provost, Dr. Herman Berliner, was shocked when I suggested we change the model.

"You would agree to that?" he asked me.

I explained that it would give the athlete the opportunity to do the course work needed to bolster his grades with the incentive of returning to the team. It would also improve his chances of earning a degree, even if he never returned to competition. I told Dr. Berliner how important that was to me and how I believed it would benefit the program in the long run.

After a few months, the change was made.

A short while later, I was called to the office of Hofstra's football coach, Joe Gardi. Coach Gardi was the main event on campus then, a former New York Jets defensive coordinator who had the Pride rolling in Division I-AA. He was an old-school Bear Bryant type of coach, and even though he was from New Jersey, I swear I heard a southern drawl when he spoke. The football program was king at Hofstra then, drawing great crowds and putting players like Wayne Chrebet into the NFL. Coach Gardi exuded toughness, and he was always very good to me, but I knew my place in the pecking order. When we would do alumni functions, his line to the crowd was: "Jay Wright might be the man, but I'm the show."

On that day in his office, Coach asked, "Son, what do you think you're doing?"

Nothing got done in the athletic department without his consent. So there were times—such as this one—when I would be summoned and, in a grandfatherly and polite way, be reminded to stay in my lane.

I explained my position. I honestly felt it was more important to encourage our players to keep their grades up and get their degrees than it was to punish them financially—and potentially make it even harder on them academically—than to continue to benefit from their play on the court or on the field.

It took some time, but a few years later, Coach Gardi came around to my way of thinking.

As for our performance on the court, one thing was clear: I wasn't focused on winning championships as much as building a culture. When I got to Hofstra, we were listed 295 out of 302 teams in the Division I RPI. We had good, blue-collar, New York City Catholic League players like Jim Shaffer and John Mavroukas and three or four more players from California. All were terrific kids, and we had energetic practices. We played hard and hustled. Everyone was impressed with that.

But we only won thirty-one games in our first three seasons.

In fact, there's one moment that highlights just how zeroed in I was on that long-term view. One day in the fall of 1997, while sitting in the living room of a recruit's home in Queens, one of the recruit's parents said, "We hear you might be fired."

We all had a bit of a laugh over it, and I told them I hadn't heard anything about my job being in jeopardy. And that was true! I had an assistant coach with me, Tom Pecora, and when we left that day I said to Tom, "Can you believe someone told them we might get fired?" And he said, "We might! We haven't won in four years!" He said it in this funny, New York sort of way, but he was only half kidding. And I'll admit, I was shocked.

Honestly, it had never occurred to me. Looking back on it now, it's fair to say I was naively focused. Our overall record entering our fourth year was 31–46, but somehow I wasn't worried about it at all. But then it hit me, and I thought, *Well, if we go down, we're gonna go down our way. I don't want to be out of coaching, looking back and thinking, I wish I had done it my way.* And my way was very much the Villanova way: Focus on the players as student-athletes—students first, athletes second—with Coach Mass levels of attention, meaning the sort of care I would give to my own family.

We may have had a losing record, but we were going in a good direction. We were getting good kids, and those kids were all graduating. These were young men who knew that there was more to life than just basketball, and the skills they had could help them be part of something bigger. So I knew we were getting there with the culture. It was just taking time.

The idea of building a culture isn't unique to me, or to Villanova, of course. I've looked to all sorts of role models, both college and pro, to help shape my understanding of what building a culture means to any program. I've looked at what Pat Riley did with the Knicks. I've looked at the New England Patriots. I've spent time with Al Groh, who coached the Jets before his long run at the University of Virginia. I've looked to Bill Parcells. Mike Krzyzewski built a great culture at

Duke. (A few years later, when I served as head coach of USA Basketball and the former Blue Devil Jeff Capel was my assistant coach, I jumped at the chance to interrogate Jeff about Coach K, usually over a beer and a cigar.)

I assumed everyone else around me at Hofstra understood the long-term goals of what we were building. But not all of them did. Some people just didn't get it. They just wanted to know if we were winning or not.

Patty and I loved everything about Hofstra—the people, the area, our friends, Rockville Centre. I'm proud to say that many of my ideas that were put into motion there worked and worked well. A new on-campus arena opened in 1999, thanks to some generous donations from wealthy alumni. (Of course, Speedy Claxton and his teammates had more to do with it than anyone else.) And over time, our performance on the court caught up to the improvements we were making to the culture.

In 2000, we earned the right to host the America East Championship game. At the mid-major level, that game is your national championship. In a one-bid league—meaning only the winner of the conference tournament gets an invitation to March Madness—the runner-up wasn't even guaranteed a place in the NIT at that time.

The title game was on ESPN, but what excited our Long Island fan base most was the fact that the wildly popular WFAN hosts Mike Francesa and Chris Russo, a.k.a. "Mike and the Mad Dog," broadcast the game on the radio. To many, the arrival of those New York City sports-talk icons signaled that Hofstra Basketball had truly arrived.

I was probably as nervous for that championship game in 2000 as for any game I have ever coached. We were at home and expected to win. When we did, it was exhilarating and—in our sixth year—a tremendous relief.

Winning the following year was fantastic too. Bringing home two America East titles was one of the great thrills of my life. It had taken so long to get there. And it meant the world to everyone at Hofstra to be on that kind of stage.

But the reality was I hadn't yet tested myself at the highest level.

When the Pride reached the NCAA Tournament, we had to be playing at our absolute best to hang with the highly seeded teams we faced in the first round. For all the gains we had made on Long Island, it felt like there was more out there.

The dream of returning to Villanova never evaporated, of course. I continued to follow the Wildcats closely. On recruiting trips, my assistants knew that the car radio had to be tuned to 1210 WPHT, the 50,000-watt Philadelphia radio station, whenever a Villanova game was on. We even maintained a summer basketball camp in Bucks County.

Yet I didn't spend a lot of time thinking about coaching at Villanova any time soon. Steve Lappas had succeeded Coach Massimino and had put together a lot of 20-win seasons. I would always be a fan of the 'Cats, but professionally it felt like my future would take me elsewhere. That's not unusual in college athletics. You go where the opportunities are. It's rare when the stars align to give you the chance to go home.

I fully understood that. I also realized that much of my career track and life track were attributable to faith. God's got a plan, and I came to believe that it's my job to give my best effort. That's it. *Wherever God decides my life should go, I'll deal with it.* That's the way I've always coached too. As long as we were making our best effort, that was what counted the most.

As I was about to learn, staying true to that attitude can sometimes lead you to exactly where you want to go.

Prayers Answered

Over the course of a few days at the conclusion of the 2000–2001 season at Hofstra, shortly after UCLA knocked us out of the NCAA Tournament, things began to move rapidly. Our success had attracted the attention of some programs in leagues like the Southeastern Conference and, yes, the Big East. I had been labeled a "hot" coach, which struck me as ironic since only a few years earlier people speculated that our staff might not survive at Hofstra. But that's the life of a college coach.

Bob Mulcahy, the athletic director at Rutgers at that time, is a Villanova alumnus and a friend. The Scarlet Knights were in the market for a new head basketball coach, and it seemed like a natural fit for me. The school is located in Piscataway, New Jersey, less than an hour's drive from Bucks County. Rutgers was then a member of the Big East (it has since migrated to the Big Ten), and Bob made a convincing pitch about the future he envisioned for the basketball program.

Patty and I had agreed to come to campus for a meeting, and it felt like we were moving down the road to an agreement. Then, on a Friday afternoon, word came that Steve Lappas was leaving Villanova. (He would accept the head coaching position at the University of Massachusetts a few days later.)

Before I knew it, I was seated in a New Jersey restaurant with Villanova's athletic director, Vince Nicastro. By Tuesday afternoon—March 27, 2001—we were in the Pavilion for a press conference introducing me as the head coach.

I will be forever grateful for the gracious manner in which Bob Mulcahy handled the news. He couldn't have been classier about it. I think he understood that if not for the Villanova job becoming available, I likely would have moved over to Rutgers.

To call this my dream job is an understatement. I felt as if I had come home.

The tall twin spires of the St. Thomas of Villanova Church, the stately stone buildings and winding paths—all of it was comforting as I confronted the nerves of what, for me, amounted to stepping into Coach Mass' shoes. And those were some massive shoes to fill! But perhaps the most comforting factor of all was the presence of Father Lazor. I was so glad he was still there.

Sadly, Father Lazor's health began to fail not long after we returned to Villanova. He was getting up there in age, and yet even as his body was in decline, his mind and will remained strong. I still have vivid memories of that time and some of the unforgettable messages that Father Lazor had for our team. He was especially thrilled to show us around Rome during a foreign tour we took shortly after I started—even though he was mostly confined to a wheelchair.

As a young Augustinian, Father Lazor had spent several years of his ministry stationed at the Vatican. When we reached the Holy City, Father wasn't about to let a wheelchair diminish the moment. He was utterly determined to show our players and staff the Vatican City he had come to love as a young priest. When our official tour ended, Father motioned for Jair Veldhuis, a 6'9" forward, to wheel him to an area where he could address us. He stood up from his wheelchair and proceeded to share what it had meant to him to live so close to the epicenter of the Roman Catholic faith.

I know that our players cherished seeing his joy in that moment just as much as I did.

As a team, we cover some miles during the basketball season. Father Lazor never backed away from the challenge of that, even though he was suffering. When he was saying Mass near the end of his life you could see the pain he was in. Still, he wouldn't give in. Even when it came to simple things, like climbing the stairs onto the bus, Father Lazor accepted help reluctantly.

When it came time for Father to retire from his duties as team chaplain in 2005, I was concerned. I couldn't imagine how we could ever replace him, and I had a hard time envisioning how our program would move forward without Father Lazor holding his seat on the end of our bench.

My worries were unfounded. The man who would teach us all the important lesson about sunsets and sunrises was about to come into our lives.

Before he retired, Father Lazor introduced us to one of his Augustinian brothers and his ultimate successor: a man named Father Rob Hagan, O.S.A. It didn't take long for us to realize Villanova Basketball had been blessed yet again.

We quickly learned that Father Rob was a local product, the pride of St. Dorothy Parish, Cardinal O'Hara High School, and, of course, Villanova class of '87. We heard all about his law degree and his time spent in courtrooms and were surprised to learn that he had just been ordained as a priest in September 2003.

Of course, those details fell far short of taking the measure of the man, but we discerned that pretty quickly as well.

The power of that introduction was not lost on me.

Getting through big transitions—realizing that after losses, even personal losses and sad moments, sometimes great things occur—seemed to be a recurring theme in my life. In fact, it's a theme that would come about a full ten years down the road, as we headed into our 2015–2016 season—when after the crushing loss to NC State, we would suffer yet another unexpected blow.

4

Be Here Now

―――――――

THE SURPRISE CAME early one morning, in the quiet of my office.

After a tough loss, it's customary for me to sit down with each of our guys. I usually wait a bit, until we've all had a little time to decompress. That second-round loss required a lot of decompression. There were two weeks' worth of NCAA games left to be played, and our early exit was brought up every time someone talked about the biggest upsets of the tournament.

We all dealt with it differently. Some guys avoided watching the games or reading about them, although that's hard to do in the age of social media. With no practices to attend, the players have more time on their hands too. They can feel the disappointment in the hearts and minds of the other students they walk by on campus or sit next to in class.

After the NC State loss, I met with the whole team several times before I started doing the individual sit-downs. I just wanted to make sure our guys felt good about themselves as a group. They'd given us more consistent effort on every single night than maybe any team we'd ever had. It was important to me that those guys knew how proud I was that they'd come to work every day—and knew that they could do that in the real world too. They *brought it*. With great attitudes and commitment.

When the private one-on-one sessions started, I expected to hear some honest feedback. We put everything on the table in our program. I want to hear from them—raw, real—and I always share my thoughts and feelings openly too.

What I didn't expect was for Dylan Ennis, the lovable, fearless player who'd taken that last shot in our last game—the shot that didn't drop—to walk in and tell me that he wanted to leave Villanova. He said he planned to graduate in May and then complete his final year of basketball eligibility as a graduate transfer at another institution.

I was absolutely stunned.

Dylan had transferred to Villanova in the spring of 2012 after a strong debut at Rice University. His desire then was to get closer to his family in Brampton, Ontario, and to play on the stage of the Big East. We were in a transition period at that time after a 13–19 season and eager to add to our guard corps. When we inquired about Dylan, the word was he was a terrific young man. Our visit with him went well. We were sold.

Dylan picked Villanova and gave us all a boost. Even though we knew he would have to sit out a year before becoming eligible to play in games (an NCAA rule), we were happy to have another guard of his skill level in the program. (We were hearing good things at that point about the recovery of our incoming freshman guard, Ryan "Arch" Arcidiacono, who had back surgery during his senior year of high school, but we couldn't be entirely sure how long it would take him to get back to full speed.)

Over the next three years, Dylan Ennis turned out to be everything we want a Villanova Basketball player to be. He came here with great enthusiasm during a period when we were trying to climb back into Big East contention. Even in 2012–2013, when he was sitting out as a transfer, he had a great impact on our team in practice with his vigor and work ethic.

We tell all of our players that they are very fortunate to be a part of this student body. The Villanova players live on campus all four of their years here because we want them to be a part of the community. We encourage them to give back to the student body because their classmates are the ones who fill that end-zone section of the Pavilion at every one of our home games, bringing energy to our home floor. The best way to return that favor is to be approachable and outgoing and to develop relationships with students who aren't on the basketball team. Dylan did that so well.

As a student, he was well respected by the faculty. He is a sociable and engaging guy with a knack for making friends wherever he goes. His fellow students and our fans loved him. In a lot of ways, he was a shining light for us on campus.

And on the court, he just kept getting better. He didn't have quite the sophomore season he'd hoped for, but by the time he reached his junior year, he was an elite defender. Some of his blocked shots were unreal. I don't know if anyone his size (6'2") has blocked as many shots for us as he did. In the summer and fall of '14 he shocked a lot of people—even our staff, to some degree—when he beat out Josh Hart for the open spot in the starting lineup vacated by the graduation of James Bell. Josh played well that pre-season, but Dylan was outstanding. We had to pick a starter, and the consensus among the staff was that Dylan's experience and intangibles, along with his talent, earned him that spot.

Thanks to his infectious personality, Dylan was on track to become one of our captains in 2015–2016, alongside Ryan and Daniel. I had that conversation with him numerous times during his junior year, and he seemed eager to assume a leadership role. I stuck with him late in the NC State game even though he was having a tough shooting night because I believed in him, and I knew his teammates had confidence in him.

So when Dylan told me of his plans to transfer, it was nothing we had prepared for. I had thought it might have been a possibility a year earlier, after he struggled offensively during his first season with us and would still have two years of eligibility remaining if he had transferred. But given the impact he had on our team in 2014–2015, it felt to me like he was all in.

"Why?" I asked him.

"You always tell us that if we don't feel like this program is going to get us to be the best man we can be, the best student we can be, or the best player we can be, we should go elsewhere," he replied.

He was right, of course. I did tell my players that. And I meant it.

Dylan's goal was to become a pro point guard (like his brother Tyler, who had played a season at Syracuse before being drafted by the Phoenix Suns), and he felt like our style of play wouldn't allow him to get to where he wanted to go. Since he was on target to graduate in May, he felt a different college program would give him a better chance to showcase his talent during his final year of eligibility.

In our program, we share the basketball. That's just what we do. And it works for us. I didn't think that would hurt Dylan's prospects. I thought he would get the chance to be a pro point guard if he remained with us, but I respected everything about how he handled this decision. He was open and honest with me. He was logical in his thinking. He had a clear objective and a path he wanted to take to reach it. In his three years with us, Dylan had done everything we'd asked him to. He had grown into a great man and become a better player. So I told him that we would help him find a new home, and that's what we did. He wound up transferring to the University of Oregon.

Even though I respected Dylan and his choice, it crushed me. The contributions he made to our team were not going to be easily replaced. I believed he was set to become one of the best guards in the country in his final season of college basketball, and I didn't see how we could recover from his absence. Yes, we had a couple of really talented incoming freshmen, Jalen Brunson and Donte DiVincenzo, set to join us. But as good as Jalen and Donte were, they would be freshmen. Instead of three senior starters, we would only have two.

How could we get back up and compete the next year after losing an integral part of what made us Big East regular season and tournament champions, with a team that felt too young?

In hindsight, I was clearly focused on the "sunset" part of what was happening.

After Dylan transferred to Oregon, I stayed in touch via text and was glad to find that he was still very supportive of our team. Unfortunately, he suffered a foot injury that caused him to miss most of the 2015–2016 season, but we were more than happy to write a letter on his behalf to the NCAA, in support of his request for a sixth year of eligibility. (The request was granted in June 2016.) By the time you read this, it is my hope that Dylan will have had a phenomenal season with the Ducks and will be well on his way to earning his master's degree.

We would use Dylan's case as a positive example to our players too.

Dylan thought his best chance to go pro was to go elsewhere. We of course want our guys to believe that their best chance to be a pro is to stay here. But we can honestly say to our players, "If you don't think that's the case, we'll help you find the right place for *you*. We have done it before." Having that kind integrity with our guys gives as much back to us as it does to them, because we know that anyone who stays here truly believes that this is the best place for them to be.

Opportunity Rises

With Dylan's decision set, we looked once again at our roster. Roster management never really stops in modern college basketball, and in our program, Baker Dunleavy keeps us on course with the aid of Ashley Howard and Kyle Neptune. Our staff is plugged-in, which is a must if we want to be ready when opportunities arise.

Just as we came to grips with Dylan's news, we got word that a gifted young wing player we had previously recruited might be able to join us at Villanova after all.

Eric Paschall is a 6'6" guard from Dobbs Ferry, New York, who had played at the St. Thomas More School in Connecticut, the alma mater of some outstanding former Villanova players, including Gary Buchanan, Dwayne Anderson, and Antonio Pena. While he was at St. Thomas More, Eric decided to attend Fordham University to play for Tom Pecora, my former Hofstra assistant who, in his own direct and witty way, had opened my eyes to the possibility of our staff getting fired at Hofstra. I met Tom at the Villanova Basketball camp back in 1985. We had worked together at Villanova and UNLV for Coach Mass, and then side by side during my seven years at Hofstra. Tom succeeded me as the head coach at Hofstra when I returned to Villanova in 2001. In 2010, he took the top spot at Fordham, where my son Collin would attend college beginning in 2012.

We'd been in the early stages of recruiting Eric for Villanova before he announced his choice of Fordham. Tom had been on him early and developed a great relationship with Eric and his parents. When Eric decided to go with Tom I was a little ticked at myself for not having pursued him more vigorously. As disappointed as we were at Eric's announcement, I at least felt good that he would be with someone I really respected as a coach and friend.

With both Tom and Collin at Fordham, we followed the Rams as closely as we could. Our family watched their games on television in 2014–2015, and we could see how quickly Eric had become a great player. None of us were surprised when he was named the Atlantic 10 Rookie of the Year.

During those months, I would occasionally ask Collin about Eric. Did he know anything about him? What was he like? Collin told me that he didn't know Eric well, but that he had a reputation as one of the nicest kids on campus. People seemed to love the guy. Those words really struck me. I was happy for Tom that he had a talented kid, a Rookie of the Year, who was an outstanding young man. I knew Tom would get the best out of a player like that, and I was sure Eric loved Tom as his coach.

So it came as an unpleasant surprise to learn that Fordham decided to let Tom go after the 2014–2015 season. He had all these great young players who had come there for him, and I believe he would have had them positioned to be a good team again soon.

A few days later, Tom told me that he didn't think Eric would want to stay at Fordham to play for a new coach. When Tom suggested that Eric would be a great fit for our program, I immediately thought back to those conversations with Collin. We made contact with Eric, and he seemed receptive to us. But we also knew that schools like Florida and Kansas were interested too.

We hosted Eric and his parents, Juan Eric Paschall and Cecelia Brooks-Paschall, for an official visit. They were so humble, and given how well Eric had played as a freshman, we asked ourselves as a staff: Is this situation too good to be true? At Villanova, we haven't pursued many transfers. Dylan Ennis and Tony Chennault are the only transfers we have brought in during our time here. Yet we worked as hard on Eric as on any player we have ever recruited.

In the recruiting process, everyone tells you the player you're after is a great kid. But you can't always be sure that these sources appreciate the same values you're looking for in a young man. In this case, though, our two key references were a great friend and my son, both of whom had spent a year on campus with the kid. It was the best kind of validation you could get.

By this time, I *really* wanted Eric on our team, so when he visited the University of Florida, we were worried. Billy Donovan was still the coach (he moved to the Oklahoma City Thunder a short while later), and that's tough competition. Billy is a New York guy who knew the family and was close to Tom too. But, as it turned out, that visit to Gainesville worked to our advantage. Eric decided he wasn't eager to go through the recruiting process any longer, and he wanted to be closer to home. If he had visited Kansas or any of the other big-time places, who knows what may have happened? When we got the word from Eric that he was in, it was a great day to be a Wildcat.

Eric would have to sit out the 2015–2016 season as a transfer, but I knew he would still play an important role in our success. Whether a guy is redshirting or transferring in, his year of ineligibility is extremely valuable. It allows him to become immersed in the Villanova culture. He gets to learn our system without having to deal with making mistakes during games, and I believe our coaching staff is as good as any in the country at developing players. Strength coach John Shackleton, Baker, Ash, and Kyle all do sensational work with these players on a daily basis.

I also knew that adding a teammate who was so clearly well liked by his peers would serve our team well, helping to fill the void that Dylan's absence was sure to leave.

And just like that, we were whole again.

Honor Those Who Came Before You

With our 2015–2016 roster set, we turned our attention to the next major event on our calendar. Each April we host what for years was known as the Basketball Banquet but is now called the Basketball Awards Ceremony. Since 2009, it has been held on the floor of the Pavilion, and it has become an evening where all of Villanova gathers to salute both the season just passed and our heritage.

When I came to Villanova as an assistant in 1987, one of the things that hit me was the amount of passion former Wildcat players had for this program. I got the chance to meet a lot of the alumni whom I had watched growing up in the area: Wali Jones, Bill Melchionni, and so many more. I saw how successful these men were in their careers, both in basketball and after their playing careers ended. It blew me away.

> **BEYOND BASKETBALL**
>
> *Tradition Never Graduates*
>
> We all need to appreciate that, as part of any organization or team, there are those who have laid the foundation for us. Recognizing the organization or individuals who came before us is an acknowledgment that our success is their success too.

When I went to Hofstra in 1994, I immediately noticed that we didn't have that with the Pride. That passion from the program's heritage was missing. We talked about it as a staff, and we decided that if we wanted to grow, we needed to build that kind of connection to the past. We reached out to everyone we could who had played basketball for Hofstra and honored some of the successful teams they had there. There were a handful of them, including one coached by the great Butch van Breda Kolff, and another from the 1976–1977 season (23–8) that we brought back all the time.

In contrast, Villanova had somewhere between twenty and thirty teams that were worthy of special recognition. When I took the job here I knew that the greatest asset this program had was its history and its basketball alumni. I have always believed that the best college programs in any sport have tradition. I wanted to do everything we could to make sure that the alumni knew how important they were to Villanova and, most important, that our current players respected our history.

I recall in the summer of 2001 being at our camp and asking some of the current players if they knew anything about the men whose jerseys were retired in the Pavilion rafters. Some of them didn't know who Paul Arizin or Keith Herron were. We made a point then to bring the current players to the Pavilion, beneath where those jerseys hang, and explain to them who each of these men were and some of the great things they had done in college basketball.

We tried to set up every event possible—alumni games, a summer golf outing, a gala—to remind our players of this history. I can still recall when the late Howard Porter, who lived in Minnesota, visited us for practice and a team dinner in the Pavilion Press Room in the mid-2000s, not long before he died in 2007. Prior to his arrival, I took a few minutes in the locker room to share with the players what Mr. Porter had meant to this program. He wasn't just an All-American but was also generally viewed as one of the best to have ever played at the school—and there are some who will tell you he *was* the best.

Then, when the guys had a chance to meet Mr. Porter, they saw his humility and grace. Here was a player who helped lead Villanova to an NCAA Finals appearance, and yet he conducted himself as a gentleman with no airs about him.

Those are the kinds of moments that are so valuable in reinforcing our culture.

This is why the awards banquet is so important. Forty to fifty former players attend each year, and we introduce every one of them to the audience. These basketball alumni help us present the awards from the podium, and we always make sure to honor those former players or coaches who have passed away in the preceding twelve months too.

Coach Jack Kraft, who won more than seventy-one percent of the games he coached at Villanova from 1961 to 1973, died in 2014 at the age of ninety-three. That was a huge loss for our program, and for me personally. As a kid I attended the Jack Kraft Basketball Camp. I also knew that he had a home in Stone Harbor, New Jersey, along the Jersey Shore. When our family would vacation nearby, I would walk up and down the street where he lived, just hoping to catch a glimpse of him. He was that much of a giant to me.

I never saw him. I remember thinking, *How can you have a house at the beach and never be there?* Now that I'm a head coach myself, I can appreciate that. But I try to always remember what a thrill it would have been for me to have seen the Villanova coach when I was a child. When I see children now I do my best to stop and spend a minute or two with them because I know what that would have meant to me.

It was thrilling for me to finally meet Coach Kraft when I joined the staff as an assistant coach here in '87, but it wasn't until I took over as head coach that I really got to know him.

A few days after I was introduced as the new head coach of Villanova, I received an invitation from Bernie Schaffer, a great basketball alumnus from the class of '66, to attend a lunch and golf outing at the Waynesboro Country Club. We were joined by a group of basketball alumni from 1962 to 1966—and Coach Kraft was there as well.

That day brings a smile to my face when I think of it now. I realized that those players hadn't come just to meet the new coach. They'd come to see their old coach. The love and esteem they had for Coach Kraft was immediately apparent, and it reminded me just what a special place I had been lucky enough to return to.

Jack Kraft was such a humble man. The respect he had for people, be they his players, me as the new head coach, or the staff serving us lunch, was so impressive. He was a Villanova icon. It was so rewarding to see that someone I admired as a kid was all that I had imagined him to be—and more. (It was the same way when I first met Coach Mass.)

When we spoke that day in 2001, I told Coach Kraft that I wanted him to be a big part of what we were doing as a program. He told me that he would do anything we needed him to. He said: "I'll always be there for you, but I don't want to be in the way." Any event we asked him to come back to he attended. Never did he ask for any accolades or special treatment. He simply got into his car, drove the hundred minutes (or more) to Villanova from Avalon, New Jersey, attended the event, and then got behind the wheel for the long ride home.

Coach Kraft passed away on Thursday, August 28, 2014. Labor Day fell on Monday, September 1. His funeral was held in Avalon on September 4, and while a lot of his former players were able to be there, there were more who couldn't make it on short notice at such a busy time of year. So we thought it would make sense to have some kind of memorial service for him. With so many alumni planning to attend the Basketball Banquet the following April, one of Coach's former players, Jim McMonagle, came up with the idea of holding a Mass in his honor before the banquet. We consulted with Father Rob and were able to make it happen.

I'm so glad we did. The St. Thomas of Villanova Chapel was packed. Our university president, the Reverend Peter M. Donohue, O.S.A., served as the main celebrant along with university vice president the Reverend John Stack, O.S.A., on the altar. It was one of the most beautiful moments I have witnessed at Villanova. The president of the university was saying a Mass to honor the memory of the former basketball coach with a chapel jammed with the Kraft family and many of his former players. Fran O'Hanlon, the great Wildcat point guard who now coaches Lafayette, delivered an unforgettable eulogy. The late Howard Porter was there in spirit, represented by his wife, Theresa Neal.

You could just feel the love and respect for Coach Kraft, for Villanova Basketball, and for the university in that ceremony. It moved me then and still does now.

All of us who attended the Mass then made our way from the center of campus to the east side, where the Pavilion and the Jake Nevin Field House—the 'Cats homes during Coach Kraft's tenure—sit in adjoining buildings.

To me the awards banquet is less about the season just passed, no matter how successful or unsuccessful it may have been, than it is a celebration of Villanova's tradition. There are season awards given to the current players, and we take pride in those. But we want everyone on the floor of the Pavilion to appreciate how fortunate all of us are to be a part of this tradition.

The most moving portion of the banquet always comes near its end, when each graduating senior offers a few remarks. (This includes walk-ons and a representative of our student managers too, since they all play such important roles.) During our days at Hofstra, we conducted a banquet with the same kind of format. The first few years, the lineup had me speaking after the seniors offered their comments, but each time I tried, my emotions overwhelmed me and I struggled to say what I wanted to. Lesson learned: no words from me after the seniors address the crowd. Instead, I now introduce them—which I still find difficult—and watch them deliver their thoughts.

Without fail, each senior speech brings home to me the love and respect they have for the staff, the program, and the people who make up this campus community. That's more important to me than any wins or championships.

When JayVaughn Pinkston stood up in front of a crowd of more than nine hundred people that night, he said, "I came here a boy. I leave here a man." It just put the cherry on top of how he had come to the end of his Villanova journey. He was set to graduate a few weeks later, and while his road had been winding at times, he had reached the destination we all were working toward—no one more so than JayVaughn himself.

As we left the Pavilion that night, having honored the past, it was time to turn our attention firmly to 2015–2016. We resumed workouts with the returning players while Darrun, JayVaughn, and Dylan worked individually with our assistants to prepare for the next phase of their basketball lives.

Each year, when the NCAA crowns a champion, we see it as an opportunity to measure ourselves against what that team achieved. That season the champion was Duke. We took a long look in the mirror and asked ourselves: *How far are we from that level?*

There is a basketball axiom that can be boiled down to this: Everyone tries to get better from November to March, but the time when there are really strides to be taken is from April to October, when the only ones watching are your teammates and coaches. Don't worry about being a showman when the lights are on. Strive to be better in the present and the rewards will come. It's a theme we touch on all the time: Be here now.

We would soon say goodbye to Darrun, Dylan, and JayVaughn. But for the returning players the time to improve was *now*. Our first steps would be just as important as the ones we would take twelve months later in Houston.

No time like the present—even in April.

5

The Real Progress Comes When No One's Watching

———

WHEN WE FIRST pull the team together for practices in April, the following season seems a long way off. The school year is winding down. Spring fever is in the air all over campus. It's easy for the guys to want to slack off a little bit or allow themselves to lose focus. So there are a couple of stories that Father Rob uses to help keep our players sharp and get them fired up.

Father Rob's versions of these stories are drawn from the Bible (Mark 12:38–44 and Luke 9:10–17, for those interested in reading the actual passages), but their power has nothing to do with any particular religion.

"The first story goes like this: There is a poor woman who sits at the table every night, praying she wins the lottery," Father Rob says. "There are bills to pay and she arises each morning and prays, 'Dear God, I have to pay my children's tuition. Help me win the lottery.'

"She arises the next morning and prays, 'Dear God, I've got to make my car payment. Help me win the lottery.'

"She arises the next morning and prays, 'Dear God, I've got to pay my mortgage. Help me win the lottery.'

"The next morning she arises and prays, 'Dear God—' and before she can finish, God interrupts her and says, 'Work with me here: *You have to buy a ticket!*'"

The guys all laugh at that, of course. It's funny because we know in our guts that it speaks to something true.

"It's good to ask God for help," Father Rob explains, "but we also ought to be willing to put forth the effort each day."

That sets him up for the second story. "We can also recall the poor widow in the synagogue," he says. "People were putting large sums in the collection basket and she may have felt embarrassed putting in her only two cents. But then Jesus holds her up as an example and applauds her contribution. 'It may have been small in the eyes of the world,' He says, 'but what mattered most was the love with which she offered it—and that it was all she had to give.'

"When we give of ourselves, our two cents can often be a difference maker. Let's not expect others to do what we ourselves could have done had we pulled together and all put our two cents in."

If that was where he ended his talks, it would certainly have had an impact. But Father Rob always takes it someplace deeper. I recall him expanding on these two stories on a few occasions to make his words resonate with exactly what some of our players were feeling. In those April 2015 practices, these lessons were particularly poignant given how the season had just ended and how closely our team would be scrutinized the following year.

"Sometimes we don't believe we have enough," he said. "We convince ourselves we're not big enough or strong enough or smart

The Reverend Rob Hagan, O.S.A., our team chaplain, is officially Villanova's Associate Athletics Director in charge of Sports Medicine and Strength and Conditioning. But we just call him Father Rob. Here he is alongside his mother, Marilyn Hagan, as well as Patty and me.

enough for the task we are faced with. Often we come to Villanova and are surrounded by so much talent that we begin to wonder if we're talented enough. So we wait for others to step up while all along we had something meaningful to offer.

"Don't ever think that what you have to offer is insignificant," he said. "Don't be afraid to put your two cents in. Everyone has something to give and it has value. Let it not be said that we could have given more for each other, or that we held back and expected it to come from someone else.

"Step up, trusting and believing that when I give my all for my brothers and sisters, God's grace can help ensure that my two cents combined with yours is enough to tip the scale and move mountains.

"When we follow this example," he concluded, "we can be at peace with the result. We may not hit the lottery, but our whole two cents will always produce a winning ticket."

Our April workouts aren't the same types of sessions we have in-season. They are shorter and more focused on skill development than our game preparation, when we're worried about a specific opponent. But the first order of business was spelling out our expectations for our seniors-to-be—primarily Ryan Arcidiacono and Daniel Ochefu in their roles as next men up on the long roll call of Villanova team captains.

To us, the seniors are an extension of the coaching staff. They've been around for three years and offer extremely valuable input. That was especially true for Arch and Daniel, who had actually spent more time in the program than two of our assistant coaches, Ashley Howard and Kyle Neptune, who joined us in 2013. Arch and Daniel brought great understanding of the values we prize most.

But assuming that new role isn't merely a matter of flipping the page on a calendar. When you are an underclassman, it may seem like the status that comes with being a senior is nothing more than a perk of continuous service. Up close, it looks much different than that. I think the new seniors realize quickly that they are now being counted on to contribute their thoughts on the team to us regularly, and there is a great responsibility in that.

At Villanova there have been a lot of guys who have finished their careers with a flourish in their final season. The incoming seniors want to live up to that. It can cause them to feel pressure. That's something we try to work through in the spring and summer, and we were very fortunate that one of our key seniors knew a little something about leadership already.

The first time I met Ryan Arcidiacono, he was just beginning ninth grade. His father, Joe Arch, as everyone calls him, was a former Villanova football player who had played alongside Howie Long, the future NFL Hall of Famer, on the Wildcats' defensive line from 1976 to 1980. Ryan's mom, Patti, is also a Villanova graduate. We later discovered that she and my wife had mutual friends during their time as undergraduates.

At the time, we were recruiting a gifted guard at Pennsbury High School named Dalton Pepper, who would later go on to play at West Virginia and Temple. Jason Donnelly, who was then part of our coaching staff (and is still a key part of our team on the development side as the Executive Director of the Villanova Athletic Fund), was with me. Adam Bowen, who had volunteered as a manager for us in July 2007 while we were preparing to lead a USA Basketball team to the Pan American Games in Argentina, was coaching in Bucks County and pointed to Ryan, telling Jason and me that Ryan was "the next great Villanova guard."

We hear that kind of statement often while recruiting, especially when we're near home. Friends and fans of the young players are excited about what they see. But as coaches we have to make a more detached evaluation, and be careful about allowing too much sentiment to creep into the process. It sounded like the makings of a great story, but we needed to be certain that Ryan fit at Villanova.

By the time he was a sophomore at Neshaminy High School, Ryan had begun to receive some regional Division I interest. We monitored his progress but weren't yet prepared to offer a scholarship—in part because it's different when you bring in a local kid who the community believes will be a star. If for some reason the player doesn't have the college career we all hope he will, there is a lot of potential for hurt feelings.

So I was cautious—and it almost cost us.

During the summer between his sophomore and junior years, Ryan's recruitment took off. Billy Donovan, who'd been a great guard himself during his career at Providence, was all in on Arch. (As you can tell, Billy and I have similar ideas about what makes a great basketball player.) He had begun flying in via private jet to catch Ryan's workouts during evaluation periods. North Carolina and Kansas were in the mix too.

A turning point for me came when Jason and I were at an AAU game in Neptune, New Jersey. One of the challenges in evaluating Ryan was that in high school games, teams were double- and triple-teaming him because he was so dominant. That can make it tough to get a feel for how a player fits at our level, where defenses can't afford to put their entire focus on one guy. But in this setting, Ryan was competing against a number of prospects who were headed to high-major college programs. It figured to be a good test for a player who was known as a prodigious scorer. I was eager to see how he would perform.

Ryan couldn't make a shot that day. His attempts were long, short, and wide. His dad knew we were there, and I could see him wince every time one of Ryan's shots clanged off the rim. The Arch family probably thought they were going to need to start piling up air miles for flights to Gainesville, home of the Florida Gators.

By the time the game ended I had made a decision: I wanted Arch to be a Wildcat.

It sounds counterintuitive, I realize. But this gets right to the heart of what we value at Villanova. On a day when he couldn't make a basket, Arch did everything else a player could do. He found his teammates with crisp passes. He dug in defensively and dove for loose balls. He kept his composure. He never gave up. In short, he demonstrated every trait we want to see in a Villanova player.

Now we just had to see if we could get him in what quickly turned into a recruiting dogfight.

There was no doubt Arch had made a connection with Billy—and Billy had a lot to offer. He had won back-to-back national championships in 2006 and 2007. He's obviously a terrific coach and had done a lot of work to establish a rapport with Arch. Thankfully, we had a few intangibles working to our advantage, most of them having to do with Arch's close-knit family and its proximity to Villanova in Langhorne, Pennsylvania.

As a parent, when your son or daughter is making a decision on which college to attend, you're put in an interesting spot. It's really the first major adult decision the teenager is making, and you want them to have the confidence to make the final call. At the same time, you have the benefit of life experience they simply can't draw on. It's very tempting to try to make the decision for them, but if you do that you run the risk of them purposely choosing a school you aren't crazy about to demonstrate their independence.

Patty and I have been through the process twice with our sons, Taylor and Collin, both of whom made wise decisions: Taylor graduated from Brown University, and Collin got his degree from Fordham in the spring of 2016. Our daughter, Reilly, was a high school senior who was getting ready to make her decision as I worked on this book.

Ryan took a long look at the University of Florida. We knew he was serious about it and so did his family. Joe and Patti Arch were in that odd parental place of hoping Ryan would end up at Villanova but reluctant to try to impose their will on him. Patti Arch told me flat out at one point that we needed to do a better job of recruiting her son so he would end up where he needed to be. We also felt like Arch's oldest sister, Sabrina, who was very close to her brother, wanted Ryan at Villanova, and she was able to say that to him in a way that his parents really could not.

As we headed into the fall of 2010, Ryan was a priority recruit. I attended every workout of his that NCAA rules permitted me to attend. We had the sense that we were nearing the time when he would make a decision, so we invited Ryan to be our guest at Hoops Mania, Villanova's version of Midnight Madness. Each year the Villanova students pack the Pavilion, and we do our best to give them a good show, capping it with a performance from a musical artist. Past performers have included 50 Cent, Drake, and Nicki Minaj.

Fabolous put on a show that Friday in October, and that hip-hop star's name could not have been more fitting, given how things went. Ryan seemed to have a blast. We were beginning to believe the tide could be turning in our favor.

A few days later, Arch called me to say he was coming to Villanova.

And yes, you *bet* I was fired up when he did!

Only, it wasn't exactly clear sailing from there. Ryan injured his back prior to his senior year of high school. It kept him out of AAU action that summer and probably prevented him from becoming an All-American. The issue lingered into the fall of 2011, and in December it was decided that he would undergo surgery. He missed his entire senior season of high school basketball, save for a ceremonial appearance on Senior Night. The doctors believed that the injury wasn't career threatening, but the back is a tricky area for a basketball player.

As much as we loved Arch, we had to consider the possibility that he might not return as the player we had recruited. That uncertainty contributed to our decision to bring in Tony Chennault, a Philly native and graduate of Saints John Neumann and Maria Goretti Catholic High School, as a transfer from Wake Forest at the end of the 2011–2012 season.

Arch's recovery went according to plan. Once he came to Villanova for the first session of summer school in June 2012, he began to work with Jeff Pierce, our outstanding athletic trainer, who introduced him to a stretching regimen that really helped him over the next four years.

Although Arch had a clean bill of health, we tried to ease him into our routine—much to his dismay. He kept telling us he was fine, but in our minds there were still doubts about whether he could play with the same kind of all-out fervor he did in high school.

Our answer to that question came in one of the first summer team workouts we held in the Davis Center.

JayVaughn Pinkston stood 6'7" and weighed a solid 240 pounds at that point, after having spent a year developing his body in the weight room with Coach Shack. Ryan is 6'3" and was only in the early days of trying to build strength after being limited by nine months of post-surgery rehab.

So when J.P. came barreling down the court with the basketball on a fast break and Arch stepped in to take a charge, every coach in the gym held his breath. JayVaughn plowed into him like a running back making a push for the goal line.

Arch absorbed the blow and bounced right back up.

We all exhaled as quietly as we could.

A few plays later, Arch was leading a fast break and made a move toward the basket. JayVaughn quickly moved his feet in an effort to block Arch's path. Arch lowered his shoulder and knocked J.P. back. I could tell immediately that J.P. had tested the freshman point guard and walked away respecting him.

Not for the last time, I thought that I liked having Ryan Arch on our side. By the midpoint of his freshman season, we promoted him to captain's duties alongside Mouphtaou Yarou and James Bell. Although records weren't kept until the 1970s, we're pretty sure he's the first freshman in Villanova history to earn that honor.

One of the cool things about Ryan coming to Villanova was that he had the same kind of affinity for the Wildcats that a football player from Alabama might have for the Crimson Tide. Ryan grew up watching Randy Foye, Allan Ray, Kyle Lowry, Scottie Reynolds, and the other guys from our teams in the mid- to late 2000s, and he played with the same reckless abandon those guys did. I thought that was special and rare in the Northeast, where there are so many schools with loyal followings. From day one, Arch took more pride in putting on a Villanova jersey than any player we've ever had.

Daniel Ochefu, meanwhile, became a captain in the more customary way, as an upperclassman. It was a new role for him and something he had earned with steady progress.

Like Arch, Daniel became a prospect in our backyard. He attended the Westtown School, a thirty-minute drive from campus in West Chester, Pennsylvania. We liked Daniel when we first saw him as a ninth- and tenth-grader, but his basketball skills at that point were raw. His passing ability was certainly intriguing for someone who would grow to be 6'11". But this was a case where we were monitoring his progress early in his career instead of jumping in feetfirst.

We learned quickly that Daniel was a very good student and that his mother, Elizabeth, was a devout Catholic. Her main priority on Daniel's official visit was not to see our offices, meet the staff, or tour the Wells Fargo Center. She wanted to meet Father Rob.

At that time, she told us that it was her belief that Daniel would one day become a Catholic priest.

Daniel's game really blossomed as a high school junior, and we became convinced that he was a good fit for our program. He was an intelligent guy and had unique skills for a forward. It was not unusual to see Daniel on the perimeter, handling the basketball against the press and finding the open man. It gave him a very well-rounded game.

We probably had a harder time convincing Elizabeth that Villanova was the right spot for Daniel than we did the player or his father, Hassan. But Father Rob and the Augustinian values of our university ultimately spelled the difference for us, even with teams such as Temple, Georgetown, and Texas hoping to land him.

A few months after Daniel came to us in the summer of 2012, we kind of got the sense that becoming a priest was not where he envisioned his life going. He was everything we thought we were getting—outgoing, smart, fun-loving, thoughtful, and a hard worker—but in our conversations you could tell that he didn't feel a calling to the priesthood.

One of the big challenges for the two of us during Daniel's fresh-

FIVE TIPS FROM FATHER ROB

Villanova's team chaplain is a source of constant inspiration to the Wildcats. Here are a few of his key messages.

1. To win the lottery, you have to buy a ticket. In other words, you have to be willing to put forth the effort to get the result.

2. Give your two cents. It doesn't matter how big your contribution is: What matters is how much heart you put into it.

3. In the words of Saint Augustine, do not be content with what you are: Push to become what you are not.

4. Do not have a stiff neck. Allow yourself to look around for the larger picture and opportunities to grow.

5. There is a sunrise after every sunset. Eventually you'll see the lessons you've learned from disappointments.

man year was how he was going to address this development with his mom. He fretted over it for a long time. Finally he told her, and I followed up with Elizabeth after they had their conversation. I think Hassan always knew that Daniel didn't feel called to the priesthood, but it took some time for his mother to let go of a dream she'd been carrying for years. Once that issue was resolved, you could see that Daniel felt less pressure.

We used Daniel regularly as a freshman even though we already had a 6'10" senior starting for us in Mouphtaou Yarou. We were able to do that because of Daniel's basketball IQ and the comfort level he had playing away from the basket in the high post. It also allowed Mouph to act as a mentor to Daniel.

Mouph is a unique guy. He came to the United States in 2007 from the Republic of Benin, a nation located on the west coast of Africa. As a kid he had mostly played soccer before being introduced to basketball by his brother. His ability and size gave him an opportunity to come to the States to live with a host family while pursuing academics and basketball. We saw him at Montrose Christian School in Maryland, and he agreed to come to Villanova.

Despite a bout with hepatitis that cost him much of his freshman season and negatively impacted his development, Mouph turned into an important player for us. It took us some time as a staff to identify the best way to use him, but once we did, he played an important role in helping us upset three top-ranked teams during his senior year of 2012–2013.

He made another, less appreciated contribution too.

Mouph was big, strong, mature, and committed to what we were doing when we encouraged him to guide Daniel. They were both really bright guys, but from a basketball standpoint, the greatest gift Mouph gave Daniel is he competed at a high level *every day*. Most high school big guys don't have to bring it daily because they can rely on their size and strength to carry them. But if Daniel tried to take it easy against Mouph in practice, he would get embarrassed. Daniel is very competitive—and was determined not to be embarrassed. He knew he had to be ready every time he stepped onto the court, and that really boosted his development as a young player.

During my time as head coach we've developed a reputation for prioritizing quickness and shooting ability over height, but in 2012–2013 we often started Daniel at 6'11" and Mouph at 6'10". We also had 7'0" Maurice Sutton in the rotation. The fact that those three were going against one another in practice each day helped all of them.

As a staff going into 2015–2016, we felt good about Daniel stepping into a leadership role for a number of reasons. Among them was that he had learned from Mouph, so when Daniel assumed this new role, respect was never an issue. The rest of the guys had seen his work ethic and belief in our value system over time. Even so, it was an adjustment for Daniel. Thinking about everyone else was difficult for him in the beginning. Daniel is very driven to be the best player he can be. Yet even in those first few weeks, Daniel developed an understanding of how the actions of every single player impacted the team—and that made me proud.

We were in the early stages of forging our new identity as the 2015–2016 Wildcats, a group that would be younger than we originally envisioned. There was no doubt that we would be relying on Arch and Daniel as our captains, and there was a perception that they were the only locker room leaders we had.

Given that a lot of fans focus only on the games, I suppose that perception made sense. But that's not quite the complete picture.

Senior Class

There were actually five seniors on our roster heading into 2015–2016, including Patrick Farrell, Henry Lowe, and Kevin Rafferty. All were what are known in college athletics as "walk-ons," meaning they did not enter the program on scholarship. (By NCAA rule, Division I men's teams are allotted thirteen scholarships granted on a yearly basis. We don't always utilize the full allotment of scholarships and award these to walk-ons when available. In 2015–2016 Pat and Henry received scholarships, so they were technically not walk-ons any longer.)

Pat and Henry were in their fourth year on the team in the spring of 2015. Both walked on in the fall of 2012, joining Arch and Daniel as members of the class of 2016. Each came to us from the New York metropolitan area—Pat from Rockville Centre, where Patty and I resided during our tenure at Hofstra, and Henry, or "Hank" as he came to be known by the guys, from New York City.

The freshman foursome of 2012–2013 entered the program as we were trying to bounce back from a season in which we had finished 13–19. There were no seniors on that team, and it forced our junior class of Maalik Wayns, Dominic Cheek, and Mouph to carry a heavy leadership burden. That was on me. Maalik and Dom both took the chance to enter their names into the NBA Draft pool in 2012 and I totally understood. Both of those guys were trying to take care of their families.

We slowly became a better team over the 2012–2013 season thanks to a number of factors, including leadership from Mouph and James Bell, who helped fill the gap created when Dom and Maalik moved on. Tony Chennault added some valuable experience in the backcourt where we needed it, and Arch demonstrated his knack for making big shots early on, draining a three from the corner after Mouph got an offensive rebound to force overtime against No. 5 Syracuse in a game we eventually won.

During the stretch when we began to stamp ourselves as legitimate contenders for an NCAA Tournament bid in January, the television cameras would sometimes focus on the end of our bench. Pat, Henry, and another walk-on, junior Nick McMahon, were coming up with some very creative ways to cheer on their teammates. They soon had their own nickname, "the Bench Mob," and were lauded by the Nova Nation and fans across the country on Twitter.

At first, I wasn't sure how to feel about these celebrations. We loved their enthusiasm but struggled with the thought that they were perhaps caught up in drawing attention to themselves. In the end, I concluded that this team, still looking to create its own identity, needed this visible passion. It was youthful enthusiasm in its purest form, and if it gave their teammates confidence, so much the better.

We did return to the NCAA Tournament that year as a No. 9 seed. We were beaten in the Round of 64 by North Carolina, but had won twenty-two times in a solid bounce-back season.

I sat down with Pat and Henry after that season and told them we appreciated the energy they had delivered to us while not in the lineup. The Bench Mob had played an important role in our revival. But as we moved forward, I thought it best we leave it behind.

Pat and Henry were on board with that. Both are terrific guys and exceptionally bright. They embraced our core values and never lamented losing the spotlight that had come their way.

In 2014–2015, we added another walk-on, Kevin Rafferty, a local product from Malvern, Pennsylvania, who had played college basketball at Tufts University before deciding to transfer home. When he chose to depart from Tufts, he knew there were no basketball guarantees but worked his way onto our active roster after spending the 2013–2014 season as a practice player (meaning he was on the practice court but didn't suit up for games).

As is the case with most walk-ons, the minutes Pat, Henry, and Kevin saw were limited, generally coming long after the outcome had been decided. When any of them entered a game at the Pavilion, the student section inevitably roared. The crowd always urged each of them to shoot whenever the ball came their way, but their charge is no different from anyone else's on our roster: Stay true to our core values by playing for their teammates and coaches.

But to me, the appreciative cheers weren't just about rooting on the little guy. I believe the student body was invested in these guys because they knew and liked them. You could sense the respect level for each one of them, and it was well earned. Their teammates felt the same way.

It was remarkable to me that a few years earlier, we'd had zero seniors in our midst, yet in 2015–2016, we would have five such veterans—five men who were greatly respected in our locker room. They were all still busy adjusting to their roles as we came to the end of the spring 2015 semester, but it was clear to our staff that the ingredients for an impressive leadership group were firmly in place.

Those seniors represented a huge building block, and once again,

Father Rob found just the right words to help inspire them—and all of us—for the journey we'd only just begun.

"In the words of Saint Augustine," he told us, "'Do not be content with what you are if you want to become what you are not yet. Where you have grown pleased with yourself, there you shall remain. Keep pushing forward.'"

6

From Many Good Players, One Special Team

IN THE LIFE of a university, there is no weekend quite like Commencement, when students, faculty, and staff come together to honor the achievements of the graduates and their families. As a basketball program we could not be more proud to be a part of it, especially because of one remarkable fact: Every player who has spent four years in our program over the last forty-plus years has earned his degree.

Weather permitting, the official Commencement ceremony takes place at 4 p.m. on a Friday afternoon in Villanova Stadium, the 12,000-seat home to our terrific FCS football team (2009 NCAA National Champions). Each year, our colleague Arleshia Davidson, whose official title is Special Assistant to the Head Coach but whose duties extend throughout our program, puts together a pre-Commencement reception for our seniors and their families that is beyond awesome. The families are encouraged to bring everyone who can make it, and it creates a beautiful, chaotic scene with upwards of forty people crammed into the office lobby of the Davis Center, spilling over into the adjacent team cinema, where we watch game tape during the season.

After a rain-soaked 2014 Commencement Friday, the 2015 version offered ideal spring weather: sunny skies with temperatures in the mid-70s. By 1 p.m., the Ennis, Hilliard, and Pinkston clans were all present with family members ranging in age from small children to grandparents. We toasted the seniors with apple cider (that's another one of our traditions) before we headed over to the ceremony. I made sure to get a photo of Patty and me with Dylan, Darrun, and Jay-Vaughn in their caps and gowns.

It's not often a college student goes through four years without a hiccup or snag, and that's true for our athletes too. Each one of these graduates endured some low points during his time at Villanova. But in the end, each found a way to the finish line. They were leaving Villanova with what they came for. We would have loved to have written a better ending for

> ## BEYOND BASKETBALL
>
> ### *Be the Connector*
>
> Organizations are dynamic entities. Talented people will come and go. It is a leader's role to be the connective tissue, introducing newcomers to the culture and taking every opportunity to welcome back those who have moved on.

their college basketball careers than a second-round loss at the start of March Madness, but there was no discounting their achievements.

These were successful young men, not just successful basketball players. To us, that's what this monumental day is all about.

Graduation also serves as the start of a new relationship with our graduates. We meet some of them when they are fifteen or sixteen years old. We share a journey together. When they take the final step on that path, we feel a sort of parental pride in seeing them off to begin charting the course of their own lives. If we've done our jobs, they will be able to adapt to any challenge and overcome any obstacle with clear hearts and minds.

In this case, it wouldn't take long for each one of these graduates to confront a new challenge in his basketball career—and to provide inspiration through his mature handling of everything that would come his way.

When Dylan enrolled at Oregon as a graduate transfer, the expectation was that he would fill a key void in Coach Dana Altman's lineup. When I ran into Coach Altman later in the year, he raved about Dylan's work ethic and the kind of young man he is. But in the end, the broken foot he suffered in the fall allowed him to play only two games for the Ducks. It was a shame the folks in Eugene didn't get to see all that Dylan brings to a team, but he kept his spirits up and decided to keep fighting.

Meanwhile, JayVaughn made a strong impression with his toughness and skill leading up to the NBA Draft in June. Even though he wasn't one of the sixty players selected, he earned an invitation to play for his hometown Brooklyn Nets in the NBA Summer League. The communication we had with the Nets indicated that they liked what JayVaughn brought to their franchise. As a former marketing man, I'm also willing to guess that the folks on the business side liked the idea of having someone who grew up a short drive from the Barclays Center on the team.

One moment on the court changed the forecast: Just a few days before his Summer League debut, JayVaughn tore his anterior cruciate ligament during a Nets practice, ending his 2015–2016 season before it began. His first year of professional basketball would be spent rehabilitating his knee.

I was crushed for JayVaughn. The recovery period for that kind of injury is nine to twelve months, and it's a slow, grueling process. As a player, you're cut off from the game that you love and, in a lot of ways, your identity. It's even worse when you aren't yet on the official roster and are without a guaranteed contract.

We were all worried for JayVaughn.

But we didn't give him enough credit.

JayVaughn confronted his injury head-on. He took a disciplined and sensible approach to his recovery, and we knew this because we saw it on a daily basis. Why? Because, in a decision that was reminiscent of the one he made when the university suspended him for getting into a fight during his freshman year, he chose to do his rehab right here at Villanova.

Back in 1988, near the end of my first year as an assistant to Coach Massimino, I was assigned to help compile the field of candidates for the position of athletic trainer. (The legendary Jake Nevin, who had filled that role for decades and helped inspire the 1985 national champions despite being confined to a wheelchair, had died in 1986.) Among the candidates was Jeff Pierce, a graduate of West Chester University who had worked with the Philadelphia Eagles. I recommended Jeff to Coach Mass, and he got the job. He's held it ever since.

One of the things I respect most about Jeff is the bond he shares with our players, especially those who have endured painful and lengthy rehabilitation stints. Early in my tenure as head coach he spent long hours with Jason Fraser, who underwent six surgeries during his college career, and Curtis Sumpter, who had two major knee surgeries in less than a year. Jeff made a powerful connection with those guys and many others over the years. Jason and Curtis trusted him and were able to return from significant injuries to play well in their senior year at Villanova (though Curtis had to be deferred a year to 2006–2007).

The door to Jeff's Davis Center training room remains open to our former players who become professionals, who often elect to work with him when they are faced with lengthy post-surgical rehabilitation efforts. Allan Ray and Mike Nardi both worked their way back to action alongside Jeff while sidelined long after their Villanova careers had ended.

So when JayVaughn decided to spend his rehabilitation with Jeff, we were pleased.

Although we wished JayVaughn were healthy and out chasing his dream, we considered ourselves blessed to see him most days inside the Davis Center. It couldn't have been easy for him, but it was somehow comforting to know one of our captains was close by. Hearing J.P.'s booming voice echo up to our offices on the second floor was music to my ears, and we were all happy to see his positive attitude carry him through that rough patch.

Our other departing captain, Darrun Hilliard, provided inspiration of another kind: He overcame every obstacle in his time at Villanova to wind up being a sought-after NBA Draft pick.

When we first began scouting Darrun, he was a thin and wiry wing player at Liberty High School in Bethlehem, Pennsylvania, an hour's drive up the northeast extension from Villanova. Even though he was beloved in the Lehigh Valley, there wasn't a lot of hype around his recruitment, in part because he hadn't played much on the summer basketball circuit, where national reputations are often made.

As was the case with Arch, we took our time evaluating Darrun.

Everyone we spoke with lauded his character. He was polite and quiet in our conversations, and we had no doubt he would be a terrific teammate. We just had to be certain that his physique (and his psyche) could take the pounding at our level, which is substantial. There is a trait of physical toughness we seek out in players. A player doesn't have to be at a certain weight or muscle ratio, but he does have to possess a desire to use his body and initiate contact at the appropriate times. If we can see that he's trying to avoid contact in games, that's certainly going to factor into our evaluation.

Physical toughness comes in all sizes. You obviously see it in larger forwards we've had, like JayVaughn, Mouphtaou, and Daniel. But it also comes in smaller packages. Mike Nardi had one of the leanest frames we've ever recruited—he was listed at 195 pounds but wasn't nearly that—yet he never backed down from anyone.

Which brings me to mental toughness, which is even more important. You have to be able to handle any situation—success, failure, a mistake by a teammate—and be able to move past it immediately so you can focus on the next play.

Early in his career, Darrun was definitely lean and needed to get stronger. But when he accepted our scholarship offer, we thought he was a great addition to our program—even if some of the recruiting pundits weren't sold. The recruiting rankings often seduce coaches and their staffs. During my time at Villanova, I've come to understand that, for us, the fit stands above all else as we evaluate a young man.

We are most interested in young men who are basketball players rather than someone who views himself as a "point guard" or a "two guard." We also seek individuals who want to constantly improve as a basketball player. If their quest is to become a great rebounder, shooter, or passer, we are only too happy to do all we can to help them achieve that. The guys who display an inner push and are willing to put in the lonely hours with only a friend or student manager rebounding for them, to get an extra five hundred shots up, are the individuals we tend to be drawn to as coaches.

On the flip side, we're generally less interested in a player whose approach is, "This is what I do. You need to fit me in here."

On that count, Darrun was a player with great promise who would require some patience but had all the tools to succeed.

Prior to his freshman year in 2011, we considered redshirting Darrun. He was still only eighteen at the time and young for his class. But we were in a transition period with an inexperienced team and felt like he could help us. He was frequently in the starting lineup in November and December and made a huge steal to help us grab an overtime win over La Salle at the Pavilion. But, as the season progressed, he wore down, his minutes dipped, and so did his confidence.

It isn't uncommon for a young player to make his biggest leap between his freshman and sophomore seasons. Darrun offered a classic example of that: His tenacity in the gym and weight room in that span helped instill a new confidence in him as a sophomore, and from that point forward he never looked back. He was a three-year starter whose steady improvement culminated with him earning first team All–Big East honors as a senior. His 31-point effort in a 71–68 win at Butler in February 2015—capped by a game-winning three-pointer set up by, who else, Arch—is one of the great road performances in recent Villanova Basketball history.

There is an understated element to Darrun's game that may cause people to take him lightly. But his work ethic is exceptional, and his skills make him a challenging guy to defend. At 6'6", he has length, is ambidextrous, and has developed a smooth left-handed jump shot. That's how I summed him up in my conversations with NBA personnel in the days leading up to the 2015 Draft.

We had an inkling that Darrun may have been valued more highly than most outsiders understood. Stan Van Gundy, who had taken over as the Detroit Pistons' president of basketball operations, was aware of Darrun after serving as a color analyst for NBC Sports Net and watching us play three times against outstanding competition at the 2013 Battle 4 Atlantis. There were also a couple of other Philly connections in Auburn Hills: Malik Allen, a terrific forward for Steve Lappas from 1996 to 2000, is an assistant coach with the Pistons, and one of their key executives is Philly native Arn Tellem, whom I have gotten to know through the years.

Each year on Draft Night, we gather as a team at my house to watch the national telecast. Because of the nature of travel hoops, most of our guys have a connection to someone on the draft board. It may be a player they played with or are friends with from a basketball camp. When it's a Villanova guy in the mix, well, the excitement level goes through the roof. So when the Pistons selected Darrun as their second-round pick, the thirty-eighth overall player drafted, the roar that went up in our living room was probably audible all the way down the block.

One of the common denominators among successful teams is that they usually share great chemistry. It's been no different for us at Villanova. Darrun—like J.P. and Dylan—was beloved by his teammates. While the public knew Darrun as quiet and polite, his teammates appreciated what a cut-up he could be among friends. There was genuine joy among his now ex-teammates that Darrun would have the chance to achieve what they all hoped to by becoming an NBA player.

Not jealousy or envy. *Joy.*

Of all the Wildcats who were thrilled for Darrun, I'm not sure anyone was more excited than junior Josh Hart—and that was a very good thing for us. Because in a lot of ways, we would now be asking Josh to assume some of the responsibilities Darrun had always handled so effectively.

Though they weren't identical kinds of players, Josh and Darrun shared a capacity to impact a game from the wing. Darrun's ability to defend players ranging from small guards to power forwards was a huge part of why we had been so good defensively in 2014–2015. We believed Josh had the talent to do that too, and at the same time to become the kind of go-to scorer Darrun was.

Josh's path at Villanova had been a twisty one. It began with an impressive freshman year in 2013–2014, during which he became a great energy guy off the bench and seemed ready to move into the starting lineup. Unfortunately for him (in the short-term, at least) that's not what played out on the court. Dylan Ennis was absolutely fantastic during the summer of 2014 and into the pre-season, and when it came time to choose a starter, we all agreed: Dylan had earned the nod.

Josh was disappointed and we understood that. Nothing he had done had cost him the job. In my meeting with him, I stressed that we didn't think any less of him than before. We were counting on him just as much now as we were when practice had begun.

As a coach, though, you say those words knowing full well that people on the outside are likely going to look at things differently. Friends and family, with nothing invested in the player who won the job, can turn their disappointment into anger directed at the coaching staff. It's natural, but it can complicate life moving forward if the player who didn't win the spot buys into that.

That Josh never felt that way is a tribute to both him and his parents, Moses and Pat Hart.

Moses is a friendly, low-key guy with a humble demeanor. At a moment when he could have coddled Josh or trained his fire on us, he didn't. His message to his son, described later by Josh, echoed ours: Keep grinding. Keep getting better. Keep being a great teammate, and you will get where you want to go.

That advice was perfect.

Josh never said another word to us about it. Instead he took this message from Father Rob to heart: "The word 'crisis' in Greek means 'opportunity.' So during a crisis in my life, on my team, in my business, or in my marriage, we can ask ourselves, 'Where is the opportunity in this mess? Where is the opportunity to grow stronger?'"

Josh turned his "crisis" into an opportunity, using the setback as motivational fuel to stoke his competitive fire—and it made him a much better basketball player. At the end of the 2014–2015 regular season, the Big East coaches voted him the league's Sixth Man of the Year. Five days later, Josh was selected as the Most Outstanding Player of the Big East Tournament after helping lead us to the title.

So we knew that in 2015–2016, Josh would be an integral part of our unit. A starting berth seemed certain to be his after the exit of Darrun, Dylan, and JayVaughn, and we were convinced he could handle that. But within our staff, we were less certain how Josh, along with his fellow juniors Kris Jenkins and Darryl Reynolds, would transition into supporting Arch and Daniel as team leaders.

From their first day on campus, Josh, Kris, and Darryl had been nearly inseparable. Kris and Josh had known each other as elite high school players in the Washington, D.C., area. Kris even lobbied Josh to join him at Villanova after Kris had committed to us in August 2012, prior to his senior year at Gonzaga College High School. (Josh was at Sidwell Friends School.) To this day, if you ask them which team won when those programs collided during their senior seasons, you'll get a full-scale comedy routine.

What was a dynamic duo quickly expanded to a trio when Josh, Kris, and Darryl enrolled in the summer session of 2013. Darryl is a Philadelphia native who played just down the road from Villanova at Lower Merion High School before taking a post-graduate year at Worcester Academy in Massachusetts. His friendly nature fit seamlessly with Josh and Kris. They quickly became our version of the Three Amigos.

And in their first two years they could be carefree, to some extent, content to leave the leadership responsibility to their elders: James Bell, Tony Chennault, Darrun, Dylan, and JayVaughn. They were good kids off the court and did plenty to help us on the floor too, but if Kris wasn't making shots or Darryl didn't get to a big rebound, I could look down the bench and tell one of the veterans to go to the scorer's table and replace them.

Now, heading into their junior seasons, we wouldn't have that luxury anymore. How would the Three Amigos respond to this new challenge? We'd find out soon enough.

The summer of 2015 was flying by, as summers always seem to, and we knew that our fans and the media would soon be bombarding us with the big question of the new season: How do you get past the first weekend of the NCAA Tournament?

To ignore this reality would have done us no favors, nor was it possible if we'd wanted to. So we talked about it. We discussed it during our summer workouts and into the fall. We talked about it when we gathered in the circle at midcourt. I may have even brought it up a time or two when making a point to one of the guys during a practice.

It was apparent that we were going to be ranked highly to start the year (and it turned out that we were No. 9 in the USA Today Coaches Poll and No. 11 in the Associated Press poll), and the idea that our season could only be deemed a success if we were to advance beyond the first weekend into the regional round of the NCAA Tournament was a widely expressed sentiment among some very knowledgeable basketball people.

I understood their opinions.

I simply couldn't accept them.

To view the season in that light would have meant reducing all that would lead up to that point—thirty-four games, as it turned out—to a kind of sleepy preamble. That's a perception college athletes, blessed with only four short years of eligibility, cannot afford to embrace.

If you're a fan or member of the media you may have followed college basketball for twenty, thirty, or forty years. You may have many more seasons to watch ahead of you. But as a player, you only get forty-eight months—and that assumes you are fully healthy for each of them. That is why, as a staff, every season, we embed in our guys the belief that each practice is important, each walk-through is important, and each game is important. All of us have only a finite number of those in our careers. We want our guys to find joy in every practice and every game. And, if we are fortunate enough to get past that second-round game, we'll deal with what it means *then*.

Every chance we had that summer—in workouts, in meetings, and in one-on-one conversations—we tried to hammer the message home: Even if everyone is telling you that what you do until March doesn't matter, don't believe it. Those people, no matter how well-intentioned they may be, aren't you. We only get to live the 2015–2016 once in our careers, so let's savor each step along the way.

7

Setting a Tone

SURE ENOUGH, WHEN I traveled to New York City in October with Daniel and Arch for Big East media day at Madison Square Garden, we heard one question more than any other: So, how will you get past the first weekend of the NCAA tournament this year?

What I couldn't seem to explain to anyone outside of our basketball family was, "We're not there yet." March was a long way away. This was the start of a brand-new season, and *that* is what we needed to focus on.

For coaches who have been at this awhile, the start of a new season puts you back into your comfort zone. In my case, I've been doing this as a head coach since 1994, and we've only made minor tweaks to our pre-season and even pregame routines in all that time.

On Thursday, November 12, we were 235 days removed from our loss to NC State as I walked into the hotel lobby near campus where we usually gather the night before regular season games. And with all eyes focused on our first opponent of the new season, the Fairleigh Dickinson Knights, I believed that our players were excited about the start of a new chapter. I felt no sense of external pressure or any kind of complacency. We had moved on emotionally, and after the prep we'd done that summer and early fall, I could tell these guys were eager to finally get on the Pavilion court and play a game together.

It was time for us to set the tone. Father Rob helped us to do that, as he often does, by asking the guys a question.

"How many times have I heard Coach Wright challenge you all to make sure you are in the proper defensive stance before anything else?" he said.

The guys all nodded their heads in acknowledgment.

It's true. I tell them all the time: When you're in your stance, when you establish a solid posture and your legs are solidly underneath you, you set the tone for all the other moves that you make on the court.

"Well," Father Rob said, "the same is true in the rest of our lives, including our spiritual lives."

He went on to use a Biblical passage as an example: Matthew 6:7–15, a passage in which Jesus sets the tone for His disciples and for all of us who are a part of the Christian faith. (I want to stress here that not everyone on our team is necessarily Christian, and those who aren't understand that the metaphors and lessons drawn from our particular faith—the faith upon which Villanova was founded—tend to speak to universal ideas. We don't ask any of our players to subscribe to a particular religion. It's the lessons that are important.)

We pray as a team before every game, and Father Rob reminded the guys why we do that. "We are getting into our stance," he said. "'Our Father who art in heaven, hallowed be Your name,' we pray. 'Your kingdom' is what matters and 'Your will' ought to supersede mine. Put God first in all that you do, and other things will fall into place."

After Father Rob finished we had dinner—chicken, pasta, fresh fish, veggies, and fruit, a delicious and high-fuel menu designed by John Shackleton—and then I took a few minutes to speak with the team. All these steps are part of our pregame routine, which we stick to with a consistency bordering on obsessive. The goal is that when the official tosses the ball into the air at midcourt, the mind of every player on our roster is free to concentrate solely on playing basketball. For us, that process begins on the eve of every regular season and post-season game. My after-dinner remarks are usually less about the specifics of the game than where we are as a team. We could be dealing with anything at that moment, but it's important that we get ourselves centered before game day begins.

Once I finish, we watch a video put together by one of our younger staff members in consultation with an assistant coach. Capping off the video portion of the meeting is a two- to three-minute compila-

BEYOND BASKETBALL

It's All About Values

An organization's core values are its pillars. In troubled times, they are a beacon. In successful times, they are a rudder. Core values reflect what matters most to your program or organization.

tion of clips, accompanied by music, highlighting the work of the winner of what we call the "Attitude Club." The video consists of plays we track that are not on the standard box score— screen assists, extra passes, defensive deflections. The winner gets to select the music to accompany his piece.

It's a feel-good video that fires the group up, and I'm as into it as anyone. The concept is to feature the unselfish hustle efforts by a single player and the entire team that we believe are so essential to success. When the video ends, we applaud and gather in a circle where we chant "1, 2, 3, Attitude!" before breaking for the night.

I don't specifically recall when that "Attitude" chant began for us. Like a lot of things we do, it's probably a combination of borrowed philosophies I have picked up over the years. I do know it dates to my early days at Hofstra.

Hofstra wasn't a good basketball team then. Game plans and strategic tactics were not going to turn our roster into a super-talented group. We were losing games. The one thing we could do to improve ourselves was to bring a great attitude, every day, to confront the challenges we faced.

"Don't walk around like a loser," I told the players. "Walk around with a great attitude. That's what we can control."

We were struggling so much in that first season at Hofstra, I would find myself playing Louis Armstrong's version of "What a Wonderful World" in the car just to buoy my spirits. One night, I played that song for the team in the locker room.

It probably did nothing for them. Some undoubtedly wondered if the coach was losing it. But I was trying to change their attitude because we couldn't seem to change anything else.

In the end, it worked. The only thing we accomplished during that 1994–1995 season was maintaining a positive attitude. Our record was poor (10–18), but we felt good about our effort. Seeing that a good attitude had an impact on us that year, it dawned on me that this was an idea worth hanging on to. Somehow that morphed into the chant *"1, 2, 3, Attitude!"*

It's served our teams well ever since.

Old-School

As we headed toward Friday night at 7:01 p.m., our tip time against Fairleigh Dickinson, I was excited to see where we were as a team. On opening night, for me, it's less about the result than it is about how we look. It's akin to a production debuting on Broadway. *Will things go as planned? What surprises are in store for us?*

One of the guys I was especially curious about was our sophomore Phil Booth.

In his first year with us, Phil had been one of the most efficient players we'd ever coached, connecting on better than fifty-six percent of his field goal attempts in limited minutes. Those kinds of numbers would be impressive if a forward like Daniel, who takes a lot of his shots near the basket, had delivered them. But Phil was a 6'3" guard.

One of my favorite things about our program is that so many of these young men are throwbacks who were taught sound basketball fundamentals, starting with their parents and families. Kris Jenkins has described what he does as "an old man's game," meaning he relies on concepts like footwork and shooting technique more than he does flash. Phil fits that mold too, and it makes sense: His dad, Phil Sr., grew up in Philadelphia, played basketball at Northeast High School, and earned a scholarship to play for Coach Fang Mitchell at Coppin State University.

Phil Jr. was named the Baltimore Catholic League Player of the Year as a senior at Mount Saint Joseph High School, and I saw him as a great fit to be a guard in our program.

What is a Villanova guard?

In our minds, he's skilled enough to handle the basketball—pass or shoot it. He can make plays for his teammates or create a shot for himself. On defense, he's tenacious and eager to battle with his opponent no matter if he is 5'10" or 6'10". (In our system, we rely mostly on man-to-man defense, so everyone has to be prepared to go toe-to-toe with an opponent who may tower over him or outweigh him by forty pounds.)

When I looked at Phil Booth Jr., I saw a classic Villanova guard. He was versatile enough to handle the basketball and a strong enough long-range shooter to play off of it. When he elevated for a jump shot, he was square to the basket and an accurate shooter. Plus he was a sound defender who, as he matured, had the ingredients to become a stopper on the perimeter.

But I also wondered about something. Phil performed really well in clutch situations during some huge AAU games we saw him play, but there were other times when he seemed a bit too content to defer to teammates. It was the same way when he played with Mount Saint Joseph, where he was a superstar who at times looked sort of ordinary.

What we didn't know then is that Phil has a great knack for knowing when he needs to assert himself on the floor. I would also come to realize that he is the lowest-maintenance player I have ever coached. When you give Phil an assignment, be it on the court or in the classroom, you never have to doubt that it will be completed.

Coming into 2015–2016, I thought Phil's work was solid. He was a proven veteran who knew our system cold. But Jalen Brunson, who had just joined us as a freshman guard, came in with a hunger and a healthy need to prove something to our staff. I thought that hunger gave Jalen an edge, and we elected to make him the starter. (A major contributing factor may have been Phil's left knee, which would require arthroscopic surgery after the season. But all of us were in the dark about that in November.)

When I informed Phil that he would not be a starter, he handled it perfectly. We had an honest discussion. He told me he wasn't happy with the decision, but he listened to what I said and then went to work. By the time we were ready to begin the season, he had become our clear sixth man and a starter in all but name.

Over the course of the season, I tried to remain sensitive to his situation. Phil is such a great kid that I never wanted to take his un-selfish acceptance of his role for granted. Every chance I had, I would bring him into my office to talk. He never came in to complain. He did all that we asked.

Of course, Phil comes by that naturally.

When we first met his parents, Phil Sr. and Robin, during the re-cruiting process, they told us that Phil Jr. would look at three schools (Georgetown and Indiana were the others) and pick one. "When he makes the choice," they said, "he is going to stay there for four years and get his degree. He won't look to transfer and you won't hear any-thing from us. He's yours to coach."

I had never really heard it put quite that way before. I have had parents or guardians express a similar sentiment, but not nearly so succinctly. And, in most of those cases, as time went on, we learned that the reality seldom matched the original sentiment. That's under-standable in a way, because it's just different when it's your loved one's welfare you are talking about. Parents are used to advocating for their sons.

Phil's parents fully delivered on their promise.

As a freshman, Phil was an important part of a team that had fin-ished 33–3. On almost any other team he would have played a lot more than the fourteen minutes per game he averaged for us. In our fateful NC State game, when so much was going wrong for us, Phil gave us a much-needed lift off the bench. And as we moved into the final minute with our team making a run at the Wolfpack, I gave seri-ous consideration to inserting Phil in place of Dylan, who was strug-gling offensively.

The moment of truth arrived after we forced a turnover and got the ball back trailing by two points with thirty-seven seconds left.

I decided to go with Dylan. Phil remained on the bench.

The hardcore Nova Nation fan probably wondered then, and still may now, why I went that route. To me, Dylan was a central part of our core and Phil was, at that point, still a freshman—a good one, but untested. I looked at Dylan as a future captain, a guy who would be standing alongside Arch and Daniel as a team leader in his final year with us. I thought it was important to trust him.

By now, you know the rest. Dylan's shot was no good and we lost.

It may have been the in-game decision I wrestled with more than any other in the dark hours of that Sunday morning before Father Rob's words helped me move on.

Would Phil have made the jumper to give us the lead?

We'll never know.

As a coach, that's one of those decisions you have to learn from and leave behind.

During Phil's freshman year, I was aware that Phil Sr. and Robin made the drive from their home in Maryland to every home game and some on the road. But I never saw them long enough to say anything more than hello. The first time I had a conversation lasting more than thirty seconds came at the 2015 Banquet at the Pavilion.

"Big Phil, you weren't kidding," I said to him. "I didn't see you all year."

He chuckled and said, "I told you."

Phil Sr. couldn't have been happy when we made the choice to start Jalen instead of Phil Jr., so I asked our assistant coaches to keep in touch with Phil Sr., and they did. There was never any animosity. (I know there was external speculation that Jalen had been promised a starting position during his recruitment, but that wasn't the case. It was just a close battle for the spot that Jalen won.)

The character of Phil Booth is a direct reflection of his parents'. I often note that what our players' parents and families gave to these kids in the first eighteen years of their lives is far more important than anything we could possibly teach them during their four years with us. Phil's attitude was a great tribute to that.

Phil's ability to make the same kind of positive contribution that Josh had made as the sixth man would be a vital part of our season starting against Fairleigh Dickinson.

So would the efforts of one of Phil's good friends, his classmate Mikal Bridges.

Like Arch and Darrun, Mikal was a local guy playing in a suburban setting at Great Valley High School in Malvern, Pennsylvania, less than twenty minutes from the Villanova campus. There wasn't a lot of high-major focus on Mikal early in his career, but a growth spurt helped catapult him into the recruiting mix prior to the start of his senior year of high school, in 2013–2014. Standing 6'7" with long arms, he was the classic case of a player with serious potential upside. He was also young for his grade. We landed a commitment from him, and he became part of our two-man recruiting class next to Phil.

I recall standing in the Davis Center atrium in the summer of 2014 not long after Mikal came to Villanova. At the time, he was real thin and getting knocked around in our workouts. I felt bad for him and was trying to pump him up. I told him that if he was getting physically beat up, he could consider a redshirt (a year spent practicing with the team without seeing game action).

His eyes popped wide open and an expression of sheer terror spread across his face. "Am I redshirting?" he asked me.

I assured him that nothing was yet set in stone. It was just something he might want to consider, I said. I was worried about his short-term confidence, but I wanted to let him know that I wasn't concerned about him at all in the long run, knowing he would get stronger.

As we went through September and into October, Mikal was looking very good in our practices. It got to the point where we felt like he would earn a spot in the rotation. But as we moved into the latter stages of October and November, you could see the slide beginning as the pounding took its toll. He was worn down.

We talked to him again about redshirting. I think it came down to his parents, Tyneeha Rivers and Jack Devine, who understood the value this could have on Mikal's overall experience at Villanova. It would help him become a better student, allowing him to spread out some of the academic load, which can be a lot to handle as a freshman. A redshirt year would also allow him to grow physically and emotionally. Mikal's parents were more concerned about what the finished product of their son would look like, as opposed to being laser-focused on the quickest path to the NBA. It was an extremely smart approach on their part.

When I spoke to Mikal again, he was very open to it. He told me he thought it could be helpful to his development. In the end, it took a weight off his shoulders—and ours. We knew we wanted to play him but couldn't see where the minutes would come from that season.

Redshirting is a big decision, and we only consider it if we believe the player has a chance to be outstanding. In our time at Villanova we have had just a handful of redshirts: Chris Charles, Antonio Pena, and Maurice Sutton. I think it helped all of them. (Chris had just begun playing basketball when he became our first signee in 2002. The extra year benefited him not so much at Villanova, but later in his career. He remains a coveted international player.)

The first thing I always ask a redshirt candidate is: Do you like being at Villanova? Because the reality is this path requires you to be here an extra year. If Villanova isn't for you, then a redshirt isn't an option.

I also try to share the example of those who've redshirted in the past, just to help them wrap their minds around the good things that can come of it. Yet one of the examples I used in my conversation with Mikal was Darrun. We had given a lot of thought to redshirting Darrun in 2011 because he was young for his class and in need of additional strength. But we were a very inexperienced team at that point and couldn't afford to *not* have him on the roster. When Mikal discussed the redshirt option with Darrun, Darrun told him that looking back he wondered how that extra year could have benefited his career and wished the circumstances would have made it a viable option. I believe Mikal was leaning toward the redshirt anyway, but Darrun's words reinforced his decision.

That kind of conversation between players is one of the most rewarding things about this job for us as a staff. These guys really want what's best for one another. The upperclassmen take the underclassmen under their collective wing. To the outside world, redshirting sounds like a slap to the ego. But as I've said before: Outside opinions are not the ones that count the most. People may say, "Don't let them do that to you." But the older players know what it's about, and Darrun's willingness to counsel Mikal gave him some insight into an important decision.

Mikal deserves a ton of credit for taking the long view and even more praise for his approach to 2014–2015. Instead of mentally checking out, he kept his concentration. In practice, when we asked him to play the role of Roosevelt Jones of Butler or Matt Carlino of Marquette, he was all in. During games, when he was in uniform knowing he would never enter the game, he was one of our most energetic guys on the bench. He even put together creative dances in the team huddles, just before the guys would come onto the court for introductions. One time Scott Graham, the executive producer of our TV show, *Inside Villanova Basketball,* asked him where that came from. Mikal shrugged and explained that since he wasn't playing, he was doing whatever he could to get the guys fired up.

Now, as we were set to begin the 2015–2016 season, we were really excited about finally getting to see Mikal in games. From the moment we had resumed summer workouts, you could see that he was on a mission. Everyone else was coming off a good season, but Mikal had this incredible hunger. He also had a confidence in the new body he had developed working alongside Coach Shack in the weight room. When he was on the court he was playing with a physicality he wouldn't have been capable of twelve months earlier.

There was also the basic roster math: JayVaughn, Darrun, and Dylan had graduated. Instead of there being six or seven players physically stronger than him, now there might be only three. We knew he was ready.

We didn't have to wait long to see Mikal's potential. He showed us everything he had in the opener against Fairleigh Dickinson. He came off the bench to score eight points and grab five rebounds as we defeated the Knights 91–54.

Cooking at Home

It always feels good to get the first win in the books, but we didn't have a lot of time to dwell on it. Nebraska was coming to campus four days later in a contest that would be part of the first ever Gavitt Tipoff Games, a partnership linking the Big East and Big Ten conferences in the season's first week.

One of the best parts about being the basketball coach at Villanova is the passion of the Nova Nation. Our on-campus arena, the 6,500-seat Pavilion, has been sold-out for every regular season game since 2000. And every one of those games has been an event on our campus. As soon as you pull into the parking lot and step out of your car, you feel the vibe.

The Pavilion is not the fanciest place in America, but it's an intimidating building for our opponents to come into, and our guys love playing there. *Philadelphia Daily News* writer Dick Jerardi once dubbed the place "the Ski Lodge," based on the hardwood ceiling of its original design. DJ, as he is known locally, was pretty much on target—the building did conjure visions of a Swiss Alps getaway before the look was altered in the mid-2000s by the application of a coating designed to improve the arena's acoustics.

I'm not sure there is any place quite like it.

Opened in 1986, it features a pointed roof and a series of angled corners. At one end of the court sits a giant set of portable bleachers with the capacity to hold 1,500 fans. Chair-back seating is deployed on both sides of the court and the upper stands offer bleacher seating with limited legroom. The scoreboard hangs over midcourt with two video boards on the second level, each tucked into a corner. The bright lights above the court create the sense that you are on a stage, and in a way you are.

When you turn on college basketball games from around the country in November, you often see a smattering of empty seats in the background. Football is still in season and there are plenty of places that haven't yet turned their attention to basketball.

Villanova is not one of those places.

It doesn't matter who our opponent is. Without fail, the energy inside the Pavilion is awesome. Yet you could tell that there was an extra dose of enthusiasm for this Nebraska game, with the top Fox team—Gus Johnson, Bill Raftery, and the studio duo of Rob Stone and Steve Lavin—in the house to watch us face a Big Ten team. Our players were amped up about it.

Personally, the link to the Gavitt family was important. When I was an assistant to Rollie Massimino in the 1980s, Coach Mass was at the top of the coaching ladder. The Big East was flourishing, and even as a novice I noticed the biggest names in the conference—John Thompson, Lou Carnesecca, Jim Boeheim, Rick Pitino, and Jim Calhoun—respected one another, but the competition among them was fierce and sometimes even vicious.

As far as I could tell, the only person each of those legends universally respected was Dave Gavitt.

Dave was a hugely successful coach himself at Providence College before becoming the original Big East commissioner in 1979. The league really was his baby. He envisioned it, formed an alliance with ESPN, and forever changed eastern basketball. He also had a knack for defusing any negative situation that arose in competition between these great, strong-willed, larger-than-life figures in our sport.

In my mind, Dave Gavitt walked on water.

When he passed away in 2011, Patty and I attended his wake in Providence, and the funeral home felt like a living history of college basketball. We are grateful to count Dan Gavitt, Dave's son and the vice president of the NCAA Men's Basketball Championship, as a good friend today.

So for us, that game was huge—and we were able to get the win over Nebraska. Josh scored nineteen points. Mikal came up with some big deflections and steals as we forced twenty-two turnovers in what became an 87–63 victory.

Later that week, we hosted a pair of preliminary-round games in the NIT Season Tip-Off tournament. We sustained our momentum, beating East Tennessee State and Akron to build a 4–0 record.

Home cooking is nice.

We had taken the first step and done a reasonably good job of living Father Rob's message to get in our stance and set a tone. We were ready to head out on the road for the first time in this young season—with the shadow of Broadway looming not too far in the distance.

8

A Strong Start

PART OF VILLANOVA University's mission when it was first founded was to educate the influx of Irish immigrants who had come to the United States in the nineteenth century. When those students graduated, they often returned to settle in the robust Irish communities located in the five boroughs of New York City, where many of their relatives lived—and where many of their descendants live to this day.

That link between Villanova and New York City lives on. Whenever we are in the metropolitan area to play St. John's or Seton Hall, it's an event. The Big East Tournament at Madison Square Garden is a March staple on the calendar of a lot of our alums who live in the city or its suburbs. We even host an annual New York City event to help kick off the season, "Hoops on the Hudson," in October at Chelsea Piers, and it's always jam-packed with alumni and friends.

So when the chance to schedule additional regular season games in the city is presented to us, we're always open to the opportunity.

Since 1985, the NIT Season Tip-Off has brought four teams to New York at Thanksgiving. The semifinals and finals were played at Madison Square Garden from the event's inception through 2014. We last participated in 2010, defeating UCLA in the semifinals before losing to Tennessee in the finals. While we wished the final game had gone differently—we did not play well against Bruce Pearl's team—it was still a memorable holiday that included a great view of the Macy's Thanksgiving Day Parade from our hotel in Times Square.

In 2015, the NIT Season Tip-Off champion would be crowned for the first time at the Barclays Center, the beautiful venue in Brooklyn, just across the East River from Manhattan. After starting our 2015–

2016 season with four straight victories in the comfort of the Pavilion, we were about to face a pair of tests.

The first of those would come on Thanksgiving afternoon against Stanford.

Everyone who has coached can tell you this about basketball during the holidays: If your team wins its game leading into Thanksgiving or Christmas, it is pure bliss. The players get to go home to their families on an upbeat note, and as coaches we can exhale a bit. But if your team loses that last game before the holiday, or even just plays poorly, it's a whole different deal.

On a Lark

Back in 2012, we were hit by a Thanksgiving storm of our own making.

We were in the midst of building the confidence of a young team that had gone 13–19 the year before. There were only two seniors on the roster, Mouph and Maurice Sutton, and we were breaking in two new point guards: freshman Ryan Arcidiacono and junior transfer Tony Chennault. We won our first three games and, despite being crunched by Alabama in the finals of the 2K Classic at Madison Square Garden, were feeling pretty good about ourselves.

We came back to the Pavilion to host Columbia two days before Thanksgiving. Many of the Villanova students had left campus to begin their holiday weekend, but the stands were still packed. It was the type of matchup that some fans may have shrugged at. But in coaching you know that sometimes these can be the most dangerous games on your schedule. It is perfectly natural for young men anticipating a holiday to let their minds wander a bit during that time of year. (It can also be an issue at Christmas.) But at this level, even that small bit of slippage is enough to cost you.

On that evening it did.

We ended up on the wrong end of a 75–57 loss.

Our fans were understandably upset as they headed out into the November night. The players were in shock. James Bell, who would later develop into an incredible warrior and first team All–Big East player for us, was near tears as we walked to the press conference. As a captain, Mouph felt like he had let everyone down.

In my briefcase was a DVD copy of the game. It is a ritual of mine to rewatch it with Patty as soon as I get home. (And yes, my sports-loving wife truly does enjoy watching the game tape with me—we play a lot of golf and tennis together too—even if she sometimes dozes off to sleep with a blanket draped over her.) It's especially important after a loss, when I'm itching to start analyzing where things went awry.

However, after that loss, the late-night horror show on the flat-screen at the Wrights' house would have to wait for an hour or two. I was due to appear at a postgame reception for some of my oldest friends: my fellow teammates from the Larks.

That's right, my Little League baseball team!

Every year I'm lucky enough to see some of my old pals in the stands at our home games, and this gathering is an annual tradition that dates back to my time at Hofstra. It's always a great night, yet there was a part of me that wanted to skip it and point my car toward home just so I could dissect the game and get it over with. I'm glad I didn't.

There is something really cool about decades-long friendships. These people have seen you at your best and worst. So my basketball-related misery in that moment took a backseat as we got to talking about our families and lives. My fellow Larks reminded me, just by being there, how important it is to take the long view. By the time I headed home, I felt a little better.

Jarring losses like that don't fade quickly, though. We got back to work at practice the next morning, but our next chance at redemption wouldn't arrive until after the holiday, when we went to play at La Salle. Even as I enjoyed Thanksgiving at home with my family, the Columbia game was never too far from my thoughts.

Hey, it comes with the territory. Our families are the ones who have to deal with us coaches and players when we are distracted or down after a defeat.

I am an optimist by nature—but I'm also a realist. Over that long Thanksgiving weekend of 2012, even I could never have envisioned the silver lining that would ultimately come with what felt like a devastating loss. The specter of that night remained with our players for the balance of their Villanova careers. Arch and Daniel, in particular, never forgot it. In later seasons, they referenced the loss all the time when they spoke to—and tried to motivate—their younger teammates. It was a lesson of incalculable value that would pay dividends all the way to Houston.

So, looking back, that wasn't such a bad Thanksgiving after all.

This Thanksgiving would have its own unique feel for our family and the 2015–2016 team. With John at the wheel of our bus, we made the drive up the New Jersey Turnpike and settled into our usual road-game routine. With a game on the holiday, we scheduled our basketball family's Thanksgiving meal for Wednesday night and were thrilled to host a group of more than fifty people (including our entire team as well as player and staff families) for a full turkey dinner with all the trimmings.

Our game against Stanford tipped off at 4:30 p.m. on Thanksgiving Day. Coach Johnny Dawkins had a young team that gave us fits on the offensive glass. (I was *not* thankful for that.) We were solid defensively for the most part, holding Stanford to twenty-six percent shooting and escaping with a 59–45 win on a day when we struggled to make shots.

Jalen Brunson scored eighteen of our fifty-nine points and showed off some of the offensive creativity that had helped make him a McDonald's All-American and a national name.

The next day, we were back on the floor at the Barclays Center to meet Georgia Tech in the championship game at 3 p.m. Josh and Jalen each scored thirteen points, and we pulled away from the Yellow Jackets toward the end of the second half to notch our sixth win of the year, by the count of 69–52.

Following the game, it was announced that Jalen had been named the Most Valuable Player of the NIT Season Tip-Off. He was the player requested for the postgame ESPN2 interview and the postgame press conference. To a lot of people watching on TV or in the stands, it felt like a freshman had made a statement in an early-season tournament.

All of us in the locker room, Jalen included, looked at it a little differently.

Knowing Whom to Praise

From the moment we got to know Jalen during the recruiting process, we were blown away by his maturity. I had known Jalen's dad, Rick Brunson, since his days as a standout guard at Temple, playing for Coach John Chaney from 1991 to 1995. Rick went on to a long NBA career and became a coach, as an assistant at the University of Virginia and later on the staff of the Chicago Bulls.

We were reintroduced to Rick and his wife, Sandra, when Jalen began to emerge as a major national recruit at Adlai E. Stevenson High School in Lincolnshire, Illinois. Rick is a terrific coach himself, and Sandra had been a track athlete at Temple, so they were as well versed in the recruiting process as any family we've dealt with. Even though they made their home in Illinois, it felt like we were recruiting a Philly kid, and in a sense we were: The family, which also included Jalen's younger sister, Erica, had lived in South Jersey before relocating to Illinois when Rick worked for the Bulls.

In the summer of 2014, we were battling Temple and Illinois to land Jalen and felt like we had a solid chance—except for one thing. There were reports that Rick was going to be hired to assist Fran Dunphy at Temple. But that never came to pass, in the wake of charges brought against Rick in Illinois—charges he was later acquitted of. (He is now assisting Tom Thibodeau with the Minnesota Timberwolves.)

Jalen eventually signed a letter of intent with us that November.

Because of the way he was raised by Sandra and Rick,

BEYOND BASKETBALL

Giving Credit

A team or organization performing at peak efficiency is a sign that a leader has the self-confidence to empower many members of his team. The more people there are within the culture who are impacting others positively, the more leaders you have and the stronger your organization.

Jalen, more than any big-time player we've had, got the culture of Villanova right away. He is polite, respectful, and a tremendous student. I also appreciate how open he is. With everything he went through as a high-level recruit, from schools promising him he would start to his dad's situation with Temple and the accusations against him, he was willing to discuss everything candidly. Whenever I spoke with Jalen, I felt like I was talking with an adult.

I had every confidence that Jalen came here to not only be the best player he could be, but to get his Villanova degree.

As a newcomer just beginning his college basketball career, Jalen recognized that when we got to Brooklyn, this was a big stage. The opponents were from the Pac-12 and the ACC. We were on an NBA court, playing where first- and second-round games of the NCAA Tournament would be held in March.

I think Jalen's thought process was, *Okay, this is a big-time game and I want to help the team. And the way to do that is to do what I've always done—go out and score points.*

Our more experienced players, led by Arch and Daniel, sized up that same setting and put their energy into defending and rebounding. Those two elements of the game are at the heart of our core values and had been ingrained in them over their time at Villanova.

Jalen's coaches and teammates looked at his performance, saw the rest of our guys doing all the dirty work to clear the way, and saw the irony in the praise he was receiving from everyone on the outside. At that point, his defense was still a work in progress, yet he walked out of the locker room at the Barclays Center with the MVP trophy.

The fans had to be thinking, *That's the way it's supposed to be!*

Inside our locker room, though, the reaction was barely contained grinning. Our older guys—Arch, Daniel, Josh, Kris, and Darryl—were actually laughing about it. Within the team, the celebration was for the players who had made Jalen's scoring possible by making the extra pass, rebounding, setting screens, and drawing charges.

To Jalen's credit, he never bought into the outside world's perception of what mattered. He understood that he needed some time to mesh his basketball skills into our philosophy. Ultimately, Jalen's contribution to our 2015–2016 team wouldn't be centered on how many points he could score. (We all knew he could score.) More important was how quickly he absorbed and grew in the areas of his game where he wasn't as strong—and in the process, grew closer and closer to becoming a complete Villanova guard.

He also recognized just how fortunate he was to be stepping foot onto the court in the first place.

As we walked out of the locker room to board our bus for the ride back to Villanova and the rest of our Thanksgiving weekend, one of Jalen's classmates stood out: 6'8" Tim Delaney. Tim, who had been the first member of our current freshman class to give us a verbal commitment, was on crutches.

When Tim was a recruit, we saw him as a skilled forward from a great basketball family—his mom, Jeanine, played at Saint Joseph's University. His versatility and well-rounded game aren't easy to find, and we also knew that he was an outstanding student at Pitman High School in New Jersey.

During his junior year at Pitman, Tim began to have some issues with his hip that would keep him out of a handful of games. He was a tough kid, though, and fought his way through. That pattern continued when he moved over to Blair Academy for his senior year in 2013–2014. The family had the recurring pain checked out and doctors recommended some rehab and rest at the end of his senior season, which he did.

When Tim arrived at Villanova for the two summer sessions in 2015, he was excellent in the workouts. But as the days went by, we noticed that he didn't move as freely as before. We gave him some off days, after which he would come back and look less constrained. He was tough and had proven he could play through the discomfort, but the problems persisted. Finally, we decided to have the injury thoroughly checked out by a hip specialist.

When Jeff Pierce, our trainer, walked into my office to inform me that Tim had a torn labrum in his left hip, I wasn't shocked. But when he added that Tim's *right* hip was going to be an issue as well, I was floored. In all my years of coaching, I had never heard of a player needing both hips fixed. My first thought was that it sounded career-threatening. I felt awful for Tim, who was in his second month as a Villanova freshman at the time.

The plan that made the most sense was to have the left hip operated on in October. Once Tim was recovered sufficiently from that arthroscopic procedure, there would be a second one done on his right hip, most likely in January. Not only would there be no basketball for him, but he would be spending the better part of his first year of college on crutches. At 6'8", that is no easy feat.

We were devastated for Tim.

Thankfully, he handled it gracefully. He never complained or made excuses, even as he tried to make his way on crutches from the Connelly Center to the Davis Center on icy winter days. It had to have been torture for him.

Knowing that your first surgical procedure is only going to lead to a second one makes it even tougher. I talked with Tim about it all the time. Yet every time we spoke, he professed to have an upbeat outlook. I'd walk away wondering if he really could be that positive in the face of this.

The other amazing part of Tim was how he never let his injury situation spill over into his academic work. For a player, losing the chance to do what you love every day can crush your soul. And when you get down, the other areas of your life can also suffer. Over the years I have seen more than a few guys dragged down in their academic work while they were trying to bounce back from an injury. Despite missing a number of days for surgery, Tim was an academic superstar. He registered a 3.8 grade point average in 2015–2016. His drive to succeed was incredible. There were times when he was in pain and struggling to get around, but he never let any of that stop him. To finish as he did is a testament to his discipline and commitment to excellence.

Watching Tim on a daily basis also brought home an inspiring message to our other guys. It offered them a dose of humility and allowed them to appreciate how lucky they were to be healthy. Right here in their locker room was a guy who had been on the court with them all summer. Now, at eighteen years of age, it was a challenge for him just to walk to class.

That night in Brooklyn, Tim hobbled up the steps toward the back of our team bus. He settled into his seat with a smile on his face.

Above him in the overhead bin were his omnipresent crutches. On the seat across from him was the 2015 NIT Season Tip-Off trophy. It belonged to him as much as it belonged to any of us.

As John fired up the bus engine, I knew there was still a lot of work to do. Our rebounding in particular had been abysmal. Georgia Tech and Stanford had beaten us up on the boards by a combined total of 94–63. Our defense allowed us to get the wins, but over the long haul of a season, that kind of a rebounding deficit will catch up to you in the Big East.

At the same time, we felt we had the makings of a good team. Josh and Kris were beginning to get a sense of the responsibilities that come with being a starter in our program. Daniel was growing more comfortable as a leader. Arch was Arch. And the younger players—Phil, Mikal, Jalen, and Donte DiVincenzo—had all grown in important ways through the early weeks of the season.

We weren't a finished product, but it was never our goal to be the best team we could be in November.

As Father Rob often reminds us: There are no shortcuts. Every journey begins with one step that leads to another and then another. We relish that. And even if the rest of the world was in a hurry to get to March, we would take our time.

9

How to Win by Losing

COLLEGE ATHLETICS HAVE changed a ton in my lifetime. In the 1960s and most of the 1970s, conference affiliation wasn't a prerequisite for basketball success. That was especially true on the East Coast, where there was the ACC and the Ivy League and then a whole host of schools that were in a loose alliance known as the Eastern College Athletic Conference. For the five Division I schools in Philadelphia during those decades, there was nothing bigger than one of the four Big Five games.

You can accurately say that I was raised on Big Five college basketball. As I mentioned back in Chapter 2, my earliest heroes were its stars and the five schools they represented. Any time there was a Big Five game telecast from the Palestra, usually with Big Al Meltzer on the call, I was glued to our television set.

That landscape began to shift in 1979, when the Big East opened for business. Villanova, which had been in the Eastern Eight, became a full-time Big East member in 1980, and many of the Eastern Eight teams, including Temple, went on to form the Atlantic 10. As cable television exploded, conferences became vital in securing rights deals for the membership. By the end of the 1980s, league affiliation had become everything in college hoops.

That the Big Five survived this transition and evolved over the next few decades is no small feat, given the near-total realignment of our schools and conferences during that time. The Big Five today is not exactly as it was back in that era—only a handful of the games are now played at the Palestra—but it remains vibrant. And it's no exaggeration to say there is nothing else like it anywhere in the country.

Non-conference scheduling is a challenge for every program in college basketball. When I first arrived at Hofstra, which played in the America East Conference during my tenure (and has since moved to the Colonial Athletic Association), we had no problem lining up quality major-conference opponents. That's because we were barely on anyone's radar, and the big programs were happy to host us for early-season tune-up games. But a few years later, when we were competing for America East titles and NCAA Tournament berths, we couldn't get a return phone call from a high-major school. We had become too dangerous.

Our situation at Villanova is unique. As part of the Big East, we play eighteen regular season games within our conference each year. That usually leaves us with thirteen more games to fill. Thanks to Villanova's basketball heritage, we receive invitations to in-season tournaments that offer terrific early-season opposition and the chance to have our players and fans travel around Thanksgiving or Christmas. In 2015–2016 the in-season event was the NIT Season Tip-Off, which accounted for four games, two played on campus and two in Brooklyn.

Other considerations come into play. Television networks are eager to set up marquee matchups between schools that don't often play each other. Those kinds of games are big for exposure, and we typically have two or three each season. You also have to leave some space for home games so you don't expose your team to too much travel early in the year and have sufficient inventory for your season ticket holders.

It becomes a real Rubik's Cube when you start factoring in strength of schedule, which the NCAA Tournament Selection Committee considers to be an important criterion as it contemplates which schools are worthy of at-large bids. Jason Donnelly, our former assistant coach and current Villanova Athletic Fund Director, did an outstanding job alongside our former athletic director, Vince Nicastro, and one of his top lieutenants, Bob Steitz, on this important task for years, and then helped bring Mark Jackson, who now oversees this area as our new athletic director, quickly up to speed. The fact that our strength-of-schedule numbers have been outstanding every year is an indication that all four of these men have done a fantastic job.

It takes so much patience and commitment from the five athletic directors and head coaches at the Big Five schools to be able to continue our beloved tradition in the face of a very different world from what existed even twenty years ago. Each school has different television partners and in-season tournament obligations, so coming up with workable dates is a time-consuming process that demands flexibility and creativity on everyone's part.

It's complex, but it's also a big part of who we are.

Thankfully, we have retained that spirit of finding ways to make this work for everyone involved. We play two of our four Big Five games at the Pavilion and the other two at the home sites of our opponents. Our fans get to see these traditional rivals on our campus, and we bring our team across the city to Saint Joe's, La Salle, Temple, and Penn (whose home court is still the Palestra). It's a source of pride for our basketball community, and I love the way we all support one another when we are playing in the postseason.

The Big Five also provides us with a mini–conference season before we get to Big East action. I have always believed that those matchups come closer to replicating what we will see in January and February in the Big East than anything else we do in the pre-season. Every Big Five coach knows exactly what his opponents have planned for his team because we're always watching one another on television. The players spend all summer in the area playing pickup with and against one another. Fran Dunphy (Temple), Phil Martelli (St. Joe's), John Giannini (La Salle), and Steve Donahue (Penn) are outstanding coaches with long résumés of successes. Their teams are so well schooled that we have to be sharp if we hope to earn the City Series championship.

December 2015 began for us in one of those Big Five cauldrons. To reach this test, we took a twenty-minute bus ride down Lancaster Avenue and onto City Avenue to Hagan Arena, home of the Saint Joseph's Hawks. It's an intense environment, with the fans right on top of you. Ninety minutes before the game, many of their students were already in their section behind one basket.

But the crowd was less of a concern to our staff than Phil's team. DeAndre' Bembry was their star, and we knew the havoc he could wreak because he wasn't just a scorer; he was versatile and skilled at finding open teammates. (Seven months later, the Atlanta Hawks would use their first-round pick to draft him.) Isaiah Miles was also having a great senior year, and the rest of the guys followed their leaders. Plus, this would be our first true road game of the season.

Our guys kept their cool even as Daniel got into early foul trouble that limited him to four minutes in the first half. When Kris made a layup with 2:02 to go before halftime, we had a 42–27 lead.

We knew Saint Joseph's would keep coming, and they did. With 14:08 left in the second half Miles drained a three-pointer that pulled the Hawks to within 54–49, and the crowd was making itself a major factor.

But we have faith in all of our guys. And if you were among the 250 ticketed Villanova fans in the building, you kind of had a hunch who would step forward. On the next possession, Jalen found Arch for a three-point attempt from the right side, and he stepped into the shot in rhythm. When it fell through the net, the lead was back to eight, and it felt like we had weathered a storm. We ended up with a well-earned 86–72 win.

After the game, Arch made sure to point out to the media that he was actually in the wrong place on that sequence: "Jalen just found me with an amazing pass."

Some people on the outside might interpret that as sloppy play, followed by a little luck. It showed me that even when things didn't go as planned, our guys were finding ways to improvise, adjusting to every moment on the fly, and figuring out how to get the win.

Hoops on Hallowed Ground

Our short drive to Saint Joseph's was a far less taxing trip than what we had planned next: On December 3, we would board a flight to Los Angeles, a pit stop on the way to our next game, which would take place in Hawaii—in the historic setting of Joint Base Pearl Harbor-Hickam on the seventy-fourth anniversary of Japan's surprise attack on the United States.

The idea for the Pearl Harbor Invitational came from Fox's college basketball producer, Steve Scheer. We had gotten to know Steve over the years when he was a key behind-the-scenes guy on CBS national games. He even coaxed me into having a camera follow me on a run the morning of our Final Four game in 2009. Steve is passionate about what he does, and every time we see him, which is frequently since he moved over to Fox in 2013, he has a new thought he wants us to consider for that telecast. I usually tell him no—he's got some real outside-the-box suggestions—but this one appealed to me from the moment it came up.

We were in the early stages of the Big East's relationship with Fox, and we knew this partnership would be good for our league. Fox executives, led by president Larry Jones, were bringing the *Fox NFL Sunday* show to Honolulu for this weekend and wanted to create a major college basketball doubleheader as well. In addition to the compelling games, this would be a tangible way for all involved to say thank you to the members of our armed forces stationed at Pearl Harbor.

Before the trip, I gathered all of our guys together in our cinema to watch *Lone Survivor*, the 2013 film about a team of Navy SEALs led by Michael P. Murphy, a young man who was posthumously awarded the Medal of Honor for his heroism during an unsuccessful mission to track and kill a Taliban leader in Afghanistan in 2005. The film was certainly a strong look at teamwork, brotherhood, and commitment. It's a film we would wind up referencing often. But for this particular occasion—this trip to Pearl Harbor—it would come to hold a very special meaning that none of us would fully grasp until we got there.

I knew this was going to be a great trip from the start, but when I learned that our opponent would be Oklahoma, I got even more excited. The Sooners' coach, Lon Kruger, was bringing back an experienced unit that was projected to be one of the Top 10 teams in the nation. It was the kind of test we felt would ultimately help us grow toward our goal of being at our best in March and (hopefully) April.

After the stop in Los Angeles, where we played an open scrimmage followed by a reception for our Southern California alumni, we landed in Honolulu and were taken to a downtown hotel housing all four teams—and one of the first people we encountered was Dylan

Ennis. Oregon was to face Navy in the second game of the double-header, and the guys were excited to see Dylan wearing that ever-present, effervescent smile—even if he did look a little odd in the Ducks colors of lime green and bright yellow. The walking boot on his foot was a reminder that Dylan wouldn't get to play in Pearl Harbor, but it was nonetheless a treat to get a moment to say hi to him as we focused on our preparations.

We squeezed in an afternoon practice, then made our way to a reception held for all four teams on the base. Our hosts were admirals from the United States Navy, and the setting was a covered veranda overlooking the Pacific. By the time the reception was over it was nearly 8 p.m. local time, which was 1 a.m. on our internal clocks, and we were all pretty spent. Part of me wanted to skip the tour we had scheduled for the team that evening, especially since I knew I'd be leaving the hotel the next morning at 5:15 a.m. for an appearance all four coaches were making on *Fox NFL Sunday*.

> ## BEYOND BASKETBALL
>
> ### Change It Up
>
> Life experiences can sometimes be the best teaching tool. Inspirational stories, culled from movies, books, or people you may have encountered beyond your team, have a way of touching everyone and can help to clearly illustrate a key point in an unexpected way.

I will be forever grateful we decided to take the tour instead of stealing a few winks of sleep. We took a bus to an area of the base where the Navy docked an impressive-looking guided-missile destroyer. It was a gleaming, nearly new ship that had just been launched in 2011—the USS *Michael Murphy*, named for the real-life hero of *Lone Survivor*.

As we stepped off the bus, members of the ship's crew greeted us and took us on board for a sixty-minute tour. I can say without hesitation that the tour turned into the highlight of our trip.

Our group, which numbered more than forty and included the president of Villanova, Father Peter, and other university officials, was split into two groups. And at one point, someone in my group asked our guide how old he was.

While in Hawaii for the Pearl Harbor Invitational in early December 2015, we had a chance to meet Howie Long (in the striped polo shirt), the NFL great and Villanova alum. On the left is the Reverend Peter M. Donohue, O.S.A., the president of Villanova, with the players (from left to right) Henry Lowe, Patrick Farrell, Ryan Arcidiacono, Kevin Rafferty, Josh Hart, Mikal Bridges, Darryl Reynolds, Jalen Brunson, Daniel Ochefu, and Phil Booth. And that's the top of my head behind Patty.

When he replied, "I'm twenty-one, sir," it hit all of us.

These men and women who were serving our country were our players' contemporaries. Their peers. To witness the respect the United States Navy had for Michael Murphy and that group of men who lost their lives serving in Afghanistan was beyond powerful. And to see these crew members in the flesh only strengthened our team's bond and brought home the reality that these young Americans on board the USS *Michael Murphy* are doing the hard work of protecting our freedom—so that we can play our game. The game we love.

We're just coaching and playing basketball. The fact that these good people would take the time to show us around and share their experiences with us was both humbling and an honor. It was a moment none of us will ever forget.

Two days later, on December 7, 2016, as I stepped onto the bus for the ride to the base, I was so pleased with where we were as a team. The guys were appreciative and grateful for the experiences we had shared in Los Angeles and Honolulu. At the same time, they were dialed into our game plan and excited for the basketball challenge the Sooners would present.

I couldn't wait to see how it unfolded.

By 2:15 p.m., with a national television audience watching on FS1 and the sun peeking through the top of the open-air arena, we were on our heels, reeling from what Oklahoma had thrown at us. We fell behind early, and I realized that Oklahoma's speed, quickness, and assertiveness were going to be a handful for us that day. Lon had five seniors, including eventual All-American and Player of the Year Buddy Hield, who together formed a highly functioning machine.

I knew Oklahoma was good before the game began. Yet I was stunned at just how good they were—and how far we were from reaching that level. We gave great effort—Daniel wound up playing through heat cramps—but our execution and precision did not even come close to matching theirs.

We trailed for most of the first half, made a run right before halftime, and felt like we were in decent shape, trailing 35–27 after the first twenty minutes. But in the second half they did what great teams do by clamping down defensively and owning the glass. In the end, we absorbed a 78–55 loss.

It was ironic that we were in the same building with Dylan that day, because our loss underscored how much we still missed the senior class of 2015. Dylan, Darrun, and JayVaughn had been our three best perimeter defenders and rebounders. We were concerned about our ability to defend and rebound when we began the year, and Oklahoma exposed that weakness. Our attention to detail and cohesiveness defensively that day was poor, and it affected us on the offensive end. We became three-happy—too enamored of the three-point shot—because our guys sensed that we weren't able to stop the Sooners, which meant the only choice was to outscore them.

As consumed as we were with trying to find something that worked against Oklahoma, we couldn't help but take pride in the pageantry of the event. In the stands, among the current and former military personnel, were survivors of the 1941 attack. During each mandated break to allow the network to go to commercial—there are nine in every televised NCAA game—a survivor was introduced to the crowd onsite and shown on the broadcast.

Everyone in the building, players and coaches included, paused to applaud each Pearl Harbor survivor.

In more than three decades of being in sports, I have never been through an experience like that—as a player, coach, or fan. As participants, we were all stopped in our tracks at each of those breaks by the emotion and sense of pride we felt as Americans. Just being on that hallowed ground with those survivors, on the anniversary of the attack, was a great reminder that we are part of something much larger than any game.

> ## BEYOND BASKETBALL
>
> ### *Respect Everyone.*
> ### *Fear No One.*
>
> There is only one goal—to give your greatest effort. If someone else gets better results than you, honor them. But maintain your own self-respect for offering your best. This will give you confidence against any foe.

Still, the bus ride from the base back to our hotel felt much longer than the forty-five minutes we sat in Honolulu traffic. When you get handled like that, you tend to retreat to your own thoughts, and that's what we all did during the ride. It was dead silent. After all the early-season winning we'd done, it felt like a massive blow. So much so that none of us were in the mood to do much of anything fun with our free evening in the beauty of Hawaii.

It's been a long-standing tradition that when FS1 analyst Bill Raftery is on the call for a Villanova game, our coaches and staff join him for a postgame meal or beverage. Trying to describe our relationship with "Raf"—or, as he is known to a lot of his many fans, "The Governor"—isn't easily condensed to a single paragraph. He is a larger-than-life figure in our game, with a gentleman's touch that makes him one of the most beloved guys in all of sports.

It's always a joy to be out with Raf, and I had never passed up an invitation from him, even after some crushing home losses over the years. But in this case I broke with tradition and went to a quiet dinner with Patty instead. I just couldn't get my mind around what I had witnessed that day against Oklahoma.

I wasn't upset by the loss as much as I was surprised by the distance in precision between us and the Sooners. I believed we could get to that level, but it appeared to be a much greater distance than I had imagined before we left Philadelphia.

Always a Sunrise

Prior to the game, Patty and I had arranged to have a car pick us up at the hotel on the morning of December 8, ahead of the first of our two flights back to Philadelphia. Walking out of the hotel into darkness at 4:30 a.m., I wondered why we had agreed to this. But as the car took us out to the North Shore of Oahu to see the World Surf League and its president, Paul Speaker, a Villanova alumnus who'd invited us to be his guests, those thoughts evaporated.

My wife and I love the beach and the ocean. Like a lot of Philadelphians—and New Yorkers—we've got our favorite getaway spot at the Jersey Shore. Being there with my family in the summer is my favorite form of relaxation.

So when we arrived at the beach on the North Shore, home of the Banzai Pipeline and many other world-class surf breaks, at 6 a.m., I finally began to let the Oklahoma game go. During our breakfast with Paul, we met some of the surfers and quickly realized they had no idea who we were or that there had been any sort of a basketball game played on the island the day before. The reality that the whole world didn't focus on our team or that loss helped bring me back to center.

By the time we returned to the hotel for the ride to the airport, I felt rejuvenated.

At different points on our long journey home, I had a chance to speak with some of the guys individually. I was positive with all of them. Attitude is everything, and since we had a lot of time to spend around one another—waiting to board in Honolulu, in flight to Los Angeles, and then on our red-eye from Los Angeles back to Philly—

I used that time to remind everyone what a great season we were hav-ing so far, despite the Oklahoma game.

"We'll get there," I told the guys. "Just keep at it. Just stay focused."

I took some time to speak with my assistants, Baker, Ash, and Kyle, to start to define the work we had to do. We tinkered with details like our shot selection and how we defended the three-point shot. We reviewed our player rotation.

I also came to grips with the fact that Daniel dealt with heat cramps during the game, in what was essentially a covered outdoor venue with no air-conditioning. It compromised his effectiveness. I didn't want us to use that as an excuse publicly, yet it was a factor, and I had to incorporate that into my evaluation.

The other lingering takeaway was what the video revealed about Oklahoma. This wasn't just a good team but a legitimate NCAA Championship contender. Lon is a coach's coach, one of the best in our game, and I felt he had offered me a lesson. It wasn't in any way fun to endure, but it gave us a road map, something to steer toward. If we could build the kind of cohesion and trust in one another we saw from Oklahoma, we had a chance to get where we wanted to go.

The sunrise out the window of the plane as we began our descent into Philadelphia reminded me that this was a new day, bright with promise and possibility.

10

Up and Down and Up Again

I WASN'T THE only one to tell our players that the loss we'd endured was something that could turn into a positive for us in the end. That game in Hawaii was the only game all year that Father Rob had to miss, but he was right there upon our return, ready to teach us all a little something about perseverance. He doesn't rely solely on the Bible for inspiration. Sometimes he turns to the church of pop culture.

"In the movie classic *The Shawshank Redemption*," Father Rob began, "Andy Dufresne, the character played by Tim Robbins, is doing hard time in prison for a murder he did not commit. He manages to persevere and maintain a tough attitude focused on his freedom despite the hardships he has to endure. He builds friendships, relationships that sustain him all along the way, as he stays focused on where he is going, though he is not there yet. His journey to freedom literally takes him through a sewer hole full of filth, but he goes through it anyway on his way back to a better life.

"So much of our life calls us to go through things, situations, hardships, and trials that we would much rather avoid or simply go around, but we cannot. That requires us to bear down, focus, and try to find meaning out of the experience as we journey to where we are meant to be."

As he always does, Father Rob found a second story to back up his point, and this one came straight from a more traditional source.

"In the gospel [Luke 9:51–56], we hear how Jesus and His disciples were on a journey to Jerusalem. What is most telling here is that Jesus takes them on a route that goes right through Samaria. History tells us that the Samaritans despised those in Jesus' community, and the feeling was mutual. There are those who would have said that this was also like going through the sewer. There was conflict, tension, and discord between people who were unwilling or unable to see past their differences.

"Most, if not all, would have found an alternate route around Samaria. But in this case Jesus—knowing full well that there would be those who would not see eye to eye, who may ridicule and persecute them—takes the chance anyway and walks right through Samaria in an effort to build relationships, heal division, and make new friends. And He *does*. He didn't avoid the hardship. He embraced it in an effort to help everyone find something better.

"Sometimes we are all asked to journey through something, not around it, in an effort to arrive where we need to or are called to go. Mom or Dad holds down two jobs on the way through to a better life for the family. The struggling law student goes through his third bar exam on the way to helping others find justice. As athletes, we go through rigorous practice on the way to better habits. And sometimes, we need to go through a loss to learn how to win."

As usual, Father Rob was talking my language, sharing the exact same positivity I was trying to impress upon our team as a coach.

"Villanova's own Jim Croce sang that there's no rainbow without going through the rain," he added. (Bet you didn't know Jim Croce was a Villanova guy, did you?)

With his gaze up over our heads toward heaven, Father Rob concluded his homily by saying, "With the spirit that fills and unites us, let's gather the strength to go right through those things that stand between us and the rainbow: A better life for our loved ones. A better world for all those around us.

"Go through the struggle of class to the joy of graduation and the opportunities that accompany it.

"Go through the minor leagues to realize professional dreams.

"Go through the tough rehab workouts to discover renewed strength.

"Let's remember we go through nothing alone. We go together. When we go with God, we find ourselves on the other side of trial only to find our destiny."

. . .

As we stepped back onto our practice court after a day of rest, I wasn't sure what to expect. Air travel takes a toll on athletes and, as a coach, you understand it may show up when you get back out on the floor. Even if the mind is willing, fatigue can lead to sloppiness.

It didn't take many minutes of observation before I was able to dismiss that fear.

Despite the disappointment, we all seemed to be of the same mind: The trip—and, yes, the loss—was a positive for us. The life lessons were invaluable. To be on that destroyer and see the professional way the young servicemen and -women conducted themselves gave us such perspective.

The only negative to that first practice was that we were down a man. Our freshman guard, Donte DiVincenzo, reported to Jeff Pierce that he was feeling discomfort in his foot. An X-ray discovered a fractured bone, and the official prognosis was that Donte would be sidelined for four to six weeks.

Though Donte wasn't playing heavy minutes for us yet, we liked everything we had seen from him thus far. Donte was a rock star of sorts in his home state of Delaware. He had enjoyed an outstanding career at Salesianum School and developed a large following with his parents, John and Kathie, front and center. He was 6'5", and we knew he had the tools to play well for us, but what we couldn't be sure of was how long it would take him to adjust physically to the college game.

We were startled at how quickly he adapted. He immediately showed that he was going to be a great defender and rebounder from the guard position. We were excited about him—and very sorry to see him hit a setback. We could only hope that he took Father Rob's homily to heart.

Outside our locker room, the take was that we would have to play without a guard who averaged less than seven minutes and two points per game. In other words, no big deal. On the inside, we considered it a significant blow. We had seen in practice what Donte was capable of, the kind of impact he could make on our team. No one else had seen what we had. Most of all, we were disappointed for Donte. He was so excited to be here, playing at Villanova less than an hour's drive from his home.

When La Salle came to the Pavilion on December 13, Donte was dressed in what would become his game-day attire for the foreseeable future: a dress shirt, tie, and slacks with a black walking boot on his right foot.

The Explorers are coached by John Giannini, a friend whom I had gotten to know well during his days as head coach at the University of Maine. The Black Bears were one of our America East rivals during my tenure at Hofstra, and John had previously made his mark in the Philly area coaching at Rowan University in South Jersey. John and his staff were sure to have taken careful notes of how Oklahoma had succeeded in frustrating us.

Our guys have learned that if you aren't prepared for a Big Five game, you will get beat. We were locked in from the start of this one and prepared for everything La Salle threw at us. By Sunday night, we had our second Big Five victory and eighth of the season.

It's always good to get back into the win column after a tough loss. What made this one extra satisfying was the timing. On top of the long round-trip to Hawaii, we had just entered exam week. It's a stressful time for our players as they work to complete projects and prepare for their end-of-semester tests. The fact that we were able to turn in a solid effort in the midst of all that was a good sign.

When Villanova's exam period ended, we were faced with a test of a different sort.

The University of Virginia Cavaliers were hearing some of the same kinds of questions we were. Tony Bennett has done a tremendous job in building a hard-nosed, tough, and talented squad during his time in Charlottesville. In 2014–2015, Virginia earned both the ACC regular season and conference tournament championships, only to get knocked off in the NCAA Round of 32. There were those who considered that to be a disappointment.

We know how hard it is to win a regular season conference championship, and our admiration for their program was off the charts. This was a terrific defensive team that prized the same qualities we do. Scoring points against the Cavaliers would be a chore, especially in John Paul Jones Arena, their building. It was a challenge we relished.

For most of us, playing at UVA was something new. It was my first time there—but not so Jalen Brunson. During Rick Brunson's tenure as an assistant coach at Virginia, Jalen was one of the ball boys.

Prior to our practice, I chatted with one of the arena staff members whose duties back then included oversight of the ball boys. When I asked him about Jalen, he replied that even during that time frame, circa 2008, Jalen was conscientious. He also mentioned that at halftime he could always count on Jalen sneaking over to a nearby practice court to get some shots up.

I chuckled and told him that sounded about right to me.

ESPN analyst Jay Bilas was among the small group who observed our practice that day. Jay would be calling the game the following day and watched closely as we went through a brisk workout. When practice was over, we sent the team and the rest of the coaching staff back to the hotel while I stayed behind to tape a segment with Jay that would air in the coming week on ESPN.

Jay is always a great barometer for me. He's honest, and by the questions he asks, you get a good sense of how he feels about your team. As a former player and assistant coach, he gets what we are doing. He's also not a schmoozer who's looking to pump you up. Jay knows that as a coach, you want to hear the truth.

By the time I walked up the arena stairs to the concourse level and caught a ride back to the hotel with our radio play-by-play voice, Ryan Fannon, I was feeling good about where we were. Jay and I got to spend a few minutes chatting after we taped the segment, and it was clear to me that he believed we had a very good team. He told me as much, while echoing our thoughts that Virginia was also terrific.

Part of my discussion with Jay centered on the number of three-point shots we had attempted thus far in the season. We had taken a lot of them, particularly in the loss to Oklahoma. I told Jay that as a staff, we weren't worried about those numbers. We knew that the advanced metrics that have become such useful tools in our game over the last decade suggested we were overly reliant on the three-pointer. But we were taking the longer view on that.

Our philosophy, especially early in the year, is that we want our guys to be aggressive. We urge them to look to make scoring plays in order to build their confidence. If the time comes when we have to dial that back, we will.

Two Steps Back

We couldn't wait to get to noon on Saturday to play this one. As a team, we were convinced that we had made important strides in the thirteen days since the Oklahoma game. Virginia had our full attention and respect.

The atmosphere inside John Paul Jones Arena was electric. Even though it was still December, you could tell everyone considered this to be a big-time game.

The forty minutes of basketball didn't disappoint.

I liked how our team approached the game and how they handled the circumstances that sometimes arise when you face an outstanding opponent on its home court.

On the whole, I believe the Big East has the best officiating in America. The supervisor of officials is John Cahill, who had a distinguished career as a referee before moving into his management role. John does an excellent job in balancing the pressures on both officials and head coaches.

That said, we all have our moments.

One of those came in the first half. Josh Hart was whistled for a foul by one of the three refs assigned to the game. I felt it was a really bad call. It was Josh's second foul of the period, and our approach in that case has generally favored removing the player for the rest of the half, though we do judge it on a case-by-case basis.

I took Josh out—and it hurt us.

We hung in there with Kris enjoying an explosive afternoon at the offensive end. Josh dealt with the foul trouble and gave us a lift in the second half. We never gave up on that game, but Virginia was able to pull away over the final three minutes when we were forced to foul. We lost 85–74.

There are some defeats that are easier to accept than others.

This was one of those.

We had made incredible strides in less than two weeks. I was proud of our forward progress and the work ethic it took to get there. All of those gains were reinforced as I watched the replay of the game on my laptop during the return flight from Charlottesville.

To some, our 9–2 record suggested we were a good team but maybe not a great one. In our two most high-profile tests, against Oklahoma and on the road at Virginia, we had lost by double digits.

Yet I felt confident that we had just seen a great team, our second in as many weeks, and that the rate of team growth we had just witnessed meant our ceiling was high—maybe higher than it had been a year earlier, when our more experienced roster gave us less room for improvement over the course of the season.

Off the court, this was a period of transition for us. Exams were over. We were into winter break, when most students return home to their families for the three-week hiatus until the spring semester begins in January. The campus gets much quieter. Our players are part of a small group of students who remain.

We have always tried to bridge this gap to make sure our players aren't off by themselves. Our centering event is the annual team Christmas party that Patty and I host at our home. The players are joined by coaches, staff, and their families. Coach Shack even relaxes the dietary rules a bit so the guys can grab a holiday dessert or two.

I just love having the team in our home right before Christmas. It gets us away from basketball. The conversations are about our families instead of jump shots. There is no shortage of laughter around the Christmas tree. We see a lot more of the players' personalities show through as they take turns busting one another's chops.

We also ask the guys to do something else.

With pens at the ready, we ask each player to write a Christmas thank-you letter to three people who have impacted their lives positively. The notes don't have to be lengthy. A simple Merry Christmas and thank you usually gets the job done. But it brings us all back to the notion that we aren't in this alone and that we have had help getting where we are.

After two tough losses in our first ten games—first to Oklahoma, then to Virginia—it felt good to head into the Christmas break with a win over Delaware.

JERRY MILLEVOI

We remained in that upbeat frame of mind as we prepared for our final game before Christmas, at the Pavilion against Delaware. This is always a special night at Villanova as we make an effort to welcome back our basketball alumni. Many of our alums in the area are regulars at our home games, but we work hard to make this night extra special. At halftime, former Wildcat guard and current radio analyst Whitey Rigsby introduced more than fifty basketball alums. Since this game takes place over the holidays, when most students are home with their families, we're able to offer the unused student tickets to the alumni, so more members of their families can be on hand. The older the former players get, the more pride they take in bringing their children and grandchildren to the game and the reception we host on campus afterward. It's just a wonderful time to be a member of the Villanova Basketball family.

Entering the Pavilion that night, I was especially enthused. The alumni were in the house, and I was convinced that one of our key juniors, Kris Jenkins, had taken a critical step in his own development during the game against Virginia.

We had first encountered Kris during his spectacular career at Gonzaga College High School in Washington, D.C. At the time, Kris was living with the Britt family, which included Nate Britt Sr. and his wife, Melody, along with their standout guard of a son, Nate Jr. We were recruiting Nate Jr., and welcomed the entire Britt family, Kris included, to campus on what is known as an unofficial visit.

Back then I did not have a sense of the complexity of Kris' family situation. I knew that he lived with the Britts, but it wasn't until later that I came to appreciate how close they were. This wasn't some kid who had moved in twelve months ago. Kris was family.

Our staff was certainly aware of Kris' skill. His shooting stroke is one of the purest we have seen at Villanova, and he has an extremely high basketball IQ. Coming out of Gonzaga, we felt he would be prepared for the academic demands at Villanova. My concern was his frame.

At 6'6", Kris would play in college as an undersized forward. His weight at the time was north of 280 pounds, and we wondered about his stamina. We want our guys to be in outstanding condition, and it was clear to us that Kris would have some ground to make up in that area.

When we met with the Britts in my Davis Center office, both Kris and Nate Jr. were there. A lot of the time was spent talking to Nate. To me, Nate possessed the tools to be an outstanding Villanova guard. Other schools thought so too; he was being recruited by a lot of the big-name programs.

I told Kris my staff thought the world of him. The honest truth, though, was I needed to take a longer look at his game to see if he was a fit for us. And I was also clear that if he wanted to come to Villanova, he would have to want to get into better condition. He would need to essentially remake his body under the direction of John Shackleton, who would tailor a specific plan for him.

In essence, I said, you will have to change your diet and lifestyle.

It wasn't much of a sales job. On the contrary, it was the kind of blunt talk that would have discouraged ninety-five percent of the kids hearing it.

We spoke to Nate Britt Sr. a few days later and asked how Nate Jr. liked his visit to Villanova. He responded that Nate liked it. Then he added, Kris *really* liked it.

That was not the response I anticipated.

I knew at that moment this was a young man I had to seriously evaluate with my own eyes.

I watched Kris often in the summer of 2012 on the AAU circuit. As that summer wore on, we began to get the sense that Nate Britt Jr. was focused on North Carolina. The more I watched Kris, the more eager I was to have him become a Wildcat. We pursued Kris with great intensity through July, and he gave us a verbal commitment in August.

Part of our excitement about Kris was the young man he is: polite, quick with a smile, and very respectful. As we got to know his mother, Felicia Jenkins (a former player), and father, Kelvin Jenkins, you could see how that came to be.

The relationship between Kris and the Britt family grew out of a difficult medical crisis in the Jenkins family. Back in the mid-2000s, Kris' younger sister, Kori, was battling DiGeorge syndrome, a disease that would ultimately take her life at eleven months. The best available treatment option was in Baltimore, and the Jenkins family made multiple trips there from South Carolina. While in the area, Kris began to play with the D.C. Assault, a prominent AAU team coached by Nate Sr. Since Kris and Nate Jr. were the same age and quickly formed a bond, Kris spent much of the summer living with the Britts.

Felicia, meanwhile, was working as a coach herself. Felicia and Kelvin appreciated how comfortable Kris felt with the Britts, and soon the families agreed that Kris would spend his high school years in Maryland with them. (Felicia and Kelvin later divorced.)

It was both a selfless and organic decision that worked because both families put Kris' welfare first.

Felicia balances her love for her son with a no-nonsense approach to basketball that has benefited Kris. When he visits her, she keeps him on a workout and diet regimen.

Kelvin Jenkins is a former player too. He works as a referee. This is a good, solid man who remains a big part of Kris' life.

Even though Kris' family situation is unique, it actually gives him something wonderful in that he has four great parents whose impact has helped make him the fine man he is today.

What You Do Speaks Loudly

In his first year with us, in 2013–2014, Kris made good on his promise. Working with Coach Shack, he dropped forty pounds, and that translated directly to the court: He was an explosive weapon off the bench. Toward the end of his sophomore season in 2014–2015, he reached a milepost in our program that may have gone unnoticed outside it. In the Big East Tournament Championship game, he did an exceptional defensive job on Xavier's outstanding center Matt Stainbrook, who stands a good four inches taller than Kris.

By that point, he had become one of our most trustworthy defensive players, and everyone in our program respected the work he had put in to get there.

Off the court, we couldn't have been happier with Kris. He retains a trace of the southern accent he acquired while spending his early years in South Carolina. On campus he was a hit, and the Nova Nation adores his ability to sink three-pointers with a quick-release stroke that appears almost effortless.

In the fall, Kris had moved into the starting lineup, but he endured some ups and downs through the first five weeks of the season. We place a lot of responsibility on our starters to set a tone for their teammates. We want our players in the habit of performing at a high level immediately in whatever they're doing, not building toward it. For example, when we start a drill, we expect our guys to run to the starting point. When we step into a team meeting, we want everyone quiet and his eyes locked on the speaker, whether it's me, an assistant coach, or someone else addressing the team. Once we begin, we don't want anyone joking around or staring at his phone.

Starting strong is paramount for us, and that effort level needs to be displayed at every practice, in every drill, and on every possession. This can be an adjustment for guys accustomed to bringing energy off the bench. And even though Kris had come a long way, there were still bouts of inconsistency as he settled into the role of a starter.

The way Kris had played against Virginia was a major breakthrough for him. It had been a monster effort as he established a new career high with twenty-three points. This wasn't just a game that got the fans excited. It got our team fired up. Athletes understand that for a teammate to have that kind of day, in a hostile environment against one of the nation's top teams, is really special. It cements their respect for him as a big-time player who can produce in the toughest situations. We all walked out of John Paul Jones Arena that Saturday feeling like Kris was on the verge of becoming a force for us.

Then, in the first half of the game against Delaware, which we would go on to win 78–48 in front of the alumni-packed crowd, Kris fell to the floor grabbing his right knee. After he was assisted off the court and into the training room, I got the sign from Jeff Pierce that Kris was done for the night. His knee was wrapped in ice as he took a seat on the bench.

Suddenly, there was a dark cloud hovering over the Pavilion. Knee injuries have the potential to ruin seasons and, in the worst cases, careers.

When the game ended, I met with Jeff and Dr. Mike Duncan, our team physician. They were concerned. No definitive diagnosis could be made until an MRI was performed on Kris' knee, but there was a clear vibe that this could be a significant setback for Kris. The fact that he had just enjoyed such a breakout game made it all the more disquieting.

The final game before Christmas usually brings a short break in our season. We would not play again until December 28, which allowed us to give the players the chance to return home for a few days to celebrate the holiday. Many of our guys left with their families directly after the alumni reception that followed the Delaware game.

Kris would have to delay his departure until after the MRI

> ### BEYOND BASKETBALL
>
> #### *The Invisible Contributions Can Matter the Most*
>
> Try never to overlook the humble efforts made by members of your team. It is a leader's job to identify those instances that others might not see and emphasize that a seemingly simple gesture can generate many positive ripples.

was completed the next morning. Our coaching staff made sure to text Kris that night because we know how difficult a period this can be. As an athlete, when your body has been potentially compromised, all sorts of dark thoughts can creep into your head.

What we didn't know at the time was that one of Kris' teammates had his back.

Rather than go to his family's Philadelphia home that night as planned, Darryl Reynolds elected to stay on campus so that Kris wouldn't have to spend the night alone with his worries. It was a small gesture, and one that our staff was totally unaware of.

We always tell the players: What you do speaks so loudly, we can't hear what you say.

What Darryl did was show his character when no one—staff, teammates, or anyone else—was watching.

In the accounts of the Delaware game, there was little mention made of Darryl's four points and six rebounds in twenty-two minutes. But his small gesture of kindness was its own kind of leadership. Leadership that we all respected.

Kris had his MRI the next morning. Following the appointment, he hopped in the car with Nate Britt Sr. for the ride home to Maryland while they awaited the results. During that ride, Mike Duncan and Jeff called me with what we would come to call our Christmas gift: The MRI revealed no ligament or cartilage damage. Kris had suffered a right-knee sprain and would be officially listed as day-to-day.

I couldn't wait to get ahold of Kris and tried to reach him to no avail. I then tried the Britts' home phone number, thinking that perhaps they had already arrived. Melody answered, and when I gave her the news, she cried. I asked Melody to have Kris call me as soon as he got home, which he did a little later.

When I gave Kris the news, we all exhaled.

As a coach, you understand that the wrong twist or turn of a joint can totally alter the look of a season. It's why we say that we're never quite sure what twists and turns a particular season will offer.

Kris' knee would require only rest, and the timing was perfect: That's exactly what he'd get over the three-day Christmas break.

For a few hours, we were reminded that adversity can crop up at any moment. In this case, it lasted less than twenty-four hours. It was nonetheless an intense and stressful time for Kris, his family, and his teammates and coaches.

As we settled in with our families for Christmas Eve, we reflected on the obvious blessing that Kris was going to be okay. But I also thought we had been blessed in another way by Darryl's selfless act of friendship.

All of those little things began to build the love, respect, and unity we shared as a team. We had taken another seemingly inconsequential step that had more power than anyone beyond our family may have realized.

11

In the Zone

BACK ON VILLANOVA'S still-quiet campus a few days before New Year's, we hosted Penn and its new coach, Steve Donahue. Steve is a local guy who returned to coach at Penn after taking Cornell to the NCAA Tournament and later becoming the head coach at Boston College. The Quakers were making progress in Steve's first season, and we knew they would have a good game plan for us.

Penn worked extremely hard to take away our three-point shooting game and succeeded in the first half—we missed all six of our attempts from deep. But we proved adaptable, connecting on eighteen of twenty-six of our shots inside the arc to build a 39–11 lead. The best news for our staff, though, was our defense. We were locked in from the start, and a lot of that had to do with Daniel. His understanding of our concepts and ability to guard on the perimeter really took our defense to another level.

So with a large halftime lead, we decided to take a look at what was, for us, something of a new wrinkle.

One of the questions I am often asked is how my style differs from that of my mentor, Coach Massimino. Everyone knows what I think about Coach Mass. He's a basketball genius. I discovered early in my head coaching career at Hofstra, though, that I couldn't try to duplicate exactly what Coach Mass did. Believe me, I tried. But it didn't feel real to me or, I suspect, our players.

Coach Mass employed multiple defensive tactics. Some trips down the court we would be in a man-to-man defense; some we might come at you with a 2-3 zone; on occasion we would utilize a 1-3-1 full-court press to disrupt the opponents' timing.

I have always preferred man-to-man defense.

Nova Nation fans who recall the success Coach Mass had shifting defenses have prodded me to consider using his approach. But to me, man-to-man defense fits the personality I want our team to have as an aggressive unit that dictates the tempo of a game. When we have occasionally used zone in the past, it too often felt to me like we became more passive at both ends of the court.

Like anything in life, to excel at something you need to work at it. On those rare times we tried a zone over the last decade, we weren't very good at it, and I quickly lost my patience with the experiment.

Now, thanks to some fresh prodding from my assistant coaches, Baker, Ash, and Kyle, I began to reconsider my resistance. As a leader, unwavering rigidity can often get you nowhere. You have to be ready and willing to adapt as circumstances change. And this 2015–2016 team was exceptionally bright. Its capacity to absorb information quickly and successfully gave us a chance to implement a new twist on defense. So we started to spend more practice time on it around the holidays, and with a 28-point halftime lead against Penn, we decided to see how our zone looked.

It wasn't pretty. Penn shot fifty-four percent from the field and scored forty-six second-half points. You could hear some restlessness in the Pavilion as they carved into our lead. Jalen scored twenty-two points, though, and our first-half work gave us enough of a cushion to post a 77–57 victory.

Earlier in my career, that second-half defensive effort may have caused me to mothball the 2-3 zone. Yet I have come to take to heart the words of our good friend George Raveling, a 1960 Villanova Basketball alumnus who went on to become a successful coach and director of international basketball at Nike. George likes to say that we should all be "lifetime learners," and at seventy-eight he is one of the most vibrantly curious people I know. To keep growing in any line of work, you must keep evolving.

We weren't giving up on the zone.

The Big Five win over Penn closed the chapter on the City Series for now. (The final game against Temple had been moved to February for ESPN.) We were 3–0 against our Philly rivals and 10–2 overall.

The Big East regular season was about to begin.

Next Man Up

We had two days to prepare for a date with a Xavier team that was the talk of the Big East. Since we had last seen the Musketeers, in March at Madison Square Garden, they had been on an upward arc. Xavier won a pair of NCAA Tournament games in March 2015 and was off to the best start in program history, at 12–0. The pollsters noticed, moving Xavier to No. 6 in the major rankings. (In contrast, our losses to Oklahoma and Virginia had dropped us to No. 16.)

It stacked up as a great showdown at noon in a packed Pavilion on New Year's Eve. Gus Johnson and Bill Raftery would be on hand to call the game for FS1. The Nova Nation was hyped.

We had heard the talk that the Big East was now Xavier's league. They were the undefeated team with the Top 10 ranking. There were some who suggested our time as the Big East's dominant program had passed.

All of that was interesting to me because we never felt as though we owned the Big East. Yes, we had won the first two regular season championships since the new version of the league began in 2013, but there are too many elite programs in our league to say that any one team stands above the rest. As many national champions as the Big East has had, what really has set it apart from 1979 through the present is the depth of quality teams. That's as true today as it was in the 1980s.

We always take the approach that we have to prove ourselves. Every year. So all that was said and written about where we stood relative to Xavier or any other program didn't bother us. In the end, it all comes down to what you do on the court. We want to be the best team we can be at the end of the year. If Xavier surpassed us, so be it. That's great for our league.

The one thing we never lose sight of is that the season is long. The key is how you handle the *entire* season, not how you play against this top team or that one. We learned that two years earlier when Creighton crushed us twice, but we won the other sixteen Big East games we played to win the conference title.

Whenever I can—and it happens often—I remind our guys that worrying about which player starts is mostly pointless too. During a season, anything can happen. We stress to our players that we have confidence in every one of them. I tell them that I will put them in at any time, in any game.

Our players believe that, but it never hurts to have examples crop up that can serve as concrete reminders. And while we weren't really looking for one on the eve of a new Big East season, an opportunity like this has a way of sneaking up on you when you least expect it. That's what happened on the morning of our big battle with Xavier.

As I walked through the lobby of the hotel into the meeting room where we gather, I learned that Jalen Brunson's status for the game was in doubt due to a virus that had kept him up most of the previous night, unable to keep food down. To fans, this news was cause for instant concern. Jalen was growing more comfortable by the day and had led us in scoring against Penn.

Yet within our family, one of our mantras is "Next man up"— so we inserted Phil Booth into the starting lineup. I didn't see

> ## BEYOND BASKETBALL
>
> ### *Change Is Inevitable*
>
> The only certainty in life is change. Core values are essential yet we also have to remain open to the new, lest we risk becoming stagnant. A willingness to reflect can produce new wrinkles that will invigorate your unit.

Jalen until we were inside the Pavilion locker room. I asked him how he felt. His response was that he wanted to play and would give me whatever he could. I admired Jalen's spirit. We were short-handed with Donte still in a walking boot. Jalen wanted to do what he could to help his team. But I knew we would only be able to use him for two- to three-minute bursts before he was spent.

After some fist bumps with the staff and Father Rob, I made the short walk from our locker room under the east stands to the area in front of our bench. I went over to say hello to Xavier coach Chris Mack and congratulate him on his team's great start. As we readied for the national anthem, I felt the noise wash over me. It sounded almost like the clock had already struck midnight in Times Square.

Then the game began, and within minutes the entire tenor of the day changed.

Edmond Sumner, a Xavier point guard who had made an instant

impact in his freshman year, was driving toward the basket when he rose up to attempt a shot and collided with Phil Booth and Kris Jenkins. It happened right in front of our bench. He crashed awkwardly to the floor, with his head absorbing much of the blow. It was a clean play, but everyone inside the Pavilion froze as they looked at the freshman guard lying prone under the basket.

From my vantage point, I could see Edmond's eyes roll back. I'd never seen that before, and it jolted me to my core. The game no longer mattered. The Pavilion fell silent as Dr. Duncan and Jeff Pierce joined Chris Mack and Xavier's trainer in assessing his condition.

It was as scary a thing as I have ever witnessed at a basketball game.

For a solid ten minutes a team of doctors, trainers, and EMS personnel tended to Sumner, eventually lifting him onto a stretcher. The entire time, there was absolute quiet in the Pavilion. Finally they wheeled him off the court toward an ambulance parked outside, and as he departed, the Pavilion crowd cheered.

We would all be forced to wait until after the game to hear any more news.

When the officials put the ball back in play, there were still thirty-eight minutes left on the clock, but I think it's safe to say that no one in that building cared anywhere near as much about the outcome of the game as they had a half hour ago.

In speaking with school officials during the pause in action, I began to get the sense that the situation might not have been as dire as it looked initially. No one knew for sure at that point, but the young man seemed to be responding to Chris and his teammates, who walked over to him just before he was removed on the stretcher.

There is no question that losing Edmond affected Xavier, and rightfully so. He is an outstanding player and losing a point guard is never easy. It played a part in Xavier's committing eleven first-half turnovers. On a more human level, though, every player on that team had to be concerned about the well-being of his friend and teammate. That's a tough situation to deal with in the heat of an intense matchup.

But the game had to go on, and as the action resumed we again witnessed the incredible gift of awareness that Ryan Arcidiacono brings to a basketball court.

Arch has the rare ability to assess a situation and decipher what his team needs at any given moment. Sometimes it's defense. On other occasions it's working to get a teammate going offensively by setting him up with easy baskets. This time, I believe Arch looked at the scene and concluded that with Jalen ailing, his team needed offensive firepower. He took the game over from the moment it resumed, scoring seventeen first-half points and finishing the day with a game-high twenty-seven. Phil stepped up too, connecting on four of five field goals for ten points in twenty-two minutes. For his part, Jalen provided us nine points in seventeen gutty minutes.

In his own way, each guy stepped up to lift his teammates.

The final was 95–64.

When we met in the Pavilion cinema area, where we gather as a team after home games, we prayed with Father Rob as we always do. I praised the guys for their commitment to our values and the attention to detail that helped us execute our best game of the season. I also made clear to everyone that no matter what anyone said or wrote about us, this was one game. We were 1–0 in the Big East with seventeen more to play.

Our guys know how good Edmond Sumner is. They understood what his loss, and the way his team lost him, had meant to Xavier. We had not seen the Musketeers at their best. This Big East opener was, in our minds, an aberration.

Later we learned that Sumner had suffered a concussion—a serious injury, to be sure, but it could have been worse. Much worse. Sumner would recover. He returned to the lineup a few weeks later and established himself as one of the great young players in our league.

A champion would not be crowned for another nine weeks. We had to quickly shift our focus to our next challenge, which would come in fifty-three hours, in Omaha, against another program on the rise: Creighton.

Better Together

For us, being on the road together might be our most treasured time as a team. We revel in the challenge of traveling long distances and preparing as one to take on a formidable opponent. It's just us: players, coaches, and staff. All of our meals are shared. There are team meetings where we talk about life beyond basketball. When we dissect video, we are less concerned with the tendencies of our opponent—though we do spend time on those—than we are with dissecting how close we are to playing Villanova Basketball at an optimum level.

Road trips are one part seminar and another part retreat. If you love basketball, as all of us do, they're kind of the perfect getaway.

Given the development of Josh and Kris (and what Arch had done against Xavier), opposing teams had begun to adapt their strategy in defending us. Teams were spending more energy in protecting the perimeter, neglecting the interior in order to contain our three-point shooting. That philosophy was one of Creighton's core values already, so we anticipated that a lot of attention would be spent chasing our shooters off the three-point line.

Good teams have an answer for that. Ours was Daniel.

We had seen Daniel dominate defensively. But now we were seeing how he could take over a game offensively with his passing and interior moves.

In the past, Creighton had exposed our forwards to some degree. Their style, as I mentioned, is predicated on limiting the damage from deep. Creighton's attention to the perimeter had, in previous seasons, offered our forwards one-on-one opportunities that we hadn't really capitalized on. However, we felt like Daniel had grown to the point that we would be able to exploit the opportunities that would be available to us around the basket.

Daniel knew going into this game that it was a chance for him to show how far he had progressed. Since his first days with us, he has always been meticulous in his study of our opponent scouting reports. At the start of the game, he had great confidence. We went to him early and he took advantage.

He used every weapon in his arsenal: Low-post moves. Short jumpers. One-on-one plays. That kind of interior production is always welcome. It is especially valuable away from home. By scoring inside, a tone is set—and that's what Daniel did at Creighton. He got us off on the right foot and helped create openings for his teammates. Soon Josh was taking advantage too, slashing his way to the basket and getting to the free-throw line. He finished with twenty-five points.

Daniel and Josh combined to convert nineteen of twenty-four of their field goal attempts. We shot sixty-eight percent from the field as a team and held off Creighton for an 85–74 victory.

People were still buzzing about our win over Xavier, but we were more energized by the victory in Omaha. Arch had produced those kinds of games at the Pavilion before. He was able to lift us offensively with the crowd at our backs, and we kind of rode that wave against Xavier on New Year's Eve.

This was different.

For this team to define itself, we were going to need Daniel and Josh to take a step forward. Arch was Arch. Kris had his breakthrough at Virginia. Then Daniel turned the corner at Creighton and Josh made a big leap too (after foul trouble limited him to two first-half minutes against Xavier). By the end of the Creighton game we were running isolation plays for him, which only added to his growing confidence.

We didn't land back in Philly until 3:30 in the morning after that Creighton win. We were all exhausted. Yet, as I pulled into the driveway of my home, I felt like we were in a good place. Aside from our 12–2 record, three of our vital players—Daniel, Josh, and Jalen—had shown themselves to be the sturdy offensive weapons we would need as we moved into the thick of the Big East season.

The Tape Doesn't Lie

On the first Monday night of 2016, we wrapped up practice in the Davis Center, and I grabbed my briefcase on the way out the door.

Our radio show, *Talking Villanova Basketball,* was scheduled to start at 7 p.m., and there was little time to waste.

During my days as an assistant coach at Villanova, I inherited the role of de facto producer of Coach Mass' weekly radio show at a restaurant on the Main Line. I helped line up the guests and made other arrangements for the show, which became a meeting place for some of our most devoted fans. Coach's prominence allowed us to attract some cool guests too.

Since 2001, the radio show has been the responsibility of our staff. Several local restaurants have hosted the show, most recently J.D. McGillicuddy's in Wayne, Pennsylvania, which is owned and operated by Tom Thornton, who once served as an assistant to our iconic women's basketball coach, Harry Perretta. Tom's daughter, Michelle, was a great guard for Harry in the 1990s, and she later married a sharp-shooting former Wildcat standout, Eric Eberz, who runs the place now. Eric and his staff see to it that we have everything we need, and our audience just loves the fact that a Villanova alumnus is an integral part of that scene.

When the show ends at 8 p.m., I usually make the rounds to say hello to our guests at McGillicuddy's. The thing I love is that I hear a lot of straight, knowledgeable talk. If people like Adam "Ace" Cilli or Eric Watkins or John Gartland have a question about a strategic move we made in a game, they will ask it respectfully. I can also count on seeing my uncle Bill Long and his family—his mother, Jeannie Long, got me tickets to the Palestra in the 1970s.

On this night, there was plenty of chatter about the wins over Xavier and Creighton. But there was also healthy respect for what awaited us forty-eight hours hence at the Pavilion: our matchup with Seton Hall.

The Pirates had an outstanding sophomore class that was just beginning to get a sense of what it could accomplish in our league. When they beat Wichita State before Christmas, you could see that Kevin Willard's team was coming on strong. Sophomore Isaiah Whitehead had begun to establish himself as one of the top players in the Big East.

Even when Kevin was just getting things going in his tenure there, the Pirates were a difficult matchup for us. The Hall knocked us out of the 2014 Big East Tournament quarterfinals. On January 3, 2015, they gave us our first regular season loss (in overtime) to snap our thirteen-game winning streak to open the season.

Part of the reason they had matched up so well against us is that they prioritize defense and rebounding, areas we also take pride in. I knew this would be a test, and so did the hardcore radio show fans I spoke with that night.

Inside the Pavilion two nights later, the game became a testament to old-school Big East basketball—ugly to watch and ugly to coach. But the defensive tenacity of both teams offered a kind of beauty too.

Daniel was dominant inside, with twenty points and eighteen rebounds. That was especially critical on a night when Seton Hall shut us down from outside. We were just four of twenty-two (.186) from long range and were only able to survive because we limited the Hall to .356 shooting on the night.

In the end, we found a way to grind out a 72–63 victory—and that is why we preach the value of defense. If you have only your offense to rely on, you're in trouble on those nights when the shots won't fall. Off nights at the offensive end are inevitable in our world. Sound defense is constant.

In the big picture, as Patty and I watched the tape afterward at home, I got the sense that this was the beginning of Seton Hall's knowledge of how to defend us and attack us offensively. We had trouble scoring against the Pirates on our home court. I could see upon my review that they got some terrific looks at the basket that they are more than capable of making. They just missed them. (That can happen on the road, especially to a younger team.)

One thing all of us knew: We had played an outstanding team—and we would have to deal with them again.

After watching the tape, I took my notes and fired off a few texts to our staff on items I thought were important to stress with specific players. Mike Clark, our graduate manager, would then clip certain moments so that the assistant coaches could show players sequences where they may have been in the wrong position.

As coaches, we like to say, "The tape doesn't lie." The work we did after watching that tape, learning from our own mistakes, and continually striving to do better would serve us well.

The Gathering Storm

On Saturday we traveled to Indianapolis to prepare for a Sunday night clash at Butler, ranked eighteenth nationally.

Two seasons earlier, we helped to kick off the first season of the reconfigured Big East in a New Year's Eve game against the Bulldogs at their storied Hinkle Fieldhouse, which for years served as home to the finals of the Indiana state high school basketball tournament, which was the inspiration for the movie *Hoosiers*. The game was fantastic. It wasn't decided until we made a couple more plays than the Bulldogs did in overtime to win it 76–73.

Last season, we had a nearly identical battle with the Bulldogs, also at Hinkle Fieldhouse, before a jam-packed crowd of 9,231. Arch found Darrun on the wing for a three at the buzzer to win it 71–68.

None of us expected anything less than a fight to the final horn this time, and that's exactly what we got.

This was a game that required our guys to come up with big plays and big shots. JayVaughn Pinkston did it in 2014. Darrun did it a year later. This time, it was Josh's turn. In an environment where every basket was precious, he tallied eleven of his game-high twenty-two points in the second half *and* grabbed eleven rebounds.

We needed every one of them.

But that wasn't enough. The other essential performance of the night came courtesy of Darryl Reynolds. Since Daniel found himself in foul trouble and was only able to play nineteen minutes of the game, Darryl picked up the slack in a major way, helping us to beat the Bulldogs once again. If his five rebounds and fifteen minutes of action may have seemed ordinary, they were anything but.

Darryl's drive that night inspired the same kind of trust that grew from the way Kris had played at Virginia and from how Daniel and Josh had lifted us at Creighton. For Darryl to do it on the road in a physical battle where every possession counted, to come off the bench in an atmosphere where any little slipup could be costly—and succeed—won him tremendous respect in our locker room.

We all knew: *If Darryl can be effective in that setting, he can be effective anywhere.*

We now had six straight wins since our loss to Virginia and were 4–0 in the Big East. Two of those victories had come against ranked opponents, Xavier and Butler. The next mission was to prepare for a gifted young Marquette team that Steve Wojciechowski would bring to the Pavilion for a midweek game on January 13.

At the completion of our walk-through that day, I learned that twenty-four NBA scouts would be in the crowd that night. We're accustomed to having scouts in the house, but that's a larger number than you typically see at a college game.

The presence of NBA scouts is a good thing. It means there is pro interest in your players, as well as those of your opponent. In this case, a big part of the draw was Marquette's 6'11" freshman, Henry Ellenson, whom many observers projected to become a first-round pick in the 2016 Draft. (This proved accurate when the Detroit Pistons picked Ellenson as the eighteenth overall selection.)

Past experience told me there was no need to bring up the presence of NBA scouts to our players before the game. They're smart young men who pay attention to what's going on. I also knew that if you have bright guys, they look at a situation like this one—a bunch of scouts there to watch a player on the other team—as a challenge. The challenge for us? To play the right way—together—in order to keep the outstanding opposing player in check, rather than have any one of our players try to shut him down individually. We've been very fortunate to have players who don't get caught up in the mindset that this is some kind of one-on-one duel.

We *always* want to shut down the opponent's best player. If there are extra NBA scouts on hand to watch that, so much the better.

As such, we planned to rotate our coverage of Ellenson as the game progressed, so the responsibility wouldn't fall on Daniel alone. In the first half, however, Daniel was whistled for his second foul as he attempted to take a charge. (For the record, I thought it to be a poor call. And yes, I may have registered my disagreement with the official.) What made that sequence worse was that Daniel bruised his tailbone on the play—a nagging injury that would linger for weeks.

On Wednesday the 13th, it was a double whammy for Daniel: He was the recipient of a bad call *and* got hurt to boot.

As for Ellenson, it was hard not to be impressed. Yet even with Daniel playing through pain, we found a way to slow him down. The freshman scored only twelve points on eleven field goal attempts.

We struggled to get a handle on the rest of the Golden Eagles, though. They hit some huge threes and held a 38–37 lead at halftime. One of Marquette's young guards, Traci Carter, a local Philly guy, was so fired up he shouted in my direction after draining a three-pointer in front of our bench. He picked up a technical foul for that.

I understood. This was an intense battle.

Thankfully it was a night where our experience lifted us out of trouble. One of the qualities we grew to love about our team was its ability to adapt quickly to any in-game adjustments we had to make. We were able to make great use of the length and athleticism Mikal and Darryl offered us off the bench. They helped us disrupt Marquette's flow as we held them scoreless for more than five minutes in the second half. That gave us enough cushion to sustain a late surge by the Golden Eagles and get the win.

Tired Yet?

It was midnight when we left the Pavilion that Wednesday night, and we were slated to play again at Georgetown on Saturday at 1 p.m. Thankfully we were able to get clearance to practice on the Hoyas' Verizon Center court on Friday, which meant we were able to head to D.C. early and get some extra rest—not knowing just how much extra rest one of our key players would need.

When we met for breakfast at our hotel, not far from the White House, on Friday morning, word reached me that Daniel was now battling a virus on top of his tailbone injury. We left him at the hotel as we made the five-minute ride to the Verizon Center. The next morning, as we readied our pregame meal at 9 a.m., Daniel decided— with our blessing—to continue resting in his room.

When the lights went on that afternoon, though, Daniel was in the starting lineup. Somehow, despite his bruised tailbone and an awful bug, he found a way to give us twenty-two solid minutes against a Georgetown team that was playing well. It was the kind of ultimate-warrior effort we had come to expect from D.O.

To me, Daniel's effort was a throwback to simpler times.

There are instances these days when a senior, or any player with NBA aspirations—which is every scholarship player at this level—wonders whether it's worth risking a poor performance in front of the world and NBA evaluators by playing at less than 100 percent. There are people who advise these players to stay on the sidelines until they are in perfect health.

The fact that Daniel gutted that one out raised his locker room respect level another notch.

Daniel's health issues also allowed us to continue to expose Darryl to pressure situations—he gave us four rebounds in sixteen minutes—and get Kris some time at the five spot. When the bus pulled out from underneath the Verizon Center, we had ourselves a hard-earned 55–50 win.

All these hurdles we cleared would pay off later. They would become part of our collective consciousness.

The question was: In just four days, would it be enough to carry us through our rematch at Seton Hall?

12

Home and Away

KEVIN WILLARD AND the Seton Hall athletics staff do a good job creating a home court advantage at the Prudential Center in downtown Newark, New Jersey, partly by closing off the upper level of the arena. It makes for a pretty cool vibe downstairs with the more intimate setting—a college atmosphere in a pro-style venue.

I bring this up because the buildings we play in are a sometimes-overlooked but important extension of who we are as basketball programs. And there is no doubt that the arenas themselves can have a direct effect on the games and the players.

In the original version of the Big East, Seton Hall played its home games at the Meadowlands, in what was then called Brendan Byrne Arena. Thousands of Villanova alumni reside in New Jersey, and we could always count on them turning out in large numbers to help fill the 20,000-seat venue. Sometimes there were nearly as many Wildcat fans as Pirate fans.

In the days leading up to this latest meeting, we were undefeated in the Big East at 6–0, and 16–2 overall. It seemed the only question we heard from our fans was whether or not Seton Hall would open the upper deck at the Prudential Center in response to the demand for tickets. In the end, the Hall made the decision not to open the upper bowl, and I respected that. The home team was committed to its ticketing plan and wasn't eager to make a few extra bucks at the risk of flooding the upper deck with screaming Villanova fans.

I thought it was awesome for the rivalry—it underscored the importance of the home-and-home series we've been able to return to in the new, ten-school version of the Big East conference. This scheduling structure—every team plays every other team twice, once at home and once on the road—was how the Big East operated when I first entered the league in the 1980s. As the popularity of the league exploded, so did the number of member schools, and this expansion made playing each opponent twice an impossibility. Returning to our home-and-home roots is one of the things we've come to love since the Big East was reorganized in 2013. It breeds familiarity and a greater level of respect.

Traditionally, Villanova hasn't played well at Seton Hall, and Seton Hall has not had a lot of success at the Pavilion. After our game on campus two weeks earlier, they knew they could get us. This was their chance.

But it was not to be for the Hall. Josh continued his aggressive play, recording a double-double with fifteen points and ten rebounds, and Mikal was a beast off the bench, going a perfect four of four from the field and blocking two shots over twenty efficient minutes. In the end, we pulled out a 72–71 victory.

We were now 7–0 in our league—and we were about to get snowed.

Respect for All

Even as we battled to win at Seton Hall, our athletic director, Mark Jackson, and his staff were sizing up what to make of an impending nor'easter. The forecast called for a massive snowfall beginning in the Delaware Valley late in the day on Friday, January 22, and continuing throughout Saturday—when we were scheduled to play a nationally televised game against a red-hot Providence team at our home away from home: the Wells Fargo Center.

We play three to five games a year at this nearly 20,000-seat building in South Philadelphia. It's a tradition that took root in the 1980s, in the early days of the Big East, when Villanova began to host teams like Georgetown and Syracuse at the Spectrum, the home of the Philadelphia 76ers and the Flyers of the National Hockey League. Some of the most vivid memories of my tenure as a Villanova assistant were forged in those battles at the Spectrum.

When the Wells Fargo Center opened in 1996, Villanova moved its games across the Sports Complex parking lot to the new venue, built on the site of the former John F. Kennedy Stadium (which served as the home to the Army–Navy football game for decades). In our time at Villanova, we have benefited from a tremendous college atmosphere in that building. Our students fill the sections behind the baskets at both ends of the court, and transform a pro venue into a sensational environment for college basketball.

There is no other place quite like Villanova when it comes to our home courts. On the one hand, we have the intimate setting on campus in the Pavilion, with fans on top of you and a throng of students behind the south basket. On the other, we have the Center, a state-of-the-art NBA arena in which we draw fans from all over the region.

You can't say that about anywhere else.

We had built a nine-game winning streak since the loss at Virginia and were alone atop the Big East, but I knew from my own history with this program how quickly things could change.

Now we had this other X factor, which was completely out of our control: the question of when our next game would actually be played. The forecast was ominous, predicting somewhere between two and three *feet* of snow. After much back-and-forth between the two teams, the Big East office, and Fox, which would be televising the game, it was announced that the game would be moved back a day, to Sunday at 1 p.m.

For the team, this meant we had an additional twenty-four hours to prepare for what loomed as a major challenge. The Friars, coached by our friend Ed Cooley, were ranked No. 16 in the Associated Press poll. Their star, guard Kris Dunn, was a player-of-the-year candidate and favorite of NBA personnel executives. (The Minnesota Timberwolves would later make him the fifth overall pick of the 2016 Draft.) Forward Ben Bentil, only a sophomore, had emerged as an All–Big East caliber forward. That stung a little bit because we had recruited Ben unsuccessfully.

With the prospect of being snowbound ahead, we elected to take the team to a Center City restaurant for dinner instead of our usual suburban-hotel routine. Delmonico's Steakhouse, a famous Philly spot, was our choice and the meal was delicious. It was a great night, in part because we don't do it that way very often. I point that out because I think breaking routine is okay once in a while. These pre-game rituals of ours aren't superstitions. They're just part of the work we do in order to focus.

The next morning, we had an 8 a.m. practice scheduled at the Wells Fargo Center. At 7 a.m., George Halcovage, our Director of Basketball Operations, set up a continental breakfast for our guys at the hotel. Coach Shackleton approved the menu, and the rationale was that we didn't want the guys digesting a heavy breakfast right before they took the court for practice. A full breakfast would be served after practice back at the hotel.

When I came down to the meeting room, I immediately sensed something was off. The quiet intensity we are used to seeing had been replaced by a different, uncomfortable kind of quiet. There was very little conversation, and the expressions on the faces of the assistant coaches and some of the players made it clear that they were upset.

I soon found out why.

Daniel had arrived that morning anticipating a full breakfast. When he saw that it was lighter than usual, he reacted. Daniel is an intense young man who is laser-focused on his preparation. In his mind that focus had been disrupted. He was irritated about it, and he voiced his irritation to George, loudly, within earshot of everyone in the room.

The outburst was so out of character for Daniel. I came to believe that the pressure on him as a captain, and perhaps on everyone, had built to a point where it needed to be released. We were on a nine-game winning streak and—for the third year in a row—had targets drawn on our back in the Big East. Plus, Daniel was still trying to fight through the bruised tailbone and was only a few days removed from the virus he had dealt with at Georgetown.

It also seemed to me that Daniel felt he was standing up for his teammates. It was his view that the continental breakfast failed to deliver the fuel they needed that morning. Though we try to stay on top of these kinds of things by soliciting input from the rest of the players—often with the captains acting as spokesmen—it struck me that this was something we needed to look at.

On a lot of teams, this might not have been considered a major blowup, and it might not sound like that big a deal to you either. But in our culture, we want our guys to treat everyone with respect. As I stated back in the beginning of this book, we all have roles to play, but we don't have a hierarchy in our basketball family. Daniel's reaction, though brief, was unfair to George. He hadn't treated a member of our coaching staff with the respect he deserved. When I spoke to Daniel, he felt awful. He apologized to me and to George. And while I appreciated that, I explained that he would not start in Sunday's game as a result of his outburst. It was a consequence he accepted without debate, and he had a good practice that morning.

After practice, all we could do was wait to see what Mother Nature had in store for us.

One benefit to the extra twenty-four hours is that it allowed me to have a very good conversation with Daniel.

I told him I knew he was sticking up for his teammates. I also stressed to him that how we interact with one another is important, regardless of whatever pressures we might be feeling. I explained that any concerns he had about the breakfast menu should have been handled in a private conversation with George after practice had ended. Daniel reiterated that he would have preferred to have risen earlier and had a full breakfast before practice, and I told him we could make that kind of adjustment in the future.

When Daniel got up from our conversation, I started to think that this episode, while unfortunate, might yield some positive results in the long term. Daniel understood that he hadn't handled the situation properly, and we could see that the concern for his teammates was genuine. In turn, his teammates saw that Daniel wanted the best for them, and he felt terribly about how his concerns had been communicated.

We put it behind us and hoped for the best.

The storm turned out to be everything the meteorologists had predicted. It began Friday night and lasted into the early hours of Sunday morning, dumping 22.4 inches of snow at the airport. Philadelphia was essentially shut down.

We did our best to maintain a routine at the hotel. By 9 a.m. on Sunday, we were gathered in a meeting room to listen to Father Rob's message at our pregame meal. (This time, we made sure to serve a full breakfast!) His choice of topics was all too fitting.

"A grandfather is teaching his grandson about human nature, and he says that within every human heart there are two wolves. Those two wolves are fighting it out each day in every decision we make," he said. "One wolf says, 'Make sure you get yours. Take the shortcut, the pain-free route, and get as much pleasure out of life as you can.' The other wolf is in there fighting, saying, 'Do the right thing even if it costs you . . . time or money. . . . Make the sacrifice for someone else; it might be more difficult, but life can be more meaningful and fulfilling. Do what might be unpopular knowing it will make a positive difference in the long run.'

> ## BEYOND BASKETBALL
> ### *The Pressure of Success*
> When success comes, expectations grow. While thriving under pressure is a great quality, it also can realign your vision, if only slightly, from the values that fueled your rise. When failure does arrive, take advantage of the opportunity to reassess.

"The grandson thinks for a second and asks, 'Then which wolf wins?' And the grandfather replies, 'The one that we feed.'

"Keep feeding the good wolf," Father Rob said. "The good side of our hearts. Coach Shack shows us all the time how our body responds based on what we feed it. There is a reason why our menu has more salmon and broccoli on it and not enough cookies and ice cream! Our souls and spirits are the same way.

"So much of our lives and decisions are affected by our value system. What are we feeding our minds and hearts? What do we believe matters most? Our lives are a product of the decisions that we make, the small ones and the big ones. Those two wolves are often fed by the people, places, and things that we engage in and with on a daily basis. *Who am I hanging around with? Who and what am I listening to? What voices are important in my life?* Our answers will be revealing and help us to know which side of our hearts we are feeding."

When the meal was finished, John Mills navigated our bus through the snowy streets to arrive at the arena on time, a hundred minutes before tip-off. Many of our fans weren't as fortunate. Though the snow had been cleared from the parking lots, the roads in most of the surrounding neighborhoods were still buried. More than 19,000 tickets had been sold, but only 7,191 fans were able to make it to the Center that day.

We want our guys to block out those kinds of external factors, and we have generally done that well. One of the most-talked-about victories in recent Villanova history came on January 20, 2005, when we knocked off No. 2 Kansas while a blizzard raged outside the Center. So I wasn't really concerned about how our team would handle the quieter building. I just felt badly that a good portion of the Nova Nation missed one of the season's best games.

Providence was terrific. We designed a defensive game plan geared to stopping Kris Dunn. We would live with the consequences if his teammates beat us. Sometimes in those situations, a star player will let his ego take over and try to force shots. Kris resisted that urge and took the opportunities that were there. His unselfishness made their offense hum as he racked up fourteen assists. Ben Bentil was often the beneficiary of those passes, scoring thirty-one points to go with thirteen rebounds.

We, on the other hand, were a bit out of sync.

Darryl started for Daniel, who entered the game as a reserve. We struggled to slow their offense and had to match their firepower to stay with them. It took another huge three-pointer by Ryan Arcidiacono in the final seconds of regulation to tie the game and force overtime. At that point, I think every one of those fans in the Center thought we were on our way to another storybook ending written by Arch.

Kris Dunn, though, sank the three-pointer late in overtime that gave Providence an 82–79 win and snapped our winning streak.

Downtime

We were not scheduled to play again for seven days. Back when we had first seen the schedule, Patty and I decided for the first time in my coaching career to see if we could sneak away together for two days during that break. We'd booked a flight to leave Sunday, and that had to be rescheduled due to the storm. We finally did get to board a flight the following day, and we celebrated Patty's birthday in Florida before returning to Philadelphia a short thirty-six hours later.

When you are in the midst of a winning streak like the one we'd been on, you do your best to ignore the pressure building around you. After each victory, your concentration shifts immediately to the next game. When a loss finally comes, it's an opportunity to take a moment to recognize the way that pressure was mounting. It's a pause that allows you to refocus your mind, and your players' minds, on the small details that help you earn wins.

Ideally, though, you'd rather not take a loss with seven days until your next game.

There really wasn't much we could do about that. Looking back on it now, I think being able to hit the reset button during a slow week helped our collective psyche.

As a team, we took several days off from practice. We were beyond the midpoint of the regular season, and through the years, I have learned that you really need to be cognizant of the toll the schedule takes on the players' bodies. The Big East offers a tough, physical style of basketball, and the guys get their share of bumps and bruises. Case in point: Daniel was still not 100 percent recovered from the tailbone injury he suffered eleven days earlier.

When we reconvened later in the week to review the tape of our Providence loss, all the little details we hadn't been mindful of that day became glaringly obvious.

It was painful to watch. At the same time, this moment was an opportunity.

Essentially, this was a referendum on our attitude. If we chose to wallow and point fingers, the Providence loss could have shaken our confidence. Instead, we moved on. Daniel took responsibility for his outburst at Friday's breakfast. The players took responsibility for their own lack of attention to detail against the Friars. As a staff, we accepted that the players had needed a break, which is why we'd stayed out of the practice gym for a few days.

One of the people I heard from that week was none other than Ed Cooley. Ed is one of my favorite coaches in our league, an extrovert who I count as a great friend. We talked about the high level at which the game had been played—it garnered a great rating for Fox—and how it added even more luster to the perception of our conference. At the end of our chat, Ed told me that he had been rewarded with a new contract as a result of their win over us.

At least there is that, I thought.

I was legitimately happy for Ed, and I appreciated that he took the time to thank me. I was just glad that call came in on Thursday, when I had finally begun to shake off that loss. If it had come on Tuesday, it might have killed me.

When we got back on the court on January 29, there was a new fire in our approach. There was tremendous energy and toughness that day in the Davis Center. As a staff, we were as excited as the players were.

People sometimes wonder why coaches relish practice the way we do. My answer? As a coach, you have so much control over practice—a control you simply don't have in a game.

In practice, we strive to create the best habits we can in our players. The more gains you make in developing those, the more prepared your guys will be when confronted with difficult situations in games. From the stretching session with John Shackleton through the warm-up routine, we want our guys to be on point. If their minds are clear of what is going on around them, they will be equipped to confront the challenge in front of them. Once the game begins, you have to leave it to the players. At that point, whatever their habits are—and whatever is in their hearts and minds—is what you'll see.

Unfortunately, all of that energy the guys gave on the practice court that day had an unforeseen downside. In a battle for a rebound, Daniel caught an elbow to the eye, on a clean play. He was later diagnosed with a concussion that would keep him out of our next few games, the first of which was a road battle against St. John's at Madison Square Garden.

St. John's was in a transition phase of its own. Chris Mullin, a central figure in the rise of the conference during his time as an All-American guard for St. John's from 1981 to 1985, had returned to Queens after a long career in the NBA (first as a player, then as an executive) to succeed Steve Lavin. There hadn't been much time to restock after heavy turnover from a roster that had gotten the Johnnies into the 2015 NCAA Tournament.

This was a young team that was having a challenging 7–14 season at that point, but Chris had instilled a feistiness in his players that worried us. Those fears played out on Sunday afternoon. The Red Storm's length and defense gave us trouble. We went to the locker room with a 28–27 halftime lead, and I suspect our fans were wondering if we were flat after a week off.

Effort wasn't the issue in our minds.

Two of the qualities we value most in our players are intelligence and character. The way those things manifest on the basketball court is that we invariably respect the threat that every opponent represents, regardless of its win-loss record or perceived level of talent. If you look at the success we have had in the regular season, it's been built on our players' consistency in taking every opponent seriously and committing to the game plan no matter what the rest of the world predicts about the outcome of the game.

We tell our guys, "When we are in first place or high in the rankings, the team we have watched on film isn't the one we will necessarily see. We have to expect the opponents to come at us with increased energy and passion." Our players have learned that over the years.

Against the Johnnies, we battled in that first half and were rewarded with just a one-point lead. But in the second half, our dedication and experience carried us. Josh and Kris both grabbed eleven rebounds and we registered a 68–53 victory that was closer than the final score may have indicated.

When asked by a reporter at the postgame news conference why he was able to grab that many caroms, Kris gave a succinct and honest answer: "Going into every game, I try to focus on rebounding. I was able to get a lot more because Daniel usually grabs most of the rebounds."

One of our takeaways from that game was how our junior class was asserting itself. At St. John's, Josh, Kris, and Darryl pulled down thirty-one of our forty-eight rebounds and allowed us to out-rebound the Red Storm by a wide margin. That was the key to the win.

We had come to the end of January with an 18–3 overall record. We were 8–1 in the Big East at the midpoint of the conference season, atop the standings, and listed at No. 3 in the national polls. Arch and Daniel were our captains, yet they couldn't be expected to shoulder that burden by themselves, and increasingly our juniors were cementing their leadership bona fides. Josh had established himself as a candidate for conference player of the year. The Naismith Memorial Basketball Hall of Fame announced that he was also one of five finalists for the Jerry West Award, given to the nation's top shooting guard. Kris was on an upward arc too. He was a reliable fixture in our starting lineup who was rebounding at a higher level than he ever had before. Darryl built upon his effort at Butler, and we had reached a point where we didn't hesitate to insert him at critical moments. In our first game of February, he pulled down a career-high thirteen rebounds against Creighton as we drained sixteen three-pointers on the way to an 83–58 win at the Pavilion. It couldn't have been a better way to start the month.

We had bounced back nicely from our loss to Providence, yet the true measure of our response was still a few days away. The Friars— and seemingly the whole city of Providence—were counting the hours until we arrived in Rhode Island.

13

Humble and Hungry

―――――――

WHEN MICHAEL TRANGHESE walked into the coaches' locker room an hour before our game in Providence, I couldn't have been more fired up to see him. The man is more than a trusted friend of Patty's and mine. He's the rock who held the Big East together for two tumultuous decades after founding commissioner Dave Gavitt left to take an executive position with the Boston Celtics in 1990. When he walked into the room accompanied by another longtime friend, retired coordinator of officiating Art Hyland, it felt like my annual trip back to the roots of the Big East was complete.

In these kinds of pregame visits, the upcoming matchup is generally far down the list of topics we discuss. The conversation is light and centers mostly on our families and friends. That's true even when the world around us is going crazy about a game, as they were with this one.

Michael told me something about this meeting, though, that caught me off guard. He said, "This is the toughest ticket I've seen for a Providence home game in nearly forty years." Knowing the long and proud history of Providence basketball—Rick Pitino took the Friars to the 1987 Final Four; Rick Barnes and Pete Gillen (a former Coach Massimino assistant) had success there in the 1990s; and Tim Welsh put together NCAA Tournament teams there in the 2000s—made it hard for me to fathom. Michael had lived those last forty years of Friars hoops, so that really said something.

When I walked out from beneath the stands to our bench in the Dunkin' Donuts Center before the opening tip, I instantly understood: The fans in "Friartown" clearly couldn't wait for this one.

Daniel had rejoined us for the trip, but was still not cleared for game action after his concussion. That meant we would turn again to Darryl Reynolds as we considered ways to slow Ben Bentil.

Thanks to the success of Wildcats like Randy Foye, Kyle Lowry, Allan Ray, Mike Nardi, Scottie Reynolds, Corey Fisher, and Ryan Arcidiacono, we have been dubbed by some as "Guard U." And while we certainly have had terrific backcourt players, we have also produced some outstanding forwards. In fact, I would stack our staff's work with forwards like Dante Cunningham, Mouphtaou Yarou, and Daniel against anyone's—and I felt Darryl was well on his way to joining their ranks.

Darryl is a Philadelphia native who played his high school basketball not far from the Villanova campus at Lower Merion High School. (If that name sounds familiar, it's because it's the same high school from which Kobe Bryant launched his epic twenty-year NBA career in 1996.)

Back in the spring of 2012, the Pennsylvania high school state playoffs were held at the Pavilion. This was during a live evaluation period, so college coaches were permitted to attend. Our primary focus as a staff that night was on Rondae Hollis-Jefferson, a gifted guard from Chester, Pennsylvania, who would go on to become a McDonald's All-American and play his college ball at the University of Arizona. (Today he is a member of the Brooklyn Nets.)

Seated next to me in the stands that night was Hall of Fame coach Larry Brown. We got to know Coach Brown during his tenure at the helm of the Philadelphia 76ers in the early 2000s, when he owned a home within a five-minute drive of the Villanova campus. Having access to his coaching brilliance was like having a resident Basketball Ph.D. on call. We became friends.

Darryl Reynolds wasn't on our radar at that point, but Coach Brown leaned over to me during that night's game and pointed to him: "That's the guy that I like."

To my eyes, Darryl was a lanky kid who didn't appear to be getting a lot done on the court. He was protecting the rim, and you could tell he had a great attitude in the way he carried himself and encouraged his teammates. But there wasn't much else that drew your attention

to him. If Coach Brown hadn't
pointed Darryl out, I might have
overlooked him.

At that point, Darryl was a
senior at Lower Merion, and we
were told that he was planning
to attend prep school the next
year. We decided that Darryl
was a player we should monitor
during his 2012–2013 prep season at Worcester Academy.

In January 2013, Baker Dunleavy traveled to Worcester
to check on Darryl's progress.

> ### BEYOND BASKETBALL
> #### *More Than a Feeling*
>
> When it comes to finding the right
> people to surround yourself with,
> take notice of the intangibles,
> such as work ethic and integrity.
> When shaping a company or any
> organization, don't underestimate
> the importance of finding the
> right feeling from people whose
> values mesh with yours.

When Baker reported back, he told us that Darryl had noticeably
improved. That development had caught the attention of other college coaches, and we soon learned that Seton Hall, Utah, Drexel, and
South Carolina were interested in Darryl as well. We set up an official campus visit for him not long after our 2012–2013 season came to
an end (with an NCAA Tournament loss to North Carolina in Kansas
City).

When we had a chance to sit down and talk extensively with Darryl, we were blown away by how thoughtful and mature he was. We
knew that his high school and prep school coaches loved him. They
emphasized to us the tremendous personal character he possessed. It
was easy for us to see why. You could tell that the year in prep school
had really benefited him academically as well as athletically.

When that official visit ended, we were convinced Darryl would be
a great fit here. Now we had to sell him on that vision.

Run Your Own Race

In our recruiting, we don't spend a lot of time talking about basketball. Instead, we spend the vast majority of our time talking about all
of the other things the Villanova experience has to offer. We make it

very clear we want people who want to be more than just great basketball players. Our philosophy: Be the best student you can be. Be the best man you can be. Be the best player you can be. We believe your commitment to excellence as a man and a student enhances your ability to reach your full potential on the basketball court. We want our players to really believe in that too.

At times, this hurts us. A player who opts to go somewhere else might say publicly, "Oh, they have too many guys at my position." Privately, we know it's because some of them don't find the way we approach things appealing.

Recruiting for me is an education process. We want young men to come to Villanova and be active participants in our culture. That process can move quickly—as it did when Kyle Lowry moved up the NBA Draft charts as a sophomore in 2005–2006 and then departed to become the Memphis Grizzlies' first-round pick—or it can last the more traditional four or even five years (via a redshirt). We use the expression that every one of our guys is "running his own race."

The conventional wisdom in college basketball is that the more successful your team is, the easier it is to recruit great players. Quality finds quality and this leads to a nonstop virtuous circle of talented players and great teams. Makes sense, right? But at Villanova, it's a little more complicated than that.

After we made the Final Four for the first time in 2009, I thought we veered off track a bit. Recruiting was suddenly a little easier. Highly rated guys were clamoring to come here, and that was a new sensation—and temptation—for us. A lot of this was on me. I was excited about this higher level of pure talent we were suddenly attracting, and in hindsight, I realize that I let myself get seduced by that. I wasn't demanding that as much attention be paid to our core values. I wasn't sufficiently educating the recruits about what we expect from our players. There were guys who got to Villanova and weren't sure our culture was for them. Again, that's on me.

It caught up to us.

The challenge going forward, and the challenge I definitely took on with Darryl, was to make sure to continue to educate these guys on everything we are as Wildcats before they make the choice to join our family. To stay committed. To not get sloppy. Playing on a team that's winning can be enticing, but it's not fair if you don't explain to the recruit what it's all about.

The role Darryl would be asked to help fill may not have appealed to everyone. The likelihood was that minutes would be hard to come by in the early years of his career.

There was a time, a decade or two ago, when such a developmental period was an accepted part of growth at this level. Players and their families today, however, are better informed than they were in years past and like to see and hear exactly how we envision their on-court roles from day one.

We went through that process with Darryl. We had a sense he was the kind of kid who could take the long view, but you can never be entirely certain. Thankfully, after considering his options with his parents, Rabia Sulayman and Darryl Reynolds Sr., Darryl accepted our offer. To us, it was a major recruiting victory—even if the outside world barely noticed his addition to our lineup.

Darryl took the recruiting education to heart. He allowed the culture of our university to carry him while he developed as a player. He showed real depth of character.

I think the first time I fully appreciated this was when his stepfather passed away early in his time at Villanova. Darryl met that sadness head-on, as an eldest son often must, by looking after his younger siblings and giving them a shoulder to lean on. And the rest of our team respected how he dealt with it. It was a real-world situation that Darryl, still a teenager, handled with the maturity of a man.

Though it sounds counterintuitive, at 6'9" and 245 pounds, Darryl isn't quite the same physical presence that Daniel is, or Mouph was. It took him time to develop the same kind of strength, particularly in the lower body, that both of those guys come by naturally. But Darryl's resolve and toughness allowed him to compete inside against bigger players.

The best news for Darryl is that his strengths—rebounding, shot-blocking, and playing defense—mirror our team's priorities. Even as a freshman and sophomore, he brought us great energy when he entered a game.

Off the court, Darryl has a playful side too, which fits well with his classmates, Josh and Kris. Early in his career, he was part of the winning team at our annual Hoops Mania dance contest. You don't often see a 6'9" man able to shimmy and shake with style alongside a young lady on our Villanova Dance Team, but Darryl pulled it off.

Off the court, he was also able to engage one of our Communications professors, Hezekiah Lewis, a former Villanova football player, to learn more about filmmaking. In the spring of 2016, he produced *Phillis Pain,* a four-minute YouTube film (starring his teammate Phil Booth as a guy who keeps getting rebuffed by a girl he likes) that generated a lot of positive feedback on social media. I watched it and loved it. It demonstrated a flair for observation and storytelling (with a surprise cameo at the end) that will serve Darryl well in the years after his basketball career is complete.

I won't tell you that this was always an easy process for Darryl. While our team enjoyed success on the court, winning back-to-back Big East regular season championships from 2013 to 2015, his role was mostly that of an understudy to Daniel. He averaged 4.4 minutes in forty-eight games over those two seasons, and at the end of his sophomore year he was understandably frustrated.

The two of us spent a lot of time talking in my office that spring. Darryl had to decide whether he was better served to go elsewhere or to stick to the path he had chosen two years earlier. When Daniel decided that he would not enter the 2015 NBA Draft as a junior, Darryl could see that he was destined for another year as a reserve. He needed to factor that into his deliberations.

Thankfully for our team and Villanova, Darryl stayed the course.

He was able to appreciate the totality of what Villanova could offer him as a person. As a Philadelphian, he understood the value a Villanova degree will have for him once he graduates. He also knows the relationships he has built here can help him pursue a career as a filmmaker.

Finally, I think Darryl could see the progress he was making as a basketball player. He appreciated the role our staff played in that and believed in what we do.

Now we were about to realize the fruits of his labors.

On a huge stage, with a jam-packed house full of Friartown diehards thirsting for a win, Darryl put the rest of the team on his back and lifted all of us. He attempted a career-high ten field goals and made nine of them. We had anticipated that we would need to slide Kris Jenkins over to spell Darryl for stretches, but we never had to. Darryl played thirty-six minutes, scored nineteen points, pulled down ten rebounds, and, just for good measure, notched two steals, two blocks, and two assists. We won 72–60.

At game's end, he accompanied me to center court to be interviewed by FS1 analyst Tarik Turner. It was the first time Darryl had ever been asked to speak on camera for a national audience. Tarik spoke to me first, and when I finished, I jogged back to our locker room. Darryl stayed on the court, completed the interview, and made his way to the locker room shortly thereafter.

We were gathered in a circle, preparing to hear the blessing of Father Rob, when Darryl walked in through the heavy metal door at the front of the room.

As soon as we saw him, the room erupted in cheers.

The circle opened to accommodate him, and you could see that he was bowled over by the spontaneous outpouring from his teammates.

Darryl did his level best to remain humble. He is such a team guy that he seemed almost uncomfortable being hailed for an offensive explosion. He smiled shyly, but this wasn't a case of hubris; it was a genuine sense of pride that he had made the kind of contribution to an important victory that every player wants to make.

It remains one of my favorite moments of the entire season.

To me, that reaction spoke volumes about Darryl—and about our team. It was a manifestation of the respect his teammates shared for his commitment to running his own race. It also demonstrated their respect for his development as a player. And it was an affirmation to everyone in the locker room that our process works.

Our message to the guys is that even if you aren't on the highlights, even if you don't see your name in the headlines, on a website, or in a newspaper story, know that you are still improving. They need to trust that if they're putting their effort into making small gains each day, it will one day pay off. We don't know when that day will be, but we are confident it will come.

Darryl was the perfect example of that.

A Bumpy Ride to the Top

Our spirits were high as we made the fifteen-minute ride to the Providence airport. This was a win over a tremendous team that had beaten us on our home court. We had examined that defeat and learned from it.

For a few of us, flights from Providence to Philadelphia invoke another, more angst-inducing memory.

On January 11, 2005, we posted our first victory in Providence since my return to Villanova nearly four years earlier. The building once known as the Civic Center had been a tough one through the years for the Wildcats, dating to my first stint on Coach Mass' staff. To get a win there for our young team represented a breakthrough for us. We were overjoyed. The bus ride to the airport flew by. As we bounded up the metal staircase to our fifty-seat charter jet, snow flurries flew around us, but we thought nothing of it. The future was bright, and we were convinced it was upon us.

Within minutes, those thoughts disappeared.

Shortly after takeoff, it was clear that something was amiss with the plane. The smooth upward arc you feel on most flights was replaced by a series of rough banks and turns at lower altitude. It wasn't anything loud or overtly scary at first. But what began as mild curiosity among a few of us turned into something more when a flight attendant—not the captain—came over the intercom to inform us that there was a mechanical issue that would force the plane to return to the Providence airport. Tension grew into terror as she briskly led us through a tutorial on the proper way to brace ourselves in the event of a crash.

A rush of thoughts flooded my mind. I considered a cell phone call or text to Patty but decided against it. I spoke up and tried to calm the fears of the players seated toward the rear of the aircraft, including Mike Nardi, Will Sheridan, Chris Charles, Randy Foye, and Allan Ray. For some reason, I told them to put their coats on. Looking back, I'm not sure how helpful an overcoat would have been in the frozen waters of the Atlantic Ocean, but it seemed like a good idea at the time.

As the aircraft continued to twist and turn awkwardly through the sky at low altitude, I thought: *If this is the end, it's been a great life.*

The minutes seemed to take hours. *Where is that airport!?* When the pilot was finally able to maneuver the plane over the airfield, I could see the snow-covered ground, and that made me feel better. *At least we're over land.* But the brief comfort I felt in that instant washed away when all of us caught sight of the line of fire trucks with lights flashing, poised at the ready near the runway.

From my seat in the first row, I couldn't see what the pilot was doing to try to land the plane safely. I just knew it had to have been an All-American-level effort.

Finally, with the squeal and bump of rubber on pavement, the plane touched down—and a cathartic cheer went up from inside the cabin.

The next day, news of our experience filtered out. It became a national story and would later be featured on CBS during the NCAA Tournament. As a leader of young people, you're never quite sure what the impact of something like that will be on the group. I learned later that some of our guys were near tears while we were in the sky. A couple of coaches elected to book train rides back to Philly rather than get on another airplane.

We all kind of helped one another through that experience. It didn't define us—but it did reinforce the sense that we need to appreciate the many blessings we enjoy.

We ended that season 24–8, and I was proud of how we dealt with that real-world adversity. For some of us who remain at Villanova—including Baker, Mike Nardi, Father Rob, Jeff Pierce, and Father John Stack, a university vice president and Augustinian brother of Father Rob's who occasionally fills in for him in the chaplain's role—it's the kind of memory you never fully shake. But it's also a comfort to know we were blessed then, and we are now.

Eleven years later, the flight home from Providence after Darryl's big game was the best kind: uneventful. On the bus back to campus, a number of the players' mobile devices were locked in to other games, specifically those of the two teams directly ahead of us in the Associated Press poll: No. 1 Oklahoma and No. 2 North Carolina. If both were knocked off, we could be in position to claim perhaps the only major honor that had eluded Villanova: a No. 1 ranking during the regular season.

For all of its great history, the Wildcats had never risen above No. 2.

Kansas State defeated the Sooners 80–69. Our former Big East rival Notre Dame downed the Tar Heels 80–76.

I'm not certain how other coaches feel, but as a team we don't get too caught up in the ebb and flow of the national rankings. We understand fans and the media do. The rankings drive interest and spur debate. They're good for our game. And there is comfort in knowing some of the most informed voices in our sport—coaches and college basketball media—believe we belong in that company. But in my experience, if you spend too many hours fretting about those external elements, you get distracted from the day-in, day-out toil of controlling what's within your grasp.

We had been on this doorstep before. In 2005–2006, we knocked off No. 1 University of Connecticut and rose to No. 2 in the polls. Ascending to the top spot was all anyone in the Nova Nation could talk about. However, UConn beat us in their building later that week, and we dropped a few notches the following week.

In 2009–2010, one season removed from our Final Four trip, we began the year 20–1, led by Scottie Reynolds, Reggie Redding, Corey Fisher, Corey Stokes, and Antonio Pena. We moved up to the No. 2 spot in early February before heading to Georgetown. The Hoyas took it to us in the midst of another East Coast blizzard, 103–90. We fell in the rankings two days later.

Now here we were again.

Shortly after noon on that Monday, I received a phone call informing me that Villanova had in fact been voted the No. 1 team in the country, according to both the Associated Press and USA Today Coaches polls.

I couldn't help but consider the irony.

When we walked out of the Dunkin' Donuts Center after beating Providence, the thought of moving up to No. 1 never even entered my mind. As a coaching staff, we honestly never gave it a thought until after the flight landed and the players started talking about it.

I was proud of that.

Chemistry 101

Monday afternoon was a whirlwind. Congratulatory texts kept popping up on my phone, many of them from Villanovans. I could feel the pride they took in this. When I was in the car listening to local radio, the news was a big topic of conversation. At the conclusion of practice Father Peter came on the Pavilion court to congratulate the team.

I told Father Peter this was new for me too—I had never coached a No. 1 team.

As soon as practice ended, we climbed back onto the bus for another ride to the airport, en route to play DePaul. We flew to Chicago, landed at O'Hare, and were transported to our hotel in Rosemont, Illinois. Dinner was served, and when it ended we finally discussed this latest development in our season.

My message to the players on this frigid Midwestern night was that this was a wonderful achievement. It meant the world to Villanova University and would be something each of them could one day look back on with a smile. Yet it had never been one of our goals. Instead, it was a by-product of our continued focus on staying true to our values. With this mindset we had improved, and look where it had delivered us.

Now the challenge became, *How would we handle this?*

None of us had ever been part of the No. 1 team in the country, and I knew that one of our favorite internal mantras would now be more essential than ever: "We must remain humble and hungry."

From a coach's perspective, the timing of our ascent couldn't have worked out better. We got the news, practiced, met with the media, and then left for Chicago. Boom. Once we were on the road, we were secluded in our own little cocoon. The ranking stuff faded to the background, which wouldn't have happened if we were on campus.

As a result, in Villanova's first ever game as America's No. 1 team, the players weren't really impacted by the hoopla. Daniel returned with a bang, scoring eleven points. Darryl came off the bench to add fourteen points and six rebounds. Josh added eighteen points and three assists.

We defeated DePaul handily, 86–59. This was a good road win against a team that was improving under Dave Leitao in the first year of his second stint at the school.

Of all the impressive performances that night, the one that meant the most to our team came from Jalen Brunson. This was a homecoming for Jalen, who had developed a huge following during his time as a McDonald's All-American and state champion in high school. Naturally, Jalen's return to the area where he started was a significant story in Chicagoland. Media that had chronicled his career in Illinois were there, along with a lot of friends and family from Lincolnshire and the surrounding area.

When players return to their hometowns, everyone else on the team is aware of it. There is a natural desire on the returning player's part to show the locals just how much he has grown as a collegian. That thought process, though normal, runs counter to our approach. We address this constantly within the team: Actors play to the crowd; players play for their teammates and coaches.

I thought Jalen went out of his way to do that.

His entire focus that night was to function as a facilitator, even though he is an extremely gifted scorer. The work he did helped ignite Daniel's offense, allowing him to quickly get back into a rhythm after his three-game absence due to the concussion. And Daniel wasn't the only beneficiary of Jalen's largesse. He distributed the ball beautifully to Josh, Kris, and Darryl too.

To understand Jalen's approach, I think you also need to take a look at Arch.

The box score indicates Ryan scored only eight points on one-of-five shooting. Those are not statistics that jump out at you. Yet his mentorship of Jalen throughout the course of the season was invaluable to our chemistry.

During our recruitment of Jalen, there was conversation among basketball people about the wisdom of pairing him with Arch. In standard basketball parlance, both are considered point guards. Some were concerned that they would have a hard time co-existing, even for the one season their Villanova careers would overlap.

We couldn't have disagreed more. We loved the idea of playing those two together. Each is so smart and selfless. The possibilities were endless.

We hosted Jalen on an official visit in September 2014. Arch and Jalen made an instant connection, which didn't shock our staff because we knew the character of Arch and liked everything we had seen of Jalen as a person. The bond was such that Jalen chose to stay in Arch's dorm room on his visit rather than go back to the hotel.

That relationship never stopped growing.

In the summer of 2015, I was with Duke coach Mike Krzyzewski. Coach K told me that the bond that he had observed from afar between Ryan and Jalen reminded him of the dynamic shared by two of the guards from his 2015 NCAA Championship team, Quinn Cook and Tyus Jones. He told me how important it had been to his team that those two had become great friends right away. He added that it looked to him like that kind of connection was already being formed between Arch and Jalen.

I appreciated that comment from Coach K, and the more I thought about it, the more pumped I became. Even before Jalen's freshman year had begun, he and Arch were already close. As the months went by, I became convinced that Ryan and Jalen had two of the highest emotional IQ's of any players I have ever coached.

Emotional IQ is one of the most critical factors in someone being a good teammate. It's an understanding of the relationships we all have with people and how to react to different people and situations. That's what you confront on a team or in a workplace. This particular group—the 2015–2016 Villanova Wildcats—was blessed with that quality in spades.

Some of our players come from inner-city high schools that may not have the resources of other high schools. For our guys to emerge from there is proof of their capacity to adapt and work well with a wide range of individuals and personality types.

We have great respect for that.

Not every guy is a 3.8 student, but that doesn't mean he doesn't have a high emotional IQ.

Ryan and Jalen are similar in a lot of ways. Both have committed, deeply involved parents. Their dads were both big-time Division I athletes themselves: Joe Arch as a football player at Villanova and Rick Brunson as a great basketball player at Temple. Each of them has a mom who is intelligent, loving, and nurturing. There is great chemistry in both families.

I never asked Ryan if he gave Jalen any tips on playing in the city where he had grown into a star. As a hometown guy, Ryan would jokingly ask members of our athletics staff when we were going to schedule his "homecoming" game for suburban Langhorne. But Jalen and Ryan were road roommates all season, and my guess is that, in some way, Arch let Jalen know how much his standing would rise in our locker room if he stayed true to our values while playing in front of his hometown crowd.

When it was over, I told Jalen that what he had done that night had strengthened the respect his teammates had for him.

He looked at me and replied, "I know."

Jalen had handled his homecoming perfectly.

Humble and hungry.

That would benefit him in the long run, and it had aided us in the short term too. With all the attention paid to Jalen's homecoming, the No. 1 ranking had become almost an afterthought.

It wouldn't stay that way for long.

14

The Good and the Bad
of Being the Best

———

THE BLISSFUL DISCONNECT we had enjoyed during our thirty-six-hour visit to Chicago ended as we settled into our routine back on campus. Everyone around us was fired up about being ranked No. 1.

Our next opponent, St. John's, occupied last place in the Big East standings. Yet as I studied the game tapes of the Red Storm, it was clear they were playing well. Chris Mullin had established a confidence in them over the course of the regular season.

There were 18,052 fans inside the Wells Fargo Center on Saturday night. On our way into the building, we participated in what has become a fun experience for our fans: the "Wildcat Walk." The bus pulled up in front of XFINITY Live!, an entertainment venue situated between Citizens Bank Park, Lincoln Financial Field, and the Center. The team walked through a room packed full of Nova Nation fans before we got back on the bus and made our way inside the arena.

We appreciated the love. But I sensed that a lot of people were coming to watch and pay homage to the No. 1 team in the country more than they were there to watch a great college basketball game.

We did all we could as coaches to help our guys block out that kind of sentiment. We stressed how well St. John's was playing and the challenges they had presented to us at Madison Square Garden in our first meeting. The final score that day (68–53) had been misleading. It didn't reflect the strides that the Red Storm had made, which we were seeing on film. We reminded our players, "Tape doesn't lie."

Due to a Flyers game played earlier in the day, the temperature in the building was cooler than normal. Between the chilly building, St. John's defense, and our own inconsistency, we found ourselves exactly where we had been after the first twenty minutes at the Garden: leading 28–27.

In the second half we were better, but we never really shook the Red Storm. Daniel's work inside—he was eleven of fourteen from the field and finished the night with twenty-five points and nine rebounds—was the difference for us in what ended up as a 73–63 victory.

While I wasn't thrilled with elements of our execution, I liked the grittiness we showed. This was a hungry opponent that believed it could beat us. We had stared that down and found a way to survive.

A Winning Tradition

As soon as the press conference ended, I rushed back to the coaches' locker room, grabbed my suit jacket, and found Patty, and we made our way to the DraftKings Lounge. That's the spot down the hall from the locker rooms where we were hosting a ten-year reunion of the 2006 Big East champion Wildcats.

Celebrating legendary teams is very much business as usual at Villanova. I've mentioned this before, and it deserves mentioning again. One of our core values is, "We play for those who came before us." We are blessed with an incredible basketball legacy, so each time we have the chance to celebrate the coaches and players who helped build this tradition, it's a thrill.

This one, though, was a little more special than most. It was the first of the Villanova teams that existed under my tenure as head coach to be saluted in this way.

With the game in progress, I couldn't take part in the halftime recognition ceremony. I learned later how cool it was. A video from Kyle Lowry, who was preparing to play in the NBA All-Star Game and thus unable to attend, opened the ceremony. Public address announcer Jim Bachman then introduced staff and players from that team, including Mike Nardi, Curtis Sumpter, and Randy Foye, to the audience. Randy then took the microphone and thanked the Nova Nation.

It was the kind of goosebump moment that makes this program what it is. We could all feel the respect our fans have for these young men, now in their early thirties, who lifted that team to a 28–5 record and a spot in the Elite Eight of the NCAA Tournament. In a way, Randy, Curtis, Jason Fraser, Allan Ray, Kyle, Mike Nardi, Will Sheridan, Chris Charles, Baker Dunleavy, and Mike Claxton (younger brother of our star at Hofstra, Craig "Speedy" Claxton) were the young men who introduced the Nova Nation to our staff's strategic vision.

Ryan Arcidiacono has said that he was one of the Philadelphia-area fans paying close attention to those teams in the mid-2000s. By watching that group, Arch began to assimilate what it means to be a Villanova Basketball player. I can't overstate what that awareness meant to his college career, particularly early on.

There is no doubt that we still reap the benefits of the efforts of those guys, many of whom were willing to gamble on a young coaching staff that hadn't done anything in the Big East when we recruited them.

For Patty and me, it was nice to feel that, finally, we had contributed something to this great Wildcat tradition. It gave me a little jolt of pride.

The other special element of this particular group's return was the power it held for our 2015–2016 team. This wasn't some distant group of older men we were honoring. It was a vibrant group of seasoned professionals who have never been strangers to summer open-gym sessions in the Davis Center.

As I write this, Kyle, Randy, and Dante Cunningham are still in the NBA. Allan has enjoyed a long and distinguished career in Europe after starting out with the Boston Celtics. Chris is one of the top players in a professional league in Vietnam. Jason and Curt are now part of NBA coaching staffs. Baker Dunleavy and Mike Nardi are coaching with us.

Our players didn't have to be told how good those former players were. They have seen it and felt it while trying to defend them in practice. What they have also witnessed is the pride their predecessors take in the continued success of our program.

When the postgame reception finally wound down, it was past 11:30 p.m. I tried to spend some time with every returnee, which also included former student managers. One of those I always enjoy seeing is Christina Vuocolo, who was a senior in 2006 and later went on to serve as our administrative assistant. When she left Villanova, she did so to accept a position with the charitable foundation set up by Randy Foye to benefit his hometown of Newark, New Jersey.

I loved that.

Being a coach is not unlike being a parent: You're proud of everyone you've been blessed to coach, and everyone you've been fortunate enough to mentor in your basketball family. Each individual has charted his or her own distinctive path.

That said, I'm not sure there is anyone I am more proud of than Randy Foye.

That feeling doesn't flow just from what Randy has done on the basketball court, which would be impressive enough. At Villanova, he was a consensus first team All-American in 2006, drafted as the seventh overall pick in the first round of the NBA Draft, and has been a productive player for more than a decade in the NBA. It's more than enough! But the pride I feel stems instead from the man Randy is today.

Randy came to Villanova in 2002 from East Side High School. He grew up without the presence of either of his biological parents in a tough part of Newark. Trouble was all around him in the forms of drugs and violence. He wasn't the best student.

What Randy never lacked, however, was integrity or work ethic. He's one of the most coachable players we've ever had, to the point where he took instructions almost *too* literally early in his career.

Randy's primary job as an all-state player in high school was to score points, and few guards were better at it. There was an explosiveness to Randy's game that dazzled the crowds in New Jersey. In his first year at Villanova, we were asking him to serve as a facilitator in addition to being a scorer. Randy was never selfish; he just knew one way to play. We were certain that by diversifying his skill set and enhancing his shot selection, Randy would make us a better team.

Not long after we returned from playing in the 2002 Great Alaska Shootout in Anchorage, I talked with Randy about this. The College of Charleston had beaten us 71–69 in the final of the Shootout a few days earlier. In his fifth collegiate game, Randy had scored ten points but was only three of twelve from the field. We talked about the need for him to be more selective with his shooting and more efficient by focusing on distributing the ball.

The following weekend, we played La Salle at the Palestra. Randy was in the starting lineup, playing twenty-four minutes in a game we would go on to win 74–71. I could tell during the game that Randy was putting a lot of energy into generating chances for his teammates, but when I looked down at the stat sheet after the game, I could hardly believe my eyes: Randy had not attempted a single field goal!

That was Randy. If you gave him a certain set of instructions, he was going to do everything in his power to follow through on them. In a sense, that night's performance was on me: I asked Randy to be more careful about his shots, and he was as careful as you could be.

The academic community of Villanova has nurtured a lot of its basketball players. There are countless stories of how professors, faculty, and the academic support staff (for years led by the late Dan Regan and now run by Dr. Jeremy Kees and Jenn Brophy) have helped players reach their full potential as people. Randy's personal development is one of the best of these success stories.

When he came to Villanova, he was a shy but perceptive listener. By the time he graduated in 2006, he was a confident public speaker who quickly established the Randy Foye Foundation to give back to young people in Newark. Today he is as self-assured addressing a room full of local executives as he is talking to a coach.

At the February trade deadline last season, the Oklahoma City Thunder acquired Randy from Denver. One of my friends in the NBA confirmed what I suspected: The Thunder made the deal because they wanted to add a respected professional to the organization for their upcoming playoff run.

In September 2015, the Big East asked Randy to serve as one of the former players it brought in to speak to members of the league's incoming class in a program called "Freshmen Fundamentals." The idea is to give the newcomers tips on what they can expect as a Big East basketball player, both on and off the court. Jalen, Donte, and Tim Delaney represented the Wildcats.

The feedback I received from the Big East leadership in the room—Commissioner Val Ackerman and her colleagues in the league office, Stu Jackson and John Paquette—was that Randy's honesty and wisdom had the intended effect on the young players in the audience. Everyone I spoke with raved about his message.

That Randy came back to join us that night at the Wells Fargo Center in the midst of an unrelenting NBA schedule meant the world to us. I can't say I was surprised. He's just the kind of family man of integrity we hope all our players will one day become.

The reception with our 2006 group that night refreshed me. At a moment when we held the No. 1 ranking in the land, we got to spend time with the people who were there the first time we had reached the cusp of that achievement. I left the Wells Fargo Center hoping that all of them understood how large a role they played in us reaching that pinnacle now.

Even Rivals Are Family

We retained our place in the rankings when they were next announced on Monday, February 15. This ensured that the hype surrounding our next game was likely to rise exponentially. In two nights we were headed to North Philadelphia to face the surging Temple Owls in a matchup that always revs up fans locally. Toss in the ranking and the fact that Rick Brunson's son would be on the court at a school that had recruited him to follow in his father's footsteps, and you had all the ingredients for a Big Five classic.

It's unusual to step outside the conference schedule so late in the regular season. The date was picked in part so that it could be featured on ESPN's Rivalry Week.

One of the most unique elements of the Big Five is the relationship we share as head coaches. As residents of the same city, we often find ourselves together at media or charity functions. Thankfully, we get along well and have great respect for one another. That chemistry has been further enhanced by our work on behalf of "Coaches vs. Cancer."

Phil and Judy Martelli (St. Joe's) and Fran and Ree Dunphy (Temple) are the superstars of the Philly Six Coaches vs. Cancer movement. (Drexel University, where I once worked as an assistant coach, is the sixth school in the Philly Six alliance. Drexel didn't move into Division I until long after the Big Five formed in 1955.) The commitment of the Martellis and the Dunphys has made our chapter a national fundraising leader. There are many demands on our time as head coaches and yet Phil, Fran, and their wives have inevitably gone the extra mile for this cause.

In 2004, a great Villanovan and friend of ours, Mike Stack, was diagnosed with cancer of the esophagus. Mike played for the Wildcats from 1972 to 1976, during the early days of Coach Massimino's tenure. He and his

> **BEYOND BASKETBALL**
>
> *Appreciate Your Opponent*
>
> Competition gets heated, and on the court or in the boardroom, it's easy to view the opposition as an adversary. But sports and business aren't life: The lines between us quickly become trivial in the face of real-world trouble. Your opponent is just trying to do the same thing you are: win.

wife, Cecy, grew very close to Coach and Mrs. Mass in the ensuing years and couldn't have been more hospitable to Patty and me when we returned to Villanova. (Mike was also one heck of a practical joker.)

It was a shocking diagnosis. Mike was fifty years old.

As a local guy who starred at Monsignor Bonner High School, Mike was no fan of any Big Five team not named Villanova. Whenever the Wildcats tipped off against those teams, he was in his lower-level seats at the Pavilion cheering us on. I would imagine that with his wit and physical proximity to the court, Mike aimed more than a few barbs in the direction of our Big Five opponents.

But as soon as word reached Phil and Fran of the news about Mike, they were on the phone to me. By the end of that day, they had put Mike in touch with some of the top oncologists in the region.

Unfortunately, it was too late for even the most talented doctors to save Mike. He succumbed to his illness in the spring of 2005, and we miss him terribly. Cecy remains an ardent Villanova fan, often seated at games with her daughter Kerry and her grandchildren. But when people ask me about the Big Five rivalries, which can be heated, the response to Mike Stack's cancer diagnosis is what I always think of.

The basketball coach in me knew that we would have our hands full at Temple. Fran was doing another sensational job with his team. The Owls were 16–8 and leading the American Athletic Conference standings.

When I met with our local media the day before the game, one of the big topics of conversation was a Villanova–Temple game played twenty-eight years earlier. Back in 1988, I was on the bench as an assistant to Coach Mass when we went into 4,000-seat McGonigle Hall as the No. 18 team in the country to meet No. 1 Temple, a legendary squad coached by John Chaney that finished its Atlantic 10 season with a perfect 18–0 record. The memories of the atmosphere that night are still clear in my mind. Above the court, behind one basket was an open walkway with people packed three deep. Every inch along the retaining railing was filled with people, most of them leaning over. While seated on our bench, you could feel the shoes of the people stuffed into the first row of the bleachers behind us.

We lost 98–86, but it remains one of the most exciting games I have ever taken part in: two extremely skilled offensive teams furiously trading baskets. Mark Macon, Temple's sensational freshman guard, dropped thirty-one on us, while Doug West led the Wildcats with twenty-seven. With each tough shot the Owls made, we usually had an answer. Just not quite enough to keep pace.

Now, with us being the No. 1 team, the days leading up to the game at Temple seemed strange to me. There was a lot of national attention. Everyone locally was dialed into it. This matched or surpassed the considerable hype attached to the 1988 meeting. Like most places (but maybe even more so), Philly loves a good underdog story. Temple fit the bill perfectly.

As a staff, we knew we couldn't get caught up in anything more than executing our game plan. A Temple team coached by Fran Dunphy is always so disciplined and so sound that any weakness in your game is going to be exploited. We had not played especially well in our previous game against St. John's, and you're never quite sure where that will lead as a coach.

When the game began just after 7 p.m., the Owls did a terrific job defending us. Arch and Daniel struggled to get open looks at the basket. Josh had a hard time getting open too. As good teams will do, Temple worked to stop our leading scorers.

But Jalen would not be stopped. By the time the horn sounded, he had scored twenty-five points and we had survived the Owls, winning 83–67.

Getting out of there with the win was, more than anything, a relief. Since the schedule had been released in September, our visit to Temple, and all the stress that went with it, had been on the horizon. Finally, we could put it behind us.

If you haven't called Philadelphia home, that statement might perplex you. After all, we face road showdowns all the time in the Big East. But there is a dynamic at work in the City Series you don't find anywhere else. We all root for the same professional teams and listen to the same radio talk shows here. When we lose to Xavier or Seton Hall, we may not see those people again for six or eight months. When the loss comes in the City Series, we may not get past that night's dinner without hearing about it.

We wrapped up the Big Five title with a 4–0 record. That was important to us, but we wouldn't have time to reflect on the achievement until season's end.

One of the most emotional days of our season was less than three days away.

15

The Grind

WE WERE NOW well into February. The reality of a season is that a measure of weariness can creep into everyone's psyche: players, coaches, and fans included. There are still a few weeks until the postseason. If you accept the premise that it's all about what you do in March—we obviously do not—then your biggest games are still a few weeks away.

That kind of thinking is all around you.

We make every effort to ignore it. Our goal is to have the guys treat each day with as much importance as any other. We borrow from the great John Wooden, the coaching legend from UCLA, who once said, "Make each day your masterpiece." We supplement that unforgettable (and poetic) piece of advice with a maxim of our own, "Be here now." Stay in the moment, from the first summer workout through whenever the final horn ends our season. "Don't look at what's ahead in a week or a month," we tell our guys. "Stay away from getting caught up in the 'what may come' of the Big East or NCAA Tournaments."

This mentality also guards against something else that can happen at this time of year (which happens to coincide with the worst weather our region has to offer). Between the physical demands on the court and the mental tendency to look ahead to the tournaments, guys can let the grind of the season wear them down.

During our 2015–2016 campaign, one player who hit a rough patch in mid-February was Josh Hart. More than any of our guys, Josh has always had a tendency to beat himself up if he's disappointed in his performance. That's as true in practice as it is in games. And the fact is, when you are a part of a deep roster of talented and competitive players, you're not *always* going to have a great practice. Even as a unanimous first team All–Big East player, a guy like Josh is going to lose to a teammate in a drill or a scrimmage. When I look at Josh in those moments, I can see his frustration. He never blames his teammates or makes excuses to his coaches. He just gets upset with himself.

We knew that making sure Josh didn't slip into a funk at this point in the season was important. Awaiting us on Saturday were the Butler Bulldogs, the same gritty group that had nearly knocked us off five weeks earlier at Hinkle Fieldhouse.

One of the reasons we emerged with a 60–55 win in that game was Josh's work on the court. On a night when both defenses were locked in, Josh's ability to be active on the offensive glass and score was pivotal.

Josh had managed to carry that momentum forward for a solid month-plus of high-level offensive production. Over the first half of the Big East season, he was our leading scorer, and his points were one of the reasons we had not been too adversely affected by the loss of Darrun Hilliard on the wing this season.

Now, though, he was dealing with a new reality.

Every team we faced put Josh's name atop its scouting reports. That's inevitable when you begin to consistently produce as Josh had over the season's first few months. With it comes a level of defensive attention that requires an adjustment.

In our previous two outings, both St. John's and Temple had made stopping Josh a priority. Both teams did it exceptionally well. Josh was a combined three of fifteen from the field in those two games.

There's opportunity in every obstacle, of course. The focus on Josh gave our team other openings. Daniel scored twenty-five points against the Red Storm, and Jalen matched that number against Temple. In each case, we came up with the win and Josh never lost sight of that as our overarching goal.

But after nearly three years of watching him practice and play, I could sense a level of frustration in Josh. So we had a conversation about it.

A little history may be helpful here. When Josh starred at Sidwell Friends School (the same school attended by President Obama's daughters, Sasha and Malia), he was clearly the best player on his team. If he didn't score in bunches, it was tough for the team to win. Josh knew that better than anyone. Winning was paramount in his mind—and the way to accomplish that was for him to produce as many points as possible.

In Josh's mind, I think he still connected his scoring to the team's success at Villanova.

Earlier in the season, our opponents had been most concerned about our seniors, especially after the way Arch and Daniel had scored during our Big East opening weekend against Xavier and Creighton, respectively. Those two were our leaders, and the coaches in our league viewed them as the players whose offense most helped us win games. Josh benefited from all those eyes on Daniel and Arch.

But as Josh's profile grew, naturally so did the commitment from opposing coaches to limit his scoring, especially on the offensive glass. At any level of basketball, second-chance points are precious. Those kinds of field goals have a way of deflating teams that have worked hard to get an initial defensive stop, only to see the opponent score or get to the line anyway. Josh is extraordinarily adept at this phase of the game, in large part because he is absolutely relentless in pursuing the basketball.

But after he struggled offensively against St. John's and Temple, he seemed to think that if he wasn't scoring, he wasn't doing his job as a starter or helping his team—even though we won both games.

What I tried to explain to Josh was that we were winning because of all the other things he did for us. Everyone in our locker room valued the energy he brought every day to the practice court, let alone to games. There was so much more he did for us beyond scoring—he was a top defender, kept balls alive so his teammates could grab them, and pulled down huge rebounds.

My hope, I told Josh that day, was that he could one day complete a game and feel satisfied with a day's or night's work when he may have only scored seven or eight points. I wanted him to appreciate all the other positive ways he was impacting our team. We chart what we call "Attitude" plays, the intangibles that may not show up on the stat sheet. Josh never failed to fill up the "Attitude" categories, and I hoped he could have a better appreciation for what that means in our program.

Honoring Our Present

As we approached Saturday afternoon's nationally televised rematch with the Bulldogs, there was another element to consider: Not only would we be hosting a very good team, but we would do so surrounded by the swirling emotions of Senior Day.

Senior Day is a tradition across college athletics. At the final home game of the regular season, the university honors the efforts of its senior student-athletes along with their families.

In the early part of my coaching career, we approached Senior Day the way a lot of programs do. We honored the seniors and their families in a pregame ceremony and then did all we could to win the game

COURTESY OF JAY WRIGHT

For more than forty years, every player who has spent four years in our program has earned his degree. Here I am with the senior class of 2011. From left, Antonio Pena, Corey Fisher, and Corey Stokes.

so those players would have a special memory as their careers came to an end.

Over the years, though, we came to realize that if you're a good team, you still have quite a few meaningful games left to play before the season ends. So in the mid-2000s, we shifted our approach. Instead of looking inward, we decided to publicly acknowledge the generous support of those who surround us.

For us, Senior Day is now about *all* the senior students at Villanova and the family members of the senior players. It has little to do with the senior players themselves. This is our way of thanking the seniors at Villanova who support our program from the day they arrive for freshman orientation through the end of their senior year.

With the help of the Student Life office on campus, we host a party prior to the game on Senior Day. Each of the senior players joins me to say a few words, thanking their classmates seventy-five minutes before tip-off. It's a break from our usual routine, when I typically want our guys focused on the game at that point, but we make an exception because it's such an important gesture for us.

Another part of this day belongs to the families of our senior athletes. The parents and family members of the senior class have usually been on a great ride. This is a farewell of sorts for them as well. Family is such a vital component at Villanova, and it's essential that we acknowledge those who develop the incredible character of the young men in our program.

We also make sure to recognize the efforts of the people you don't see on the court who mean so much to our program: the student managers and office assistants. They are introduced to the crowd along with their family members before the game, and we take a photo at center court. At halftime, the senior cheerleaders are saluted. We also bring representatives from those groups onto that week's radio broadcast as a show of public appreciation.

To me, the entire event is a statement about who we are and what we value as a basketball family.

I have been through more than my share of these celebrations, and the emotion usually gets the better of me. That is especially so when the senior is someone like Randy Foye or JayVaughn Pinkston, who has come so far to gain a college education. And it was never tougher on me than in 2014, when Tony Chennault walked down through the student section for his final time as a Wildcat.

In my mind, the example that Tony created had a direct impact on every good thing we were now seeing in 2016 from Arch, Daniel, Kris, Josh, and Darryl.

When we had evaluated Tony while he starred at Philadelphia's Saints John Neumann and Maria Goretti Catholic High School, we were impressed. Tony was a classic Philly guard with toughness, skill, and leadership. Those kinds of guards have always thrived at Villanova. (Wali Jones, who starred as a Wildcat from 1962 to 1964, was one of the first to do so.)

In recruiting, though, fit is important. And when Tony was due to start college in the fall of 2010, we were already deep at the guard position. Corey Fisher and Corey Stokes, both outstanding Big East guards who had played as sophomores on our Final Four team, were busy preparing for their senior years. Maalik Wayns and Dominic Cheek were returning for their sophomore seasons and primed to play major roles for us.

BEYOND BASKETBALL

A Caring Culture

Culture is how you live together as a unit. Any leader has an opportunity to set a tone for how his group or organization lives by being positive, energetic, and invested in those around him.

We knew that a guard of Tony's caliber would have opportunities elsewhere to get significant playing time early in his career, so we were not surprised when he elected to attend Wake Forest University. It made sense. In addition to being an elite guard, Tony was an outstanding student. He immediately seized the opportunity and became a starter with the Demon Deacons.

Two years later our respective situations had changed.

After two years in Winston-Salem, North Carolina, Tony decided to seek a transfer to the Philadelphia area to be closer to his mother, Crystal Morton. Crystal was facing some health issues at the time, and the NCAA had begun considering "hardship" waivers that would allow students to transfer without the penalty of sitting out a year if the circumstances warranted it.

At Villanova, meanwhile, we were in a different place by the spring of 2012 than we had been during Tony's original recruitment. The two Coreys had graduated. Maalik and Dom had both announced their intention to forsake their senior years to pursue professional careers. Our top signee at the guard position, Ryan Arcidiacono, had missed his entire senior season at Neshaminy High School after back surgery.

We were in need of reinforcements, especially ones with experience. In two short years we had gone from no fit for Tony to a perfect one.

This was a different decision than the one Tony had made in 2009. It was now about family and the desire to take care of his mom. He also knew that the Villanova network could go a long way toward helping him realize his post-basketball dream of pursuing a career as a filmmaker and businessman.

Tony agreed to come on board once he completed his spring semester at Wake Forest, and we instantly felt much better about our roster. From a basketball standpoint, he would bring the toughness and experience we were lacking. Off the court, his maturity would be an incalculable bonus to younger players like James Bell, JayVaughn Pinkston, Darrun Hilliard, Daniel, and Ryan, who would all be stepping into leadership roles before their senior year.

We were excited. Tony was too.

Then, on May 31, 2012, everything changed in Tony's world. His brother Mike Jay, a great mentor to Tony and to his younger brother Sean, was killed by gunfire in Philadelphia. The family was told this was simply a matter of Mike being in the wrong place at the wrong time.

As a team, we joined Tony at the funeral. Seeing how he bore up to that tragedy made an impression on the rest of our guys, even as they were still getting to know Tony.

Tony brought exactly what we hoped he would to the team. Although he had been a starter at Wake Forest, he worked hard to accept the role we needed him in as a reserve. His on-the-ball defense at the guard position was vital to our improvement at that end of the court. On offense, I knew I could trust him to run the team when we needed to create extra scoring by moving Arch off the ball. His leadership alongside James Bell and Mouphtaou Yarou was instrumental to our return to the NCAA Tournament after a one-year absence.

But it wasn't always easy for him. In the spring of 2013, after his first season with us, Tony's swirling emotions brought him into my office with a shocker: He wanted to transfer again, ideally to another Philadelphia-area school where he could return to his more familiar role as a starter. It didn't seem like the best idea to me—as a transfer with only one season of eligibility and most of the area schools already set in the backcourt, his options would be limited—but we agreed to let him look. He took a few weeks, thought about it, and eventually returned to my office, this time with JayVaughn by his side, asking if he could return. We were happy to have him back on board.

Then, a few months later, tragedy struck again: Tony's mother, Crystal, passed away.

Tony was crushed. But at that time, he made the decision that the best way to help him through the grief would be to stay connected to the team and keep busy. He understood that being alone wasn't the way he needed to work through his loss.

There were times during our conversations when Tony would naturally wonder, "Why me?" Before I could even form a response, he would stop himself and say, "I know I've got other blessings. I can't go down that road."

Watching Tony conduct himself as a young man facing such adversity had an incredible impact on his younger teammates—especially Arch, Daniel, Darrun, and JayVaughn. They watched a twenty-year-old make intelligent decisions in the wake of real tragedy while conducting himself as a good man. Their respect for him was enormous.

There was another dynamic at work too. Tony stood up to me maybe a little bit more than I would have liked. One afternoon in practice, for example, I stopped play when I thought Tony was being overly aggressive on defense, as he sometimes was. I called it a "Tony mauling," which was a term we used at the time. The other guys laughed. Tony didn't think it was funny and stormed off the court. I told the remaining players that I actually respected Tony's competitiveness and we moved on. Tony returned the next day and apologized to the team. For my part, I understood that I couldn't underestimate the sacrifice he was making for the unit. And from that point forward, his approach was nothing short of sensational.

As a senior, when Tony didn't start, he understood exactly what we needed from him whenever I called upon him to enter a game. He won many games for us during that 2013–2014 season by realizing precisely what was required in the circumstance, whether it was him defending an elusive point guard or driving the basketball and kicking it back out to get one of his teammates a shot.

In the same spot, a lot of other seniors might have been most concerned with proving to me that they should have been in the game to start. Tony was not. His work ethic as a senior reserve made him a great example to the rest of the group. What Tony did for us is rare. It's not often you see a senior come off the bench and really impact the outcome in practice and games. He brought it every day—and our guys never failed to be inspired by the way he dealt with an incredibly challenging two years.

When we honored Tony at Senior Day in 2014, all of that hit me. Since his graduation, Tony has worked in community service for the Philadelphia 76ers and has crafted a reputation as a talented filmmaker. He has already produced several documentaries, including one titled *Oldhead,* in which he looked at the value of mentorship in his native inner-city Philadelphia.

This Senior Day, 2016, was tough for me too, as they all are. While the overarching focus of Senior Day is on all Villanova seniors, we still bring players and their families onto the court before the Pavilion crowd, and that tugs at my emotions. We honored Kevin, Henry, Pat, Daniel, and Arch prior to tip-off. In my role as the CEO of the program, it's important that I soak all that in. But once that group photo is taken, I have to quickly shift back into being the head coach. Butler demanded my full attention for the next forty minutes.

The game didn't disappoint.

The Bulldogs made an early run to take a 17–16 lead midway through the first half. Josh seemed to be playing with a clearer mind than he had at Temple. He helped spark a 9–0 burst that allowed us to take a 34–25 lead at halftime.

We never doubted Butler's resolve, which showed early in the second half. Kelan Martin, a terrific forward, ignited an 18–7 spurt, and the Bulldogs led 43–41 with 12:17 on the clock. We were struggling to score, and you could feel the unease in the Pavilion.

At times like this, we turn to another of our favored phrases, "94 by 50 feet." Those are the dimensions of a basketball court. By saying that, we remind our players that what goes on around us isn't important. What matters is what transpires within those dimensions.

Ironically, we probably invoke that "94 by 50" phrase more at home than we do on the road. Away from home, you are the hunted. But at home, there are usually family and friends present, which creates a different kind of pressure.

In this game of runs, we put together a great final push, outscoring the Bulldogs 36–24 the rest of the way. Josh and Kris led the charge, combining for forty-two points and eighteen rebounds to get us to a 77–67 win.

Our record was now 24–3, and the No. 1 ranking was likely to remain in place for another week.

After we shook hands with the Butler staff and players, we walked to the baseline in front of the student section for what has become one of my favorite rituals. After every game we salute the students, holding up our "Vs" to acknowledge their support. A few years ago, one more twist was added.

In 2009, in the wake of a Senior Night victory over Providence, Dwayne Anderson, Shane Clark, Dante Cunningham, and Frank Tchuisi made a spontaneous decision to climb atop a baseline press table near the visiting team bench. That "step" has become a tradition, and I absolutely love the visual it presents. Each year I request a photo, taken from behind the players with the full student section looking down from the stands, to be featured prominently in my office—and 2016 was no different.

The Great Majesty of Life

It was Sunday morning before I had a chance to go through my post-game texts. For a head coach, the volume of people reaching out via text or email spikes after a game. Many of these messages are a lot of fun to read. And one of my most faithful "correspondents" since our return to Villanova has been Mike Daly.

Mike came to Villanova in 1968 after playing basketball at Cardinal O'Hara High School. His timing could hardly have been better. Among the Wildcat icons he played with were Fran O'Hanlon, Howard Porter, Clarence Smith, Chris Ford, and Tom Ingelsby. After graduating in 1972, Mike went on to build a successful business career and has been one of our most supportive alums.

In some ways, Mike was perfectly positioned to be a generational link. Growing up in the area, he watched the Villanova stars of the 1950s and '60s, players like Jim Huggard, Jim Washington, George Leftwich, and Hubie White. He played on our 1971 NCAA Finals team. And he has watched every Villanova team since as a season ticket holder.

The respect and love for Mike was such that, when he called to encourage an alumnus to come back for a campus event, the request truly meant something. And he did that without any nudge from our staff. Mike was a bridge builder, and he is a major reason why our basketball alumni network is so vibrant. He did so much to keep all of us connected, yet at no time did he ever want to be out in front in this effort.

The text from Mike on this Sunday morning included a video featuring his two-year-old granddaughter. In it, she was singing the Villanova fight song. Mike's words accompanying the video were: "This is how you start the brainwashing in a Villanova family."

I responded with a text to the effect that his granddaughter was great and that she could soon help us out by singing the national anthem at a game. His text back to me was a classic: "She could also help you out on the sideline."

On Monday morning, around 9 a.m., I responded to Mike's text with another of my own: "I can always count on you to keep me humble."

I went about my morning and then, shortly after noon, I received a phone call with shocking news: Mike had died that morning of an apparent heart attack.

A short while later, I had to tape an interview for our television show. My guess is that anyone who watched that episode later in the week wondered where my head was. I was in shock then and even now, months later, I will still look down at my phone and think about texting or calling Mike.

This one hit me as hard as the news of any death ever has. In a lot of cases, you have a sense that a friend may be ill, so you're aware of the possibility. There was no warning for this. When last I had seen Mike earlier in the month, he had looked as robust as ever.

Mike was not what you would describe as an outwardly emotional guy. He was of that era when you let your actions speak for you. The selfless manner in which he always carried himself was his own form of leadership.

Although Mike wasn't prone to displays of emotion, there were moments I could sense really moved him, and some of those were big Wildcat wins. The one that immediately comes to mind took place in March of 2009, when we defeated UCLA in the second round of the NCAA Tournament, 89–70.

UCLA, of course, is the same program that beat the 1971 Wildcats in the NCAA Championship game. Following our 2009 win in Philadelphia, Mike and many of his former teammates joined us in the locker room. The pride those men shared in Villanova having taken down UCLA in an NCAA Tournament setting was immense.

Later Mike would type these words to me in a message: "The Great Majesty of Life." It's an expression he was often inspired to use during sentimental moments in the Wildcat program, especially when there was any kind of cross-generational meeting connecting Villanovans young and old.

Those words became a recurring theme of ours, and I still recall them often.

As shaken as I was by Mike's passing, I knew full well that his desire would have been for us to zero in on Wednesday night's rematch at Xavier. I spoke with Mike's wife, Arlene, and we did our best to let the Daly family, and the world, know just how much Mike meant to us. Steve Scheer, the Fox producer, even managed to get Mike's passing mentioned on one of our telecasts that week.

The game itself was the talk of the college hoops universe. The Musketeers were also 24–3 and ranked fifth in the country, averaging eighty points a game. Edmond Sumner had returned to the lineup after recovering from the concussion he suffered in our game against them on New Year's Eve, and he was terrific. Xavier had seven legitimate scorers we would have to account for.

For all of my grief, I also appreciated how lucky we were to be in a game of this magnitude. This was a huge night for the Big East. The two top teams in the conference were meeting in front of a packed house at the Cintas Center in Cincinnati, and it was a huge national story. A top-five clash like this was business as usual in the original Big East, so to be on that stage again, in a grouping of schools that was only three years old, felt invigorating.

I am the first to say it: This Big East will never be the same as what we had before. But that is true for every conference in America. Our sport has evolved, and so have the leagues and rivalries.

Yet this night reinforced that this new Big East is special too. We have something utterly unique in college athletics: a great basketball conference run by basketball people who possess a deep understanding of how our game works. At each of our ten schools, basketball is the clear athletic priority for the university and the fan base.

The atmosphere at Xavier was terrific. Both teams were ready to play—but they were just better than we were that night.

The final was 90–83.

Believe it or not, I left the Cintas Center feeling good about what had transpired.

Xavier wanted to beat us badly, and they were able to get it done. I respected not only what Chris Mack and his team had accomplished on the court, but the mood of the entire evening. The record crowd of 10,727 at the Cintas Center was supportive of its team while being respectful of us. No one made any effort to portray the Sumner fall in our previous game as anything more than it was: a clean basketball play. There was no nastiness.

At the end of the game, Xavier had defeated the No. 1 team in the country, yet its fans didn't storm the court. Chris and his staff were classy. So was the crowd.

I was proud of our guys too. We battled for every ball. We just lost.

We had endured an emotional seven days. The No. 1 ranking wouldn't be ours for much longer. There would be no words of encouragement for me in my text box from one of our program's great friends.

"The Great Majesty of Life" isn't solely about the good times. It's also about the perseverance needed to get through the tougher days.

16

Senior Moments

IN THE WEEK that followed the Senior Day victory over Butler, more than a few people asked me why we had not given our senior walk-ons—Patrick Farrell, Henry Lowe, and Kevin Rafferty—a start on Senior Day. (We had gone instead with our normal starting five: Arch, Daniel, Josh, Kris, and Jalen.)

I understood the question.

Whenever we held a lead during a home game in the last few seasons, it was impossible not to hear the students chanting their names. It's reminiscent of the climactic scene of the movie *Rudy*, about the hardheaded, five-foot-nothin' walk-on football player at Notre Dame who suited up and played in the final seconds of his senior season. That kind of reaction isn't uncommon; fans often have the desire to see a coach "clear the bench." But this sentiment went well beyond that.

Pat, Henry, and Kevin were beloved figures on our campus. The chanting was a tribute to the people they were, not just the role they played on our team. Our students had gotten to know these young men and respected them. And I think they also respected that when any of the trio did enter a game, even if the score was lopsided in our favor, they never played to the audience.

One of the more familiar elements of Senior Day across the country is that every senior, whether on scholarship or not, is often introduced as part of the starting lineup. In our time at Villanova, we've assessed that decision on a case-by-case basis. In 2014, for example, we held Arch out of the starting lineup for the only time in his Villanova career so that Tony Chennault could start. Likewise, Baker Dunleavy started on his Senior Night in 2006.

The decision to use the regular starters against Butler was in no way meant to slight Pat, Henry, or Kevin. Rather, our intent was to do what was best for the team in an important game that could have a major impact on our pursuit of a Big East regular season championship.

No one understood that better than those seniors themselves.

When I informed them, they didn't flinch. To a man, the response was, "We got you, Coach." They were able to put aside any disappointment they may have felt for the greater good. It was just one more example of how their genuine selflessness positively affected our team.

We had two seniors who were on the court all the time in Arch and Daniel. But we also had three other seniors who were in the locker room, in the dorm rooms, and seated near the back of the bus with the rest of the leadership on road trips.

That's rare in college basketball today.

At this level of Division I hoops, there is so much to absorb. These three became an incredible resource for the underclassmen because they had a fantastic feel for what we were looking to accomplish as a unit. This may sound strange, but it's true: Early on, our veteran walk-ons are better at executing the details of Villanova Basketball than some of our younger scholarship players are. They're able to operate as more efficient cogs in the wheel at that point. A scholarship freshman might be more talented, but his learning curve is steep enough that he often disrupts the flow of practice.

As such, if you are a Pat Farrell or a Henry Lowe, you might be tempted to teach a heralded newcomer a "lesson." You have a base of knowledge they don't yet possess, and that gives you an edge. It would be possible for you to make a play or a move on a prominent name that you could tell your family and friends about for years to come.

None of these guys ever gave in to that urge. Their only goal was to help the scholarship players improve. The walk-ons made a tremendous contribution by speeding up the learning process for guys like Phil Booth, Mikal Bridges, Jalen Brunson, Eric Paschall, and Donte DiVincenzo. As a staff, we never took that dedication for granted, and the younger guys recognized it too.

Pat and Henry like to tell a story about something that happened as they were preparing to attend Villanova in the summer of 2012. Neither had yet met their highly touted classmate, Ryan Arcidiacono, but, as students of the game, they knew him by reputation. Each of them independently did a Google search of Ryan and came upon the same scouting service report. In it, Ryan was described as something of a selfish player.

Henry and Pat wondered just what this big-name recruit would be like when they became teammates.

To this day, that report and its utterly inaccurate assessment of Arch's approach is a source of amusement to all three of them.

On some teams, there are clear lines between the scholarship players and the walk-ons. We never make those distinctions. It goes back to one of our core values. "Everyone's role is different but their status is the same."

This group embodied that expression as well as any we have ever had.

Pat and Arch discovered that they had common friends on Long Island soon after they got to Villanova. They hit it off instantly and remain tight to this day. Kevin developed a unique relationship with JayVaughn Pinkston. There were times when JayVaughn, the kid from Brooklyn, went home to spend time with Kevin at his family's house in Malvern. Tony Chennault also became close with Kevin and his family over his time at Villanova. Henry grew close to James Bell.

The respect for Pat, Henry, and Kevin developed naturally, and it only served to enhance our fabric as a group. In practice, if anyone's energy dipped, those three corrected it before a coach could—but never in a selfish way. When we put any of them into a game late, their goal was to play Villanova Basketball, not to make it about their point totals.

Together, Patrick, Henry, and Kevin combined to play eighty-four minutes over the course of forty games in 2015–2016. Yet their impact was so much greater than that. They were simply the latest examples of the lessons my father, Jerry Wright, first taught me—way back when I was a shortstop on the Larks.

Turning Weakness into Strength

In each of the last three seasons, we have faced the Marquette Golden Eagles at the BMO Harris Bradley Center on "National Marquette Day," a celebration of the school and its alumni. The buildup to this season's game, on the final Saturday of February, was all around us when we flew into Milwaukee on Friday afternoon. Our downtown hotel was overflowing with Marquette alums from around the country. A crowd of 19,043 would attend the game.

I was interested to see how our team would handle this matchup coming off the loss at Xavier, and the way the players came into practice in the days leading up to this one gave me a quiet sense of confidence. I wouldn't say that we had been humbled in Cincinnati. What I saw was more a case of renewed focus on the part of the guys.

After every loss, the coach has a certain take on what happened, born of his experiences

> **BEYOND BASKETBALL**
>
> *Listen to Your Team*
>
> Offering instructions for improvement is necessary, of course, but it never hurts to solicit input from your team. Try asking your team or your employees what they think the group could be doing better—and also where it excels. Those conversations are often illuminating.

and sense of the big picture. Yet the more time I spend in this profession, the more I have come to appreciate the value of hearing the players' take on the loss before I present mine to them. (I sometimes wonder why more CEOs and other leaders don't employ this sort of "listening to your team" approach. I wonder how much improvement they'd see in their organizational performance if it happened more often. Based on my experience, I'm guessing a lot.)

We had surrendered ninety points at Xavier, and all of that had to do with the firepower of the Musketeers. They were an exceptionally balanced and gifted unit that was humming on its home court.

Yet there were still mistakes we made in our defensive execution. Communication in a cauldron like the Cintas Center can be difficult for the visitors, and these breakdowns led to some open shots for

Xavier. We wanted to be ready for what we knew would be another difficult road environment in Milwaukee.

A year earlier, that same sort of perspective, shared with me by Arch and some of his classmates, helped me process the loss to NC State.

In this instance, we listened closely to our guys. We were all in agreement that learning from this loss was a matter of addressing some of the many small details that spell the difference between victory and defeat. To beat a team the caliber of Xavier—or a gifted and hungry Marquette team at home—we needed to be crisper in our execution.

And we were, although not in every facet of the game. Like our first matchup, this one was high scoring. We converted nearly fifty-nine percent of our first-half field goals and scored forty-two points. But Marquette was accurate too, sinking half of its attempts from the field to produce thirty-seven points over the first twenty minutes.

At the start of the second half, Arch made sure we got off to a good start. He scored five points in an 8–0 surge to open the period, and we suddenly had a double-digit advantage. But each time we would start to pull away, the Golden Eagles came right back at us.

Marquette's ability to be disruptive defensively helped fuel its offense. The Golden Eagles excelled at forcing turnovers, and we had seventeen—six more than we averaged on the season. A number of them led to easy baskets for guards JaJuan Johnson and Haanif Cheatham, who each scored nineteen points. It was one of those days when it seemed like the clock would never hit zero.

But we kept Marquette at arm's length the rest of the way, winning 89–79.

This was another day when our leaders carried us. Arch stepped up at a crucial moment. Daniel's work on the interior—he ended the day with eighteen points and twelve rebounds—created opportunities for Josh and Kris (nineteen points apiece).

In a lot of important ways, this was a real "Attitude" game for us.

February was now complete. Our record stood at 25–4 with two regular season home games remaining in the first week of March. A victory in one of them would secure the Big East regular season title for the third time in as many seasons.

During the flight home, I studied the tape on my laptop. Always working, always reassessing, and always trying to improve is a must when you're trying to be your best. When we later spoke as a staff on the ride from the airport to campus, we all agreed: Our team was developing a new dimension, something that could prove important in the weeks to come—the growing versatility of Kris Jenkins.

Over the course of the season, Kris had become a lethal threat not just from the outside but increasingly in the post. Thanks to his unique skill set, he was the best mismatch option for us, better even than Daniel. His strength made him a tough cover for smaller defenders; his perimeter-shooting touch made him a challenging foe for taller ones. And Kris' natural intelligence was allowing him to make superb decisions when he held the ball down low. If you came to double-team Kris, he would kick out to the open man beyond the arc. If a teammate was slashing to the basket, Kris could thread the needle through traffic to find him.

That comfort level hadn't been achieved overnight. Like many talented young players in the early portion of their careers, Kris was mainly a scorer. That was the skill that had made him the Washington, D.C., player of the year at Gonzaga College High School. If the ball wasn't finding him in the flow of the offense, he would look for opportunities to score rather than letting the chances come to him.

It's something Kris and I had discussed at length.

What I asked Kris to do was to trust the coaching staff. If he could take care of all the little things, we would find ways to unlock his scoring prowess.

In watching that Marquette tape, it was clear: Kris was now right where we hoped he would be. The details that mattered most to us—taking charges, playing hard every second—were now second nature to him. And we were so much the better for it.

Now we were running plays through Kris. Searching for shots was no longer part of his game. We were also taking full advantage of his skill as a facilitator. In the win against Marquette, we had delivered twenty assists on thirty made field goals, an indicator of how smartly we were moving the basketball. Seven of our eight players, including Kris, had two or more assists that day.

What had been one of our downfalls in the loss to Oklahoma back in December now felt like one of our strengths.

On Monday, the new national polls were released. With the loss at Xavier, Villanova dropped to No. 3 in the Associated Press rankings and No. 2 in the USA Today Coaches Poll. It had been a pressure-packed three weeks and our guys had handled things well. At the height of our Big East season, we had won five of the six games in that span, including three on the road. The only loss came away from home against the No. 5 team in the nation.

More important, we had kept our focus pointed inward rather than getting caught up in the hoopla surrounding us.

The final week of the regular season coincided with Villanova's spring break. We were to host a pair of home games—against DePaul at the Pavilion and Georgetown at the Wells Fargo Center. At a lot of schools, games during school recesses are a cause for concern among coaches and athletic directors because it means you will be subtracting a vital component of your support.

Villanova is not one of those places.

I never cease to be amazed by the turnout we have during these "break" games. It doesn't matter if the break is for Thanksgiving, Christmas, or spring: The Nova Nation is there in force. When you look up into the south end zone in the Pavilion or the two end zones at the Wells Fargo Center, the stands are packed. There may be more graduates than current students and more families with younger children than we typically see, but they are ready to cheer on the 'Cats.

A lot of the credit here goes to our AD, Mark Jackson, and our ticket manager, Bob Nyce. Using a model first developed by Mark's predecessor, Vince Nicastro, and Bob Steitz, a former senior associate AD at Villanova, they work to make available to the public tickets that aren't picked up by the students. The coach in me wants our guys to ignore the crowd and keep the focus within those 94 by 50 feet of court. But the basketball CEO in me thinks it's great for our players when they walk onto a Villanova home court and the arena is packed.

One of the areas I planned to pay close attention to against the DePaul Blue Demons was our defense. As pleased as we were to have the new offensive wrinkles, we also understood that the cornerstones of our program remained defense and rebounding. We had held up reasonably well in the latter category at Marquette—thanks mostly to Daniel—but it seemed to me there had been a bit of slippage at the defensive end.

In part, that was a product of being away from home and facing a couple of potent offenses. But as coaches we knew we couldn't dismiss it that simply. There were too many cases of a dribbler eluding the first defender, which breaks the rest of your defense down. DePaul and its fine guard Billy Garrett Jr. had the ability to exploit us in that way if we weren't more attentive.

Once again, Daniel and Arch set the tone.

During the first half, Daniel aggravated a left ankle sprain that had been bothering him in practice. Instead of taking a seat on the bench, though, he persevered. On this night he wouldn't be the offensive force he had been at Marquette—he ended up taking just one shot. But he gave us twenty-three rugged minutes and made certain we were dialed in defensively.

We limited the Blue Demons to sixty-two points in a 21-point victory.

Kris continued his rise, recording a new career high with thirty-one points. The 6,500 fans in the Pavilion reveled in every one of the eight three-pointers Kris made that night. Josh stepped forward with eighteen points, and Kris and Josh were the players requested to meet with the Philadelphia media with me in the press room afterward. I stressed to the reporters that the decks had been cleared for Josh and Kris by the tireless production in other areas from Arch and Daniel.

With the victory, we clinched the Big East regular season championship. But in meetings with Mark and members of our staff prior to the game, we had decided to forgo any kind of postgame celebration. There was still one regular season game left on the schedule, and that was our priority.

At 26–4 and with a Top 5 national ranking, much of the conversation around us those next few days focused on the upcoming NCAA Tournament. The East Regional Finals were to be held at the Wells Fargo Center and, by rule, we were eligible to compete at the site by virtue of the fact we had not hosted more than three regular season games there. The number of questions about the postseason and the chances we would get to play in Philly increased by the day.

In one sense, the entire 2015–2016 season had seemed less than meaningful to certain segments of the public and media. To this audience, the critical games wouldn't take place until the first weekend of the NCAA Tournament.

That wasn't our mindset, of course, but we had to be honest with ourselves too. A lot of people, even very informed ones, shared that thought. My charge was to help us deal with that sentiment in a polite way without having our team internalize it.

I'm not sure how many of the 20,173 who came to the Center on the final Saturday of the regular season allowed their minds to drift ahead. What I was most proud of was that the fourteen Villanova Basketball players on our bench that day cared only about the Hoyas and the challenges they presented to our unit.

Daniel was playing hurt but gave us ten points and six rebounds in twenty-four minutes. We built a 46–27 halftime lead and had another day of crisp passing, with twenty-three assists on twenty-seven made field goals. The Hoyas' L. J. Peak made us sweat in the final fifteen minutes—he sliced us up to the tune of thirty-one points on the day—but we closed out the regular season with an 84–71 win.

Shortly after the horn sounded, Father Peter and Mark carried out the Big East Championship trophy. We spent a few minutes sharing in the achievement with the Nova Nation, which had been right there with us throughout. Then we headed back down the tunnel to the locker room.

One of the things I wanted to do in the aftermath of that win was to make sure our staff took pride in winning the Big East regular season title: Baker Dunleavy, Ashley Howard, Kyle Neptune, George Halcovage, Arleshia Davidson, Mike Nardi, Jeff Pierce, and John Shackleton had done a tremendous job recruiting, coaching, and mentoring these young men.

We understand that a conference title probably means less to the fan than it does to us. But in our minds, the regular conference season remains the truest barometer of where your program stands. Teams get hot in the NCAA Tournament or, as we knew all too well, get knocked off unexpectedly. It's the nature of a single-elimination event.

We were proud of our third straight Big East title.

We were more proud of the five seniors who had helped lead us to it.

17

Buckets Over Broadway

My formal introduction to the Big East Tournament and all of its energy came in 1988. It was near the end of my first season as an assistant to Coach Massimino, and when the bus pulled up to the curb on 33rd Street, I had chills.

There were no fancy underground bus entries back then. The area around Madison Square Garden was jammed with people wearing gear from all the Big East schools, and as soon as you stepped off you were hit with the scent of hot pretzels from the nearby food carts. As we walked toward the loading dock for the elevator ride five floors up—the same no-frills freight elevator used for generations by pop stars and circus elephants alike—you could feel the storied history of the venue.

From my playing days at Bucknell through my work with the Philadelphia Stars and into my early coaching career at the University of Rochester and Drexel, I always found time to watch the Big East Tournament on TV. But this was something different. Being there in person, feeling that energy, I instantly understood what a huge deal this was for each school's alumni base. That is especially true at Villanova. The core of our alumni is based in and around New York City. The annual March trip to the Garden to watch the Wildcats is something they *live* for. Everyone has their favorite hotels and restaurants where they return each year. It's truly a pilgrimage.

I love the NCAA Tournament, but I believe the Big East Tournament rivals it. I say that with as much conviction as I did in 1990, 2000, or 2015. There is simply nothing like that week in New York City. All of your friends and family are there—everyone who you've come up through the ranks with. During the five-day extravaganza, we can count on seeing many of the people whose generosity to Villanova allows us to compete the way we do.

The Augustinian traditions at Villanova inspire a lot of our alumni to give back, either financially or by volunteering to serve (or both). A lot of Villanova engineers work with the Peace Corps in Africa before coming back to start a lucrative career in the States. Business students do volunteer work before they go on to Wall Street and make a ton of money. It's just a part of the Villanova culture: We want to excel and be our best, but we believe that being our best individually comes from being a part of a community. By giving back, we actually help one another to achieve the best of ourselves.

When it comes to financial giving, we have many alumni who prioritize the university's academic mission and allocate their resources accordingly. We also have a group of alumni that sees the value of our basketball program as a unique connector between Villanovans of every generation—a kind of "front porch" of the university in the public eye.

At every institution, it is important to have relationships with the donors. The best part of our situation at Villanova is that our key donors are people who I would hang out with even if we weren't connected by this program. They include people such as Bill Finneran, Villanova class of 1963, who endows the head coaching position. (In April 2016, he also made a $22.6 million gift to enhance the Pavilion.) Bill has a brilliant mind for business and organization. He's been an invaluable resource and friend throughout my tenure here. Bill Davis and Jim Davis, Villanova classes of 1985 and 1981, respectively, were the lead donors to our practice facility and remain vital parts of our program's fabric as well. Ed Welsh, class of 1966, endows the point guard scholarship. Pat LePore, class of 1977, endows a scholarship as well. These are all tremendous people who have become close friends of Patty's and mine. I love spending time with them, and every one of us affiliated with Villanova is appreciative of their love for our university.

These days, one of the most stressful parts of the Big East Tournament for me is managing our ticket requests. It's not just a matter of getting people in, but making sure they are seated in the right areas.

Tickets are valuable and people know it. The decisions you make about allocating them therefore send out signals to members of important constituencies: donors, alumni, former players, and university officials.

This is another indication that everything you do counts. You can't take any aspect of what you do as a leader and say, "This isn't important."

When we go to the Big East Tournament, every former Villanova Basketball player knows that he receives a ticket. We can preach the value of those guys all day long, but this is one of those moments when we have to *demonstrate* it. By providing them with a ticket, we prove their value.

It's essential that we take care of our own.

We made the drive from Villanova to Manhattan after practice on Tuesday, March 8. The Big East had announced the bulk of its regular season awards on Sunday and Monday, and Josh was a unanimous selection to the Big East first team, which suggested he would be a serious contender for the conference's Player of the Year award, to be announced the following day. Ryan was named to the second team.

In 2015, Ryan had shared the Big East Player of the Year honor with Kris Dunn. In one sense I was amazed when that news came in; we had a balanced roster, which meant Arch's stat line wasn't as eye-popping as those of the other candidates. To me, it signaled that the coaches in our league (who vote on the awards but cannot vote for their own players) really respected the impact Ryan had on our team.

Over the course of 2015–2016, I spent ample time telling Arch how much we admired the way he was handling the year after winning an award of that stature. I thought he went out of his way to prove to his teammates that winning an individual award again wasn't important to him. He never tried to get numbers and did all the little things—the "Attitude" plays—to make his teammates look good. In fact, Josh was one of the beneficiaries of that.

When the final results came in on Wednesday, Kris Dunn was named the Big East Player of the Year. He deserved it. I voted for Kris when I cast my ballot.

Ryan Arcidiacono's team won a third regular season championship. Never in a million years would he have traded that accomplishment to win the Player of the Year award. It's part of what makes him so unique.

I did feel badly to some extent that Josh wasn't our league's Player of the Year. My regret was mostly for his parents, Moses and Pat. They never look for personal acknowledgment of Josh's ability as a basketball player. I just know how much they love their son, and he was deserving of the award. He was the most productive player on the team that won the regular season conference championship.

In the back of my mind, though, I suspected that this was the kind of slight Josh would use as motivation—a log on his fire, as Father Rob might put it. Josh loves to use things like that to elevate his game and never allows them to circumvent our team goals. Competitive situations mean everything to him.

Speaking of competitors, I was concerned about Daniel. We were set to face Georgetown for the second time in six days in Thursday afternoon's quarterfinal opener, and Daniel was still troubled by his right ankle. No one knew how much he would be able to give us over the duration of this tournament.

No one competes harder than Daniel. I'd seen that back when he was still in high school. In all the years I have coached, I've never seen a high school player more committed to winning than he was. Recruiting rankings and scholarship opportunities weren't his priority. It's a memory I always drift back to when contemplating Daniel's role on our team. So there was no question in my mind: Daniel is all about winning. He wanted to win a Big East Championship in his senior year.

What I also understand about Daniel is he is extremely intelligent. Daniel takes my advice seriously, but he's always got his own plan.

Looking back on it now, I wonder if he wasn't a step ahead of us all during that second week of March. I think he calculated that he didn't want to jeopardize our chance to win an NCAA Tournament, which we never talked about, by pushing himself beyond the pain in the Big East Tournament.

It's probably the way a smarter coach than me would have played it.

I just believe you take things one day at a time. So that's what I conveyed to Daniel in our conversation prior to the Big East quarter-final. The plan was to have him try to play and see how he felt. If the ankle bothered him, we would remove him. We also knew there would be a period of at least four or five days to recover from this nagging injury before we opened the NCAA Tournament.

I made certain to reinforce to Daniel that if he was struggling in any way, we would take him out and sit him for the rest of the tournament. Jeff and Dr. Mike Duncan, who were both onsite with us, were on top of this.

Daniel gave me the nod that he wanted to play against George-town. He started the game, but I could tell right away he was laboring. With his mobility limited, he essentially put any thoughts of low-post offense aside and zeroed in on defense and rebounding. It was a warrior's effort.

The Hoyas gave us fits. We trailed 27–25 in the final minute of the first half before Kris drained a three-pointer on the final possession to give us a one-point lead going into the locker room.

Once again, Darryl Reynolds rode to our rescue.

With Daniel sidelined after giving us thirteen minutes, Darryl did a terrific job of stepping into the void. He contributed so much off the bench with his consistency and unselfishness. When he got an offensive rebound, he kicked it out for an open three. When he posted up and was pressured, he found someone making a cut to the basket. Most critically, he was always on the glass against a George-town team with great size. He finished with nine rebounds.

There is no easy way to calculate what Darryl's success means to his teammates. He's such a lovable guy. Everyone on the team understands his complete commitment to every other Wildcat. When Darryl shines, it lifts our entire team in a different, more emotional way than when anyone else does. In the second half, it was Darryl who created the momentum for us, just by being Darryl. Everyone fed off his energy.

We got a big boost from Josh too, who scored twenty-five points, and Arch, who delivered nineteen points, six assists, and only a single turnover. By the middle of Thursday afternoon, we had ourselves an

81–67 victory, and the guys had the opportunity to return to the hotel to get as much rest as they could for Friday night's semifinal.

After the postgame press conference, I mulled over whether to stick around to watch the second half of the afternoon quarterfinal. We would face the winner (which turned out to be Providence) in the semifinals. In tournament settings, coaches are permitted by NCAA rule to scout the opposition in person.

That kind of scouting isn't allowed during the regular season. But that rule didn't exist back in the 1980s, and that was a bit of good fortune for me.

In an era when nationally televised games were still the exception rather than the rule, the NCAA let coaches—who typically sent their assistants—travel to scout upcoming opponents. As one of the younger members of Coach Massimino's staff, that duty often fell to me. A practice would end in the Pavilion at 5 p.m. and I would hop into my car and drive as quickly as I could to the Meadowlands to catch a Seton Hall game, or to Manhattan to watch the Johnnies, or D.C. to catch the Hoyas.

I thought I was in heaven.

While there was certainly value in being able to scout a team up close, the real benefit to a novice coach was the basketball people it brought you into contact with. We were granted media credentials and seats on press row, which in those days were mostly on the sidelines opposite the team benches. Some of the best friendships I have in coaching were forged while we were seated alongside one another back then.

I always tried to stick around for the postgame press conferences too. I was amazed at the things you could learn just by listening, and some of those nuggets usually found their way into my reports to Coach Mass.

I'm not proposing we return to the rules of old. We are in a different era now. I can have an opponent's game tape available to watch within an hour of the game's completion. This is a much more efficient use of an assistant coach's time than the four to five hours it takes to reach places like Syracuse and Boston. But there's a part of me that owes a debt to that old-school model.

> **BEYOND BASKETBALL**
>
> *Find Your Leader*
>
> The best thing a newcomer to any business can do is spend time around people who are already a success in that endeavor. Listen to their perspective. Not only will it broaden your horizons, but it will also help improve your own listening, a skill that will always be an asset.

After our win over Georgetown, when offered the choice between joining the two assistants we had scouting Providence from courtside or heading back to the hotel, I elected to return to the hotel with the team. We watched the second half together on a giant flat-screen as we enjoyed our postgame meal, and I was able to point things out to our guys in real time.

Just over twenty-four hours later, we were locked in our third meeting of the season with the Friars. We would once more have to deal with Kris Dunn and Ben Bentil. Before the game, I made the decision that I wasn't going to jeopardize the prospect of Daniel playing in the NCAA Tournament to try to win this one. We had given it a shot. For the rest of the Big East Tournament, we planned to use Daniel off the bench, if at all.

Once play started, we wound up using him mostly to spell Darryl for short stints. Daniel was clearly in pain. But in the second half, his adrenaline kicked in and he was suddenly moving like he had before the injury. We didn't want to waste this chance. We knew as a staff that we had one shot with Daniel in this half. If we removed him, the likelihood was that the ankle would stiffen and that would be it. So when we saw how well he was moving, we started feeding him the ball in the post. We called every play we could for him. Daniel scored eight points and was so effective inside that he drew a fifth foul on Bentil, ending his night.

Even on half a leg, Daniel helped carry us to a 76–68 win.

The next day, we'd face Seton Hall in the Big East Tournament Championship game.

Saturday night at the Big East Tournament is always electric. Everyone in New York basketball was there. (Even the actor Hugh Jackman was there.) As we were lining up for the pregame introductions on the Garden court, the Seton Hall fans started a chant backing the Pirates. It sounded like every single one of the 19,812 fans in attendance was there to support the Hall. But when that chant faded, the Nova Nation fans filled up the Garden with a chant of their own: "Let's Go No-va! Let's Go No-va!" All of a sudden, the entire building was packed with Wildcats.

I felt my entire body vibrating with anticipation. At a moment like that, in Madison Square Garden, the atmosphere is simply overwhelming. You have to just soak it in—and appreciate how fortunate you are to be a part of it.

When the game began, Seton Hall came right at us. They'd gained great confidence since our last meeting in January. Kevin Willard—with whom I shared the Big East Coach of the Year award—had done a superb job in shaping a hard-nosed defensive unit that could also score. The Pirates, led by Isaiah Whitehead, drilled 56.7 percent of their field goal attempts in the first half and built a 40–29 halftime lead.

We obviously needed to make some adjustments.

Seton Hall was the best defensive team in our league. In the first half, it forced switches on Jalen Brunson, our youngest starter. At 6'4", Whitehead has at least an inch and a half on Jalen, and the Pirates isolated him on Jalen every time they could. Down eleven points, we decided that we would employ a taller lineup in the second half, primarily by substituting Mikal Bridges, who stands 6'7".

That plan got us back into the game. When Kris made a three-pointer with just over nine minutes to play, the game was tied at fifty. It would seesaw back and forth the rest of the way.

I was proud of the way our guys battled back. But if you put yourself in a hole like that against an outstanding opponent, you put your team in harm's way.

Whitehead made an outstanding play to score on a layup to tie the game at sixty-seven. He was fouled in the act of shooting and made the free throw to give Seton Hall a 68–67 lead with eighteen seconds left.

We called time and got Kris a contested look at a three-pointer, which missed. Seton Hall rebounded, we fouled, and Angel Delgado headed to the line with three seconds on the clock. We took another time-out to discuss what we would do after the free throws. At worst, we would have the chance to tie with a three-pointer.

Delgado sank the first free throw but missed the second. Daniel got the rebound and kicked it ahead to Arch, who dribbled over mid-court with his head up, looking to make a play. The plan was for Arch to kick it forward, where Josh was wide open. But Arch slipped on the court, and that disrupted things just enough to force him to take a contested three-pointer, which missed.

It was a great win for the Pirates.

By the time we reached the locker room, it was hard not to note the difference a year made. In 2015, we had a jubilant celebration in the New York Knicks' locker room. This time, we were crushed. Josh and Kris had a tough time composing themselves prior to the media's entrance into the locker room. When the Big East officials brought the second-place trophy inside, it sat on the floor untouched near the entryway.

This one hurt.

As disappointed as I was in the result, it forced me, as the head coach, to make decisions about how we would play in the NCAA Tournament. Kevin's brilliant game plan sent me back to take a hard look at our own.

Seton Hall's four exceptional perimeter defenders were able to contain our guards and wings. If teams were good enough to do that—as Seton Hall clearly was—we had to find a way to combat this. We could have held our breath and hoped that we would get lucky and avert that kind of opponent later in March, but that's wishful thinking. If you advance in the early rounds, you will inevitably run into a Kansas or a North Carolina team that can attack you the way the Hall had.

Through the pain, I saw some good things that day.

I loved the way our team competed from start to finish, after falling behind by double digits. I loved how Jalen Brunson handled being a star freshman who barely played in the second half. And I loved how we had executed that final offensive play. It would have generated a wide-open shot if not for the slip of Arch's foot.

We had done everything we could do.

Seton Hall played a tremendous game, and its strategy would have a lasting impact on our own tactics moving forward.

That night I received a text from Rick Pitino. This loss, he suggested, would serve us well as the public turned its attention to other "hot" teams entering the NCAA Tournament.

I wasn't sure I agreed.

But I certainly hoped he was right.

18

Opening Weekend Jitters

_____

SELECTION SUNDAY DAWNED sunny and cool outside our hotel near Central Park. By late morning, the team had made its return from New York City to campus to begin the countdown to the nationally televised program revealing the bracket for the 2016 NCAA Tournament.

Over the course of my two-plus decades as a head coach, I've seen all sides of this American basketball holiday.

In the beginning of our tenure at Hofstra in the 1990s, we were in the loneliest place of all: the outside looking in. For a coach or player, there aren't many feelings worse than the knowledge that your "bubble" has long since burst. Over time, we got to appreciate what it felt like to wake up that day secure in the knowledge that your school's name would show up on that screen, courtesy of the America East automatic bids we earned in 2000 and 2001.

During my first season at Villanova in 2001–2002, we had made a charge down the regular season stretch to put ourselves into the discussion for an at-large bid. But when Connecticut's Ben Gordon drilled a three-pointer in the final seconds of a Big East Tournament quarterfinal game to deny us the upset, we sensed we would come up just short of inclusion.

Naturally, we watched that Selection Sunday and held out hope that our 17–12 record would be enough to eke us into March Madness. But when the field was announced, we were not in it. So we were left to make the best of a bid to the National Invitation Tournament, and to the credit of that group (led by captain Brooks Sales, Andrew Sullivan, Ricky Wright, and Gary Buchanan), we won two games.

In 2008, we were viewed as a bubble team after an up-and-down regular season. Following an 82–63 loss to top-seed Georgetown in the Big East Tournament quarterfinal, our staff was convinced our NCAA Tournament hopes had slipped through our grasp. But we got a lot of help over the next three days in tournaments played around the country. A number of regular season champions in the mid-major conferences also won their tournaments and, lo and behold, we found our way into the field as a No. 12 seed.

Selection Sunday is as emotional as any non–game day we have in our sport. The television cameras love to capture the raw euphoria or dismay at the instant when a team learns its fate—for better or worse.

On the cusp of the 2016 edition, I would characterize our team's mood as ambivalent.

On the one hand, this group had completed a remarkable season. It would enter the NCAA Tournament with twenty-nine victories. A lofty seed was assured, and that's nothing to make light of. An NCAA Tournament berth is always something to be celebrated, as I note every year, when you consider that there are 351 Division I teams clawing to claim one of the sixty-eight spots.

At Villanova, we were about to make our eleventh appearance in the last twelve seasons. On each of those ten previous Selection Sundays, I'd urged those with us for the watch party to cherish the achievement and not become inured to it. It's too special to take for granted.

In the big picture, I think we all grasped that. Yet I could also sense a palpable mood of regret among our players. We were less than twenty-four hours removed from our loss to Seton Hall, and none of us had moved past it yet.

That was the backdrop as I pulled my car into the parking garage across from the Connelly Center. Multiple television trucks were parked outside the building. Inside more than four hundred of our family members, university officials, and students assembled for a buffet dinner. Two giant screens in either corner projected the CBS broadcast, which began at 5 p.m.

The team took its place in chairs positioned directly in front of one of the television screens as the hour arrived. Beneath the screen, cameras had been set up to record our reaction when our destination was revealed.

My feelings mirrored those of our players. The loss to Seton Hall still stung. But as the CEO of the program, I had to be prepared to answer the big-picture questions we were sure to hear once our spot in the bracket was announced.

Prior to the Seton Hall loss, most analysts projected us as a No. 1 seed in one of the four regions. That defeat had muddied our prospects. Some "bracketologists" still listed us as a top seed; others knocked us down to a 2. I leaned on the expertise of our radio voice, Ryan Fannon, on this topic, and he viewed it as a toss-up.

We were also on the verge of learning where we would travel. Most experts predicted that as one of the higher seeds, we would begin our NCAA Tournament at the nearest early-round site, Brooklyn, New York. Beyond that, there was speculation, particularly among the Nova Nation, that we might have the chance to play in Philadelphia if we advanced to the second weekend. The only way that could happen was if we were placed in the East Region.

Near the top of the show, the four No. 1 seeds were announced: Kansas, North Carolina, Oregon, and Virginia. North Carolina would be the No. 1 seed in the East Region.

My hope was that this wouldn't preclude us from being placed in the East Region as the No. 2 seed, but my instincts told me otherwise. I didn't believe that the NCAA Tournament Selection Committee would put the top seed in a situation where it could potentially have a road game—that is, against us in Philly—with a berth in the Final Four on the line.

I didn't, however, have much time to process the possibilities. A few minutes later, our name came up on the screen. We were the No. 2 seed in the South Region. The journey would indeed begin in Brooklyn. In the opening round, we were to face No. 15 seed University of North Carolina at Asheville. The winner of that game would play either No. 7 seed Iowa or No. 10 seed Temple for the right to go to the Sweet 16 in Louisville.

I wasn't all that familiar with UNC Asheville, but I knew very well the challenges Temple and Iowa could present. The Hawkeyes are coached by Philadelphia native Fran McCaffery. Our former assistant coach Andrew Francis was part of the Iowa staff, and we had seen firsthand how rugged this program was in the finals of the 2013 Battle 4 Atlantis in the Bahamas. Iowa had been ranked in the Top 10 for much of January and February. To me, they were under-seeded as a No. 7.

Then there was the Temple team that knew us so well. We had survived one battle with the Owls, and I knew instantly what a second encounter would entail. We might be favored, but Fran Dunphy and his team were playing at a high level. They would relish another crack at a Big Five rival on this stage.

> ## BEYOND BASKETBALL
>
> ### *Establish the Big Goal— Then Focus on the Little Ones*
>
> It's necessary to set goals for the future, but once you've set them, the only way to reach them is by focusing on what's in front of you. Stress the importance of each step as it comes. A brighter tomorrow is achieved through the toil of today.

Later on Sunday evening, we started watching film of UNC Asheville. We saw a team that had beaten Georgetown at the Verizon Center. We quickly realized that the first-round matchup wasn't going to be a breeze either.

Welcome to the NCAA Tournament.

Rather than let myself get consumed by worry, I did some deeper reflection. I recalled a lesson we learned in 2009.

When the field of what was then sixty-five teams was announced that year, we were a No. 3 seed in the East Region. The consensus among the experts was that our road to Detroit, site of the Final Four, would be as tough as anyone's. It had the potential to include UCLA in the Round of 32, Duke in the Round of 16, and Pittsburgh in the Elite Eight. As it turned out, we wound up facing every one of those teams—and made it to the Final Four.

That taught me that what your team's "road to the Final Four" looks like on paper is meaningless. The fans and media could have fun with it, but for us it was all about another one of our mantras: "Next game."

As far as we were concerned, the only thing that mattered was UNC Asheville.

When Rest Is Best

One bit of good luck to come out of Selection Sunday was that we would open play Friday instead of Thursday. At this point in Daniel's recovery, every extra hour counted. After consulting with Daniel, Jeff, and Dr. Mike Duncan, we decided to give Daniel three full days off from practice.

For everyone else, we held a light practice on Monday and then met with the media. Tuesday was another off day.

In my earlier seasons, I would have been paranoid about giving my team two full off days during the week of the NCAA Tournament. As a young coach, you want to cover every conceivable possibility, and the best way to do that is on the court. Yet I had a great deal of trust in this group's experience and ability to ready itself. In my mind, the benefit of added rest at the end of a long season far outweighed any incremental gains we might make in practice.

If I had any doubts about that decision, they were dismissed as soon as we hit the practice court Wednesday. From the first whistle, the intensity and energy were sensational.

There are four phrases painted high on the walls of our practice gym, bold enough to catch your eye from wherever you happen to be on the court: Play Hard. Play Smart. Play With Pride. Play Together.

Those phrases sum up what we aspire to as Wildcats, and they reflected exactly how our guys were performing that day.

There's one more word painted in bold blue letters, high up on the walls at both ends of the court, above all else: ATTITUDE.

After resting up, thinking back on the season, working together, and working hard, it was clear to me that our guys had taken that word to heart in every way. We'd had a strong, heartfelt, authentic hangover from our loss to Seton Hall a few days earlier, but the Big East Tournament was now behind us. We were focused.

We also got a glimpse of something we hadn't seen much in the past couple of months: Daniel Ochefu was back, not just in spirit, but at the top of his game. The series of medical setbacks that had begun to accumulate in mid-January—the bruised tailbone, the concussion, the sprained right ankle—seemed like they'd never happened. Daniel was a force, and by the end of that practice, our attitude—and everything that came with it—was as strong as can be.

"My Bad"

When we tipped off shortly after 12:30 p.m. on Friday afternoon at the Barclays Center, there was a moment in the opening minutes when our staff looked at one another knowingly. What we had witnessed in the comfort of the Davis Center was no mirage. Daniel moved easily around the court, and from the first whistle you could see the joy in his eyes. The knowledge that he was back in top form gave him such great confidence.

As a coach, it was a pleasure to watch.

UNC Asheville resembled a lot of successful mid-major programs. Its best weapons were perimeter players who made up for what they lacked in height with skill and grit. In a lot of ways, these can be the hardest teams for tall forwards like Daniel to go against, since they often wind up chasing players four to five inches shorter around the perimeter. Some big men can get caught in situations where their size is actually a disadvantage.

Part of what set Daniel apart as a junior and senior was that these kinds of matchups were never kryptonite for him. He could step out against smaller teams and hold his own defensively on the perimeter while using his height advantage to rebound and score at the other end. When Daniel was in the lineup, we were never hurt by small ball. And we weren't on this day either.

We jumped out to a 10–2 lead before the Bulldogs narrowed the gap to 28–26. Then we reeled off a 12–0 spurt just before halftime to grab a 40–26 lead. Daniel's work inside—he finished with seventeen points on seven-of-nine shooting to go with ten rebounds and three blocked shots—set up the open looks from beyond the three-point line that helped us pull away to an 86–56 victory.

The advantage of playing in the early afternoon is that, if you win, you can quickly shift your attention to the next round. We completed our postgame media responsibilities, boarded the bus, and made the ride from Brooklyn through traffic back to our hotel at the tip of Lower Manhattan, where we watched the remainder of that day's second game between Iowa and Temple.

Our entire team—save for Baker and Ash, who scouted in person at the arena—was riveted to the action on the screen. Iowa built a lead, and it felt eerily similar to 2015, when LSU established a lead against NC State in the opening round. I had wondered in the twelve months since watching that game in Pittsburgh: *Had we become too settled in thinking that LSU would be our next opponent because of the lead it held for most of the night? Did the thought creep into our minds that we had gotten a lesser team in the Wolfpack when it rallied to win?*

This time, I made sure that our players understood that this one was up for grabs, no matter what the score was. It was important that we didn't become locked in on Iowa due to its lead.

Temple did rally, which surprised none of us. We had witnessed that spirit ourselves when the Owls kept coming at us at the Liacouras Center in February.

Their game against Iowa went into overtime and wasn't decided until Adam Woodbury scored on a putback just before time expired to give the Hawkeyes a 72–70 win.

Later in the evening, we began to watch film of Iowa. One of the tapes we showed the team was the Hawkeyes' 89–61 victory at Marquette back in November. Our guys have great respect for Marquette, and Iowa just annihilated the Golden Eagles on their home court. Watching that game instilled in our players an appropriate fear of the Hawkeyes. They knew this was an experienced team with outstanding scorers in Jarrod Uthoff and Peter Jok.

Meanwhile, beyond the cocoon we had the team wrapped in, the anxiety level of our fans was undoubtedly spiking. We were preparing to play a game in the NCAA Tournament Round of 32—the round that had been our undoing in each of the previous two seasons. We had heard all about it for twelve months, and now the moment of truth was here.

That was how it was portrayed on the outside. On the inside, the vibe was entirely different.

Our approach to the loss to NC State, beginning the night it happened, was direct. We took responsibility for it. We answered every question about it politely. As a team we accepted a simple truth: There was no way to fast-forward to the Round of 32 in 2016.

We told the players that there was so much work to do to get back to that point, we didn't have the luxury of fantasizing about what we would do once we got there. We weren't guaranteed a return trip to the Round of 32, and it was imperative that we understood that. If we acted like we were entitled to this, we would never make it back.

So to finally be on this doorstep was a major triumph of its own.

At the same time, every one of us understood the reality. If we didn't come through, the same din we had listened to for the preceding twelve months would envelop us. In the eyes of the public, this was a pass-fail test based on our ability to reach the second weekend.

All year we had looked forward to this moment. Now it was here and we felt unshackled. We weren't afraid of what came next.

I rhetorically asked the guys: "What is the worst thing that could happen if we lost? Could we handle it if we did?"

We already knew we could because we had done it.

As a coach you can usually sense the mood of the group, but you can never be certain. These were such good guys. They look you in the eye and nod their assent to what you have to say. Still, it's impossible to know if they have fully internalized your message.

The one thing I knew for sure was that virtually everyone in the Nova Nation beyond our team—from Father Peter to Mark Jackson to our students and our families—was on edge. I even detected uneasiness among our local media when I met with them in the hallway outside our locker room after Saturday's press conference at the Barclays Center.

Over the years, we have had the assistant coaches lead the team on the bus back to the hotel while I remain behind after the formal press obligations have been completed. I then meet with representatives of the Philly media, usually numbering eight to ten people, who have been with us all season.

After I gave my answer to the last question, there was a long pause. I looked at a group that included Joe Juliano (*Philadelphia Inquirer*), Mike Kern (*Philadelphia Daily News*), Terry Toohey (*Delaware*

County Daily Times), and Kevin Cooney (from my hometown's *Bucks County Courier Times*). I finally said to them, "You guys seem nervous about this game."

It was Mike Kern who responded: "Please don't make us write this article."

As I walked away from that exchange, it felt to me like they were reluctant to get to game time. The idea of telling this same old story to their readers was *that* distasteful.

I turned to our graduate assistant, Mike Clark, who was driving me back to the hotel, and asked: "Am I that pathetic that these writers actually feel sorry for us?"

In an odd way, it made me feel good. We had all gone through this together, from that night in Pittsburgh till now. We had been honest with the media, taken ownership of our loss, and dealt with it. There was no animosity on either side.

On Sunday morning, I was nervous too. I knew what was at stake and what was in store for us if we came up short. That anxiety, at least for me, was rooted in my desire to see Arch, Daniel, Henry, Pat, and Kevin get past that stigma of not having advanced to the second weekend.

As tip-off neared, the team was on the court warming up. The coaches have our own set of good-luck rituals before we walk out together to the floor. Father Rob and I always hug. This time I could sense the anxiety of even Father Rob, whose great Augustinian faith usually makes him the most unflappable person in our locker room.

The only people who didn't seem angst-ridden when that game began were Ryan Arcidiacono, Daniel Ochefu, Josh Hart, and Kris Jenkins. Their clear minds and piercing eyes told me that they were absolutely convinced they were getting this done.

On the game's first possession, Kris got a look at an open three-pointer. It missed. After Iowa rebounded the ball, the Hawkeyes found Jarrod Uthoff, who came back to drain a three of his own.

The thousands of Villanova fans in the building must have been flashing back to Buffalo, where we lost in 2014, and Pittsburgh. But then we got another taste of Arch's impeccable sense of timing. Ryan scored our first points with a layup on the next possession. Daniel blocked the Hawkeyes' next shot, and Arch buried a three at the other end.

I'm not sure anyone could have envisioned what came next. We found an offensive flow and the shots kept falling. As the clock ticked toward halftime, we held a 54–29 lead. With four seconds left, Kris Jenkins fouled Uthoff. Uthoff then missed both free throws, the second of which led to the final Villanova possession of the

> ### BEYOND BASKETBALL
> #### *Don't Be Afraid to Err*
>
> Admitting a mistake isn't a sign of weakness. Errors are a universal fact of life. We all make them. Your acceptance of that reality strengthens trust and deepens the bond you share with those in your working relationships.

half. Ryan quickly dribbled up the left side before letting fly a three-pointer. Uthoff blocked the shot and the clock ran out.

The Nova Nation was on its feet, cheering our 25-point lead in a truly phenomenal performance.

But I was angry about that final sequence.

One of our core values is that we ask our guys to just make the right play. We don't want them to get hung up on being theatrical or overly creative. We ask them to keep things simple. It's the basketball flip side of the encouragement we give them away from the court to be legit—to make the right choices for the right reasons.

Over the course of our four years with Arch, we had developed a unique trust. If I sensed that he was locked in offensively and in position to take the game over, I gave him the freedom to do so. Ryan never made a show of it. Instead, he would simply walk over to me on the sidelines and say, "I'm taking this s— over."

Ryan never abused that trust, and his instincts for attacking in that situation had never been wrong.

Against Iowa, Arch was in that kind of zone. His aggressiveness was the perfect antidote to any hints of anxiety that may have lurked in the minds of our players.

On this final possession of the first half, Arch had the ball in his hands. There was a decision to make as he dribbled into the frontcourt. But in this case, he made the wrong play. He was so consumed with trying to drop a dagger into his opponent that he didn't take notice of the fact that Josh was wide open.

I let him know about it as soon as he stepped off the court.

As always, Arch reacted perfectly. He took responsibility and told the team, "My bad."

That's leadership.

One of the most important things we want our guys to learn is that we don't expect them to be perfect. They just have to give their best effort and take responsibility for their actions. When one of your best players, a guy who everyone knows is a team leader, accepts that with humility, it sends a powerful signal to the rest of the group. Ryan Arch had made a lot of great plays in the first half. For him to accept that correction, without getting hung up on all the other positive things he'd done, is pure humility and pure commitment to team.

During the halftime break, we used that final sequence as an example of what we couldn't afford to do going forward. Iowa was one of the most explosive offensive teams in the nation. If we got caught up in trying to stick daggers in them, they possessed enough firepower to rally.

We came out of the locker room eager to prove to one another that our concern wasn't the score or the outcome, but being true to our values. Arch reiterated that message to the guys on the court right before play resumed.

It worked. We went on to an 87–68 victory.

My emotions in the minutes after I shook hands with the Iowa players and coaches at midcourt could be boiled down to two words: pure relief. I was overjoyed that our seniors weren't going to be forever identified with the ghosts of NCAA Tournament first weekends. I was more than ready to have to go through that with them (again), and I knew they would have handled it with dignity.

But man, oh man, was I glad we didn't have to!

I was also happy for our administration, led by Father Peter and Mark Jackson. If we had failed to advance, I knew they would have been completely supportive. I was just so relieved that they weren't going to have to deal with any of the surrounding fallout from another loss on this stage.

In a weird way I was almost—I want to stress *almost*—relishing the chance to deal with the ramifications of a second-round defeat. If you preach "Attitude," you have to be willing to live it.

Mostly, though, I was delighted for everyone connected to Villanova. And I was simply in awe of our guys.

None of the pressure affected them at a time when it was impacting everyone else, including me. I was so impressed that Daniel, Arch, Josh, and Kris, the players who had most dealt with the blowback of the previous two NCAA Tournaments, had thrived in the face of so much scrutiny.

A full 362 days after we needed the words of Father Rob to lift us up at sunrise, we had finally cleared the hurdle that for so long had been all anyone wanted to talk about.

As the bus entered the Holland Tunnel shortly before 7 p.m. for the return ride to Villanova, the GPS noted that we were heading south. In four short days, we would meet another powerhouse, the University of Miami, with a chance to reach the Elite Eight.

19

The Sweetest Sixteen

BACK ON CAMPUS at our first media availability on Monday afternoon, the questions started flying about the prospect of a matchup with Kansas, the No. 1 overall seed, in the South Regional Final and a trip to the Final Four. I responded candidly: "Either of those outcomes would be great, but I'm not looking beyond our opponent in Thursday evening's semifinal, the University of Miami."

People always seem disappointed by that response, but my mindset never changes: *Next game*. And that couldn't be more important than it is during the NCAA Tournament.

This isn't to suggest we don't look beyond the next game as a program or a staff. In this case, Baker Dunleavy was tasked with the advance scout on Kansas while Mark, Arleshia, George, and Jason Donnelly were in constant communication to be sure all our needs were met in Louisville and, in the event we advanced, Houston. Knowing they have those matters under control means I am free to pour my energy into the next opponent.

Same goes for our guys.

Like Iowa, Miami had spent a good bit of January and February ranked in the Top 10. The Hurricanes' coach, Jim Larrañaga, starred at Archbishop Molloy High School (where he was coached by the legendary late Jack Curran, who later mentored our own Villanova legend Whitey Rigsby) and Providence. Then he began a successful head coaching career that had produced 588 victories thus far. Our paths had crossed only once before in NCAA Tournament play, when he led George Mason past the Wildcats in 2011.

The Hurricanes entered this game with twenty-seven victories.

This was a savvy, tested team that finished in a tie for second place in the ACC.

One of the story lines in our tournament so far was the offensive efficiency we displayed in our first two victories. We had scored 175 points, connected on better than fifty-five percent of our field goal attempts, and won by double-digit margins in consecutive games.

Yet as a staff, we were more pleased by what we were seeing unfold at the other end of the court.

As I've said, we strive to be a cohesive team in everything we do. But the area where we most need to be in sync is at the defensive end. Good offense can sometimes be a matter of players making shots. Superior defense is mortar for your program—always there to withstand any offensive storms you can be certain are coming.

That kind of defensive cohesion in game situations takes time to hone. Jalen and Mikal were much better defensive players than they had been in November. The speed and skill at this level no longer surprised them. Each understood where he was expected to be and how he was expected to react.

In fact, Mikal's defensive development even in the preceding ten days had enhanced our capabilities significantly. After his sterling effort against Isaiah Whitehead in the Big East Final, we knew we had to find more opportunities to use him.

We flew to Louisville on Tuesday and were checked into our assigned lodgings, the historic Brown Hotel, by 2 p.m. This wasn't Philly, but it didn't feel foreign to us either. The University of Louisville was a part of the Big East from 2005 to 2013 and was the host of the South Regional. Rick Pitino followed up on his post–Big East Tournament text to me by welcoming us to the city and offering us the use of the Cardinals' practice gym.

So from the time we arrived, we were greeted warmly.

With the game scheduled for Thursday night, Wednesday offered us a packed schedule, including an open practice and a meeting with the Turner/CBS crew of Jim Nantz, Grant Hill, Tracy Wolfson, Bill Raftery, and producer Mark Wolff. Such sessions are routine during the season, as the broadcasters look to complete their prep work with insight from the coaches and media-relations staff. For the most part

I enjoy the process. The analysts are former players and coaches whose experiences can produce valuable insight, as Jay Bilas' had back in Virginia.

Still, I was anxious to wrap it up and get back to our routines.

We had a breezy thirty-minute chat. There was even some basketball discussed, which isn't necessarily a given when Raf is in the house. (During his days at ESPN, I always felt badly for Sean McDonough, who would wearily try to steer the conversation back to basketball as the Governor held court. There was plenty of laughter, but poor Sean never gleaned much useful information beyond where Raf was planning to host his postgame "meeting.")

As we concluded the conversation, I asked Jim Nantz about the upcoming Masters golf tournament, where he serves as CBS' lead voice. It is held the first week of April, and in recent years, Bill and Jim Davis had graciously included me as their guest to attend the tournament for a day. I explained to Jim that I had made tentative plans with the Davis family to attend the 2016 Masters.

Jim smiled at me and said, "You may have something else to do that week."

Until he said that, I hadn't even considered that the Masters falls only a few days after the NCAA Final—when the winners would be taking victory laps and making media appearances.

Jim was right, and we shared a laugh about the fact that I was utterly oblivious to the connection.

But as quickly as the elevator door closed on the television crew, that thought evaporated from my head. I walked back down the hallway to our meeting room and happily sat down with our team for breakfast. To me, there was no better place to be.

The next afternoon, Thursday, before our pregame meal, Father Rob stood up to offer a few words.

"Daniel was pointing out to us earlier," he said, "the difference between talking about doing the right things and actually executing and following through on them. Our lives always intersect the gospel, and on this special night called Holy Thursday, Jesus—ever the teacher—was showing the difference between talking about love and sacrifice and service, and actually doing these things for us.

"In John 13:1–17 we find Jesus at His *own* 'team meal,' if you will. He is gathered with those closest to Him to share a very important and everlasting meal. He shared it with those who had gone through so much with Him. He could have given them a beautiful speech on the value of love and sacrifice. But rather than say, 'Do as I say,' Jesus said, 'Do as I do!' He took this last meal with them as an opportunity to solidify what it means to truly live for others, and He washed their feet in an act of humble service. By doing that, He gave us a piece of Himself for all time.

"The act of washing someone's feet was a servant's job, a fact that was not lost on His friends. Peter suggested that he should wash Jesus' feet, not the Son of God washing his. *'What God washes feet?'*

"Jesus said, 'That's exactly the point. Humility is not weakness. It is strength.' Our God places no limits on His love for us and neither should we. There was nothing He wouldn't do for us, and He was showing us that He would die for us. Ours is a God who will lower Himself to our level to help heal and assist us in any way He can out of love for His brothers and sisters. He leaves us with an instruction to go and do likewise and to do this in remembrance of Him. 'See what I have done and now do the same for each other.'"

I've said this before but it bears repeating: Father Rob's messages are based in Christianity and the Bible, but every single person in our basketball family—be they Jewish or Muslim or atheist—knows just how universal his reflections truly are. And on that day, every person in the room was tuned in to exactly what he was saying, because the values that are so essential to the brotherhood we'd built were the very same values this Biblical passage conveyed.

Father Rob being Father Rob, he also made sure to bring the story back to the lives we live today, and to put it in terms that every one of our guys could relate to.

"So much of our lives is measured in numbers," he continued. "Number of points, number of minutes, number of highlights on *SportsCenter*. Number of dollars. Jesus is challenging us to track some new numbers: The number of times I picked someone else up who was down. The number of times I sacrificed a piece of me for someone else. The number of times I asked for and offered forgiveness.

"Brothers, on this Holy Thursday, thousands of people are imitating this gesture of humility and commitment to serving others. Maybe we could join in that spirit and simply pull off a sneaker and a sock and use these pitchers of water on the table to wash the foot of the person next to us. A coach, a teammate, a manager, a trainer, a spouse . . ."

I won't deny it: I was taken aback. On this sunny Kentucky afternoon—Holy Thursday in the Catholic faith—had Father Rob just informed us that we were, as Jesus had, going to *wash one another's feet?*

We rarely discuss what he plans to say at these pregame meals, and he had certainly not discussed this with me beforehand. For a moment, I questioned whether this was going to fly with the guys.

But as Father Rob walked to the table, grabbed a full pitcher and walked in my direction, my confidence in him carried me past the misgivings that had surfaced a few seconds before.

I pulled a shoe and sock off and rolled up the pant leg of my Nike sweat suit. Father Rob took the pitcher and began to pour. The cold liquid on my foot didn't surprise me—but what I saw flowing from the pitcher did.

Father Rob had washed my foot with iced tea.

The rest of the room didn't get a clear view of this exchange. It happened below table level. If they'd seen it, the serenity of the moment may have been lost. As it was, Father Rob and I smiled at each other, but otherwise played it cool. I wiped the tea off my foot.

Arch was seated next to me. I looked at him, and without a word, he took off a shoe and sock.

I grabbed another pitcher—this one filled with water—to wash Arch's foot. And so it went, from one player to the next, on to the coaching and administrative staff. The room was silent the entire time.

As each player passed the pitcher to the next, it felt to me like we were growing incrementally stronger with each pouring. The message Father Rob had delivered—that we all should serve one another— struck a chord.

In basketball terms: We had to play not for ourselves, but for one another.

"We remember what Coach reminds us: Our roles may be different but our status is the same," Father Rob said. "Let us pray that our love will always be shown by our actions. Let us once again remember that the pathway to greatness is through service. Let's imitate this game plan for life, and let there be nothing that we won't do for those we love."

Focus

When we tipped off against the Hurricanes that night, I was reminded why experience is so vital in the NCAA Tournament. From the moment the ball was tossed into the air, the offensive fireworks began. We built a double-digit lead. Miami came storming back. It seemed like neither team had any defensive answer for the other.

There are moments during the regular season when both teams are in an offensive flow early. In those instances, you understand that the likelihood that they will continue to score at that rate is low. Typically, the hot teams cool off when faced with quality defense.

This late in the NCAA Tournament, it's a different circumstance. Only the most efficient teams remain in the field. Scoring in bunches at this level isn't a fluke and may not wane. We had learned that firsthand against eventual champions: Florida in 2006, Kansas in 2008, and North Carolina in 2009.

Seven years had passed since we last experienced this. I had forgotten what it was like. To see both teams trading blows by making skilled plays was exhilarating. From here on out, this is what we could expect to see.

Finally, in the second half, we were able to string together enough stops while still functioning well offensively to pull away with a 92–69 win. We would move on to the Elite Eight.

A few hours later, Kansas defeated Maryland and the showdown with the Jayhawks was set for Saturday. The winner would advance to Houston for the Final Four.

When we dove into our preparations for the Jayhawks on Thursday night, I thought we had been fortunate in one sense: Miami, with its size and athleticism, offered a lot of similarities to Kansas. Sometimes, in postseason play, it can take your team a few minutes of game clock to adjust to the style of a team you haven't encountered recently, if at all. The danger isn't just that you can fall behind until you adapt, but that one of your key players may fall into foul trouble or get pushed off his rhythm, never to locate it again in those forty minutes. So Miami's resemblance to Kansas was a positive for us.

On the Friday between games, our team kept to its familiar routine: meals, meetings, practice, and film. Apparently there was a concert that night featuring the rapper Flo Rida a few blocks away. As far as we were concerned, it may as well have taken place in another galaxy.

My only real connection to the outside world during these times is Patty.

As a staff, we work many hours and spend much of that time together. Whenever we are at a tournament location, Patty is the one looking out for the wives, girlfriends, and families of our staff. She makes it a priority to organize outings where they can be together while the coaches, players, and other staff are immersed in preparation. Having been the wife of an assistant coach in this program, she is cognizant of how challenging it can be for them, especially when they are raising small children.

Patty never wants any credit for this, but her gestures of kindness to the hardworking members of our staff and their families are many. It could be a spa visit for the wives and girlfriends at our team hotel. She has volunteered to babysit when a staff member's wife has been housebound for days with a sick child. During the 2016 NCAA Tournament, she saw to it that a staff member and his wife's bill was taken care of when she noticed them stealing a few minutes of alone time at a restaurant.

Most times, I'm not even aware any of this is happening. It's Patty's way of letting those around us know how much we appreciate them and her message to me that they deserve this.

Patty is the rudder of our family's ship, and also of my personal psyche. She knows me better than anyone. She is the first to detect

Patty and I with our kids at the White House. That's our younger son, Collin, on the left. On the right is our daughter, Reilly, and our elder son, Taylor.

when I am veering off course by becoming a little too competitive. (I have learned from her that this is one of my weaknesses. It's taken me a long time to have an understanding of that.)

In the aftermath of our trip to the Final Four in '09, Patty was the one who pointed out to me that I had gotten caught up in trying to be what everyone wanted me to be rather than being myself. I was receiving all kinds of requests to attend more alumni functions, charity events, and appearances on behalf of old coaching friends . . . and I tried to do every one of them. It was a case of me doing what I thought was expected of me rather than stepping back to understand that I was a father first.

When I get too committed to basketball and the team, Patty reminds me of the importance of family.

In January 2014, Seton Hall beat us in overtime in Newark. It was the kind of loss that can eat at you as a coach. We had several chances to win in regulation and couldn't make the plays we needed to. I was working through that when the two of us got into our car, which was parked in a garage not far from the team bus. My plan was to follow the bus back to Villanova. Patty had another idea.

BEYOND BASKETBALL

Show Your Humility

Within the hierarchy that most businesses maintain, there is room to show your humility. Helping someone figure out a new task or volunteering to clean up after a meeting, no matter your title or theirs, is a sign of respect that is always appreciated.

She told me that I was too wound up and impressed upon me that the best thing I could do at that moment was to step away. Poring over more game film would not solve anything.

I didn't necessarily agree with her, but conceded the point. Instead of trailing the team bus, we drove to the Jersey Shore. By the time we arrived, I had already begun to relax and I sheepishly offered Patty the answer she has come to expect: "You were right." We spent our Sunday together, away from the team, and I returned on Monday feeling completely energized.

I can get too intense and fixated on work. Patty saves me from that.

On the flip side, when the intensity is warranted—as it was at this moment—she does everything possible to help me stay focused.

For all of that, I am eternally grateful.

Patty and our three children, Taylor, Collin, and Reilly, were seated in the stands directly behind our bench for the Kansas game. Sitting nearby were great friends of ours, including Villanovans Ed Welsh, Matt Morahan, and Joe Petri, legendary Villanova guard Bill Melchionni, and my basketball godfather, Coach Massimino.

I was trying to keep my focus on the court when a voice called out my name. When I didn't respond, it called out to me again: "Jay!"

I knew it was Coach Mass, but each time I ignored his call, the subsequent call only grew louder.

Finally, I turned around.

He pointed to the pocket square on his sport coat and shouted to me, "Fix your hankie!"

It was perfect.

This may as well have been 1989. It was like I was twenty-eight years old again and still working for him. A sense of calm enveloped me.

As was usually the case, Coach was right. When I looked down, I saw that my pocket square was off center. I adjusted it, and all was right in my world again.

If you have followed my career at all, you have probably heard or read something about my "style." I get a lot of attention for the suits I wear on game days, and it began when I was starting out at Hofstra: The only honest compliment people could give me in those early seasons was that I was well dressed.

That label has proven pretty durable through the years, and I'm really not sure why.

My parents taught me the value of dressing well, and when I worked for Coach Mass, I noticed the attention he paid to wearing suits that were well tailored and sharp-looking when he stepped out on the floor. (As longtime Villanova fans know, that look usually changed quickly once the game began.)

The funny thing is, I am of the opinion that college basketball coaches should dress like most of our football counterparts do: in tech pants, athletic shoes, and golf shirts or pullovers. That would be much more comfortable. (This is one reason I enjoy the pre-season trips to places like the Bahamas or Hawaii, where we get to wear that more casual attire.)

But the tradition in our game is that coaches wear suits, and I want to honor the profession as my colleagues do. And if you are going to be dressed in a suit, you want it to look good. My friend and tailor, Gabriele D'Annunzio, takes care of me in that regard. Any credit for my suits or ties belongs to Gabe.

Frankly, I think the praise for my suit game is overstated. If you ask me, the best-dressed people on the Villanova sidelines these days are Baker Dunleavy, Ashley Howard, Kyle Neptune, George Halcovage, and Mike Nardi.

At any rate, with my pocket square fixed, it was time to turn back to the task at hand.

Our respect for Kansas was immense. Though the Jayhawks were similar in athleticism to Miami, they weren't identical. Miami offered legitimate size, but in Perry Ellis, Kansas had one of the nation's most efficient interior scorers. While we had dealt with a lot of gifted perimeter players thus far, it had been a long while since we had confronted a post threat of his caliber.

In preparing for this game, we stressed to the guys that we had to be ready to embrace what we like to call a "street fight." In our lexicon, that's code for the kind of gritty battle that isn't decided by silky jumpers or rim-rattling transition dunks. These are games where every basket is earned, every possession a struggle.

Over our first three games in the NCAA Tournament, we were shooting a shade under sixty percent (.599) from the field. From beyond the three-point arc, we were connecting on fifty-three percent of our attempts. We were averaging better than twenty assists per game. It was the kind of efficiency every coach craves.

Yet we understood that a storm was still likely to come and it might very well come courtesy of the Jayhawks.

That's exactly what this turned out to be—and we reveled in it.

Drives to the basket that may have been easy buckets on other nights were getting blocked. Passing lanes that had been wide open in previous games were now clogged. Apparent breakaway layups were thwarted by players racing back to turn the driver away.

Ellis was a defensive concern for us, to state the obvious. What made him so tough was that he wasn't just an efficient scorer but a gifted passer who could make the defense pay by locating open shooters.

In the first half, we managed to keep Ellis in check and created just enough offense to grab a 32–25 lead at the intermission.

On its first possession of the second half, Kansas executed a perfect pin-down screen to free Ellis. He scored on the play and was fouled. I turned to my staff and said, "That's why Bill Self is a great coach." Kansas had run a play to open the second half that it had not yet tried, in order to produce a basket and free throw for its leading scorer.

I wasn't happy with the result of the play, but the coach in me loved the fact we were going against the best coaches, players, and programs.

Kansas struck back in a big way early in the second half, outscoring us 15–8 in the early minutes to grab a 45–40 lead. Then, keyed by Arch, we put together a 10–0 response and regained the lead.

It was a battle to the very end.

In the final minutes, we felt that Kansas' ability to execute its half-court offense was so lethal that our best option was to employ a zone defense. It's not my favorite tactic, as I've mentioned, especially in critical situations. A zone leaves you vulnerable to offensive rebounds, which are often what do the most damage late in games. But it seemed like the best option. I know it's a cliché, but sometimes you have to take big risks in order to reap big rewards. And to be honest, I just didn't think we were good enough to stop Kansas with our man-to-man defense at that point.

We were leading 56–54 when Kansas took possession with forty-three seconds on the clock. I called for the zone. The Jayhawks ran a play where they set a screen for Ellis against the zone. Mikal Bridges came from the weak side, sniffed out the play, and stole the pass with thirty-four seconds left.

A few seconds later, he made another big defensive deflection, dove on the floor to collect the ball, and signaled for a time-out. It was an unbelievable play for a lot of reasons, and an iconic visual too: The image of Mikal on the floor, arms wrapped around the basketball, conjured up memories of Dwayne McClain in a similar spot as the Wildcats completed their epic upset of Georgetown in 1985.

Down the stretch we converted all eight of our free throws, the first four by Arch, to hold on for a 64–59 victory.

Mikal made the plays of the game.

It was the perfect representation of a player who was no longer just an energy guy off the bench. Mikal was now a big-time performer who made key contributions at critical moments. Within our team, he had solidified himself.

The celebration on the court was wonderful. We got to share it with Coach Mass, of course. And we also got a brief family moment I will always remember.

As Patty and my three kids gathered on the floor, we re-created an impromptu hug we shared after defeating Pitt in 2009 to advance to

the Final Four. We embraced and began jumping up and down together, much as a team would.

It was my favorite part of the evening.

The next morning, Easter Sunday, we stepped into the same meeting
space where we had experienced the washing of the feet. This time
family members joined us as Father Rob said Mass. There were a lot
of smiling faces, and I couldn't help but flash back to another Sunday,
fifty-three weeks earlier in Pittsburgh, where we were holding on to
one another in our collective grief over the loss to NC State.

We returned to Philadelphia by charter flight and spent the next
few days in the euphoria that engulfed our campus. There were cameras everywhere.

On Tuesday afternoon I took the short walk from the Davis Center
to Bartley Hall, which houses a satellite link that allows major networks to tape interviews with Villanova faculty, coaches, and students. On my way over, I received a flood of words of thanks and
shouts of encouragement from just about everyone I encountered. It
was awesome.

Over the next six days—between the win over Kansas and a Final
Four rematch with Oklahoma—nothing proved more beneficial to
me than the experience of our trip to the 2009 event in Detroit.

When we advanced that year, I reached out to as many friends in
coaching as I could. I picked their brains about the best ways to
handle travel, lodging, and the media. At one point I was standing in
our Boston hotel lobby with Coach Massimino, discussing this with
him. He pulled out his cell phone, punched a button, and put me on
with his close friend Chuck Daly, who had led the Detroit Pistons to
two NBA titles and coached the Dream Team. (Sadly, Coach Daly
passed away a few months later.)

Coach Daly pumped me up on that call. He kept telling me, "You're
right where you belong. You've earned this." He also gave me some
thoughts on how to keep the hoopla and noise that would surround
us from becoming a distraction. Coming from a great coach who was
near the end of his life, it meant a lot.

Before we finished, he also walked me through a version of his "press offense"—because he thought we'd been struggling to handle the full-court press.

I took every word to heart.

Yet it still felt to me that we had been less ready on game day than I would have liked. The stage of the Final Four is so enormous, I'm not sure anything can prepare you for it until you experience it yourself.

> ## BEYOND BASKETBALL
>
> ### Ask for Advice
>
> Whatever challenge you are facing, it's almost certain someone else has faced it before. Never let pride stand in the way of reaching out to people who are in a position to give you advice. There is no better salve for anxiety than being well prepared.

This time, we were armed with the knowledge of what had worked for us and what hadn't.

Wednesday was departure day for Houston. At the end of practice, Daniel asked one of our graduate managers, Ryan Harkins, if he would snap a photo for him. Then Daniel and Arch knelt on the court and kissed the V as a farewell. They would never practice on this court as active Wildcats again.

I must admit, that moment got to me.

I tweeted the image out and it went viral. (Apparently I wasn't the only one moved by it.)

Our departure ceremony was unlike anything I have seen at Villanova. The area in front of the Davis Center was packed with thousands of well-wishers. Television trucks were wedged into every corner of the driveway. A news helicopter trailed the bus as we proceeded to the airport.

Upon landing in Houston, we were greeted by members of the military. Our bus received a police escort to our hotel, where the staff lined up in the lobby as we entered. The hype was absolutely everywhere. And yet our guys were as dialed in as ever. We settled into our area of the hotel (which was blocked off by security) and entered our cocoon.

On Thursday, we got the chance to have a closed practice at NRG Stadium, home of the Houston Texans, which helped the guys adjust to the vast open spaces that are part of playing in a football facility that's nearly four times the size of a typical basketball venue.

We took care of our media responsibilities, which included being on a lighted stage with a hundred or so extras cheering us in a segment taped for Turner/CBS. It was so surreal, and far more Hollywood than I was used to. As I walked off that set, I said to an official: "Jim Boeheim is doing this?" I just couldn't picture my friend, who would coach Syracuse in the second Final Four game against North Carolina, in that setting.

We participated in Friday's open practice, and when it was over, I felt we were now comfortable in NRG Stadium. We were ready.

The fact that we would face Oklahoma again wasn't as comforting. The Sooners had become exactly what we thought they would after the beating they hung on us at Pearl Harbor. Buddy Hield was the national player of the year. Lon Kruger had done a tremendous job in guiding the Sooners to this point.

As well as we had played lately, the memory of that first meeting remained fresh in our players' minds. We knew all too well how potent Oklahoma could be.

The game was tight early. Mikal sank a three-pointer to give us a 19–17 lead with 11:25 to play in the first half. We went on a 12–0 run and found an offensive groove we never had that day in Hawaii. The lead opened up to 37–21, then 42–28 at halftime.

None of us relaxed.

Oklahoma narrowed its deficit to nine early in the period—and we answered with a jaw-dropping 25–0 run. It became one of those games every coach has lived, on both sides: One team can't miss and the other can't get anything to work. We ended up setting a Final Four record for margin of victory—forty-four points—in a 95–51 win.

I was stunned. To have played at that level against a team as skilled and well coached as the Sooners—in that setting—just blew me away.

I also understood that what came next would shape how we ultimately viewed this accomplishment. Standing in a converted football locker room before we opened the doors to the media, I reminded the guys that as well as we had played, this couldn't define us. None of those forty-four points would carry over.

Our task was simple but immense.

We had to treat the praise like perfume. "It's okay to sniff it, but never drink it," I reminded them. "Treat praise and criticism like the imposters they are."

The guys nodded. We were all right there together.

There was one mountain left to scale.

Next game.

20

Bang

WITH PATTY AT my side, I stepped out a service door of our hotel into the late-afternoon sunshine. The team bus, adorned with Villanova logos, was parked by the loading dock and nearly ready to depart. The guys were already aboard. I greeted Rick Finfrock, the Villanova Public Safety officer who had accompanied us on the trip to assist with security, and the trio of Houston police officers who had also been with us throughout the week.

Then Patty and I settled into the first two seats on the right-hand side of the bus for the twelve-minute ride to NRG Stadium.

It was April 4, 2016. The "next game" was upon us: The NCAA Championship.

The bus driver started the engine as the officers climbed aboard their motorcycles. Once their lights were flashing, our cavalcade pulled out from the rear of the hotel, passed throngs of cheering Villanova fans, and drove onto the streets that would take us to the final game of this "storybook season."

There wasn't a lot of chatter on the bus. A number of players donned headphones or earbuds, focused on their own choice of motivational music. This is traditionally a quiet time when all of us are left to our own thoughts, and there was no reason for this game to be handled any differently.

As we turned off the highway, the stadium loomed in the distance. Just beyond it I could see the now-shuttered Houston Astrodome, a building dubbed the "Eighth Wonder of the World" when it opened back in 1965. In 2016, our team would be playing for a national title across the parking lot from where the Wildcat team I revered as a kid met UCLA in the 1971 NCAA Championship game.

That led me to think of our friend Mike Daly, a member of that team who we had lost so suddenly only seven weeks earlier. I missed Mike something awful—but I also believed that he was with us as we stepped down from the bus, entered the stadium, and made the long walk to our locker room.

When you play in a dome primarily designed for football, the magnitude of everything grows. The walks from the bus to the locker room and the locker room to the playing floor take more time. The routine strolls to a press conference are replaced by long rides in a golf cart. A basketball locker room is typically designed for fifteen to eighteen people. A football locker room, by contrast, can house ninety to a hundred.

In our case, we did our best to try to keep it small, and to try to re-create the same feel we have at home. Chairs were set up facing a whiteboard at the front of the room. That's where I would address the team before the game and at halftime, and I wanted it to feel as familiar as possible.

There was nothing extra about our pregame routine. Everyone in that room knew where we were. So we focused instead on the simple things we could control. We went through our usual talks. Father Rob led us in a brief prayer.

With a little less than eight minutes remaining on the pregame clock, the players and assistant coaches headed back out to the court to complete their warm-ups. On the way out, each one of them reached above his head to tap a simple sign above the door—a piece of white tape marked in black Sharpie with one word: ATTITUDE.

I spent a moment conferring with Jim Brennan, our team performance consultant, who helps me keep my finger on the pulse of the team's psyche. Finally, just before I walked out to the court, Father Rob and I shared a quick hug, and then we both reached up to touch the "Attitude" sign ourselves.

Pressure

How can I put this?

Let's just say that the first half did not go as we had hoped.

The fact that it played out in front of a TV audience of millions and 74,340 fans in the stands wasn't the worst of it. Neither was the fact that it unfolded before a gallery of Villanova legends seated just behind our bench, including Coach Massimino, 1985 MVP Ed Pinckney, NBA All-Star Kyle Lowry, and Mike Fratello, the former NBA head coach who had once been on Coach Mass' staff.

The worst of it was that we just weren't playing our best.

There were no more games to go. No more chances to improve. Our one goal was to be playing our best at the end of the season, and this was it. We were at the finish line. And for all of our energy—perhaps because of it—we weren't playing our best. We weren't playing efficiently.

The halftime walk from the bench to the locker room seemed interminable. That is never truer than when you find yourself staring up at a deficit, which was the situation we found ourselves in after twenty minutes of action against the North Carolina Tar Heels. A late spurt had propelled Roy Williams' team to a 39–34 lead.

Were it not for the offensive heroics of our sixth man, Phil Booth, the deficit may have been larger.

During the NCAA Tournament, the halftime breaks last twenty minutes, five minutes longer than they do in the regular season. Our routine as a team over the previous three weeks was to enter the locker room, players and staff alike, and I would speak briefly to the group. The coaching staff then stepped outside the door, huddled privately for several minutes, and then re-entered, diving into the key strategic points we wanted to review for the second half.

As I approached the assistant coaches on this night, I was startled at the sight of our senior captain, Daniel Ochefu, breaking away from the rest of the team to approach me. I could tell he had something on his mind.

He looked at me directly, and with intensity in his eyes said: "Coach, I got this."

With twenty minutes left to play in his four-year career, Daniel was pleading with me to let him address his teammates—without the coaches present—before I did.

This was not a routine request. If it had come from a player twenty years earlier, during my tenure at Hofstra, or even a decade before, in my early years at Villanova, I'm not sure I would have acquiesced. (I have had former assistant coaches tell me there is *no way* I would have agreed to it.) But in this time, in this place, with a national championship on the line, it felt like the right move.

Daniel entered the locker room. The door closed behind him. Several of my assistants gave me a look that said, *You sure about this?*

> ## BEYOND BASKETBALL
>
> ### *Trust Your Team*
>
> There are moments when no one knows your team better than your team itself. So don't be afraid at times to hand control over to those you lead. Your trust in them will bolster their confidence and yours too.

The truth is I *wasn't* sure it was the best idea. But what I had confidence in was the bond and cohesion of the 2015–2016 Villanova Wildcats. That bond had been forged over the course of several seasons, and of our own public failures in the 2014 and 2015 NCAA tournaments. I trusted the commitment and leadership skills of Daniel and his fellow senior captain, Ryan Arcidiacono. No two individuals were more responsible for us having reached this point than they were.

Daniel was loud. Loud enough that we could hear him through the closed steel doors. When he had spoken to me outside the locker room, I could sense his anger at the way we'd been playing, but it was a controlled anger. If I had thought he seemed out of control, I wouldn't have let him speak. Still, I listened just to be sure.

I was pleased when his anger turned to something else. Like a good coach, Daniel showed his anger, even took it right to the edge, but never went over the line. He told his teammates that this was *not* Villanova Basketball and it was *not* what we came here to do. He said he "isn't going down this way" and, most important, "*we* aren't going down this way." And then the anger turned to focus: "We've come this far. Let's finish this playing together, our way!"

While Daniel addressed his teammates, I began studying the halftime statistics. There were a few troubling numbers staring back at me.

First and foremost, North Carolina held a 15–9 edge in rebounding. Though the Tar Heels owned a size advantage, we pride ourselves on taking care of business on the glass. We hadn't done that effectively in the first half.

North Carolina had also connected on fifteen of twenty-eight first-half field goal attempts (.536), including seven of nine from beyond the three-point arc. The Tar Heels had not been a statistically prolific three-point shooting team over the course of the season and we had game-planned for that accordingly. But on this night they had heated up from the perimeter and burned us with seven threes.

When Daniel finished his message to the team, our staff re-entered the locker room. I calmly emphasized to the players the few areas we needed to improve upon. Essentially it came down to a reliance on our core values, highlighted by defending, rebounding, and playing together.

I told the guys, "Daniel is right. What we have done all year is commit to our basic values and our scouting reports." I made it clear that we hadn't done either of those things in the first half. We had been lacking in the simple concepts of getting back to the paint on defense on the fast break, stopping easy baskets. We didn't want to run with the Tar Heels, and yet at times that's exactly what we had done. In the scouting report we had identified certain players to whom we couldn't allow open looks at three-pointers, and those guys had scorched us. Joel Berry II and Justin Jackson were a combined six of six from beyond the arc in the first half.

It was uncharacteristic of us to get caught up in the moment, I told them, and I thought we had let that happen. It was time to turn it around. It was time to focus. It was time to play the best basketball we could. Not for the fans. Not for anyone else. For us.

When the players went back out on the floor to warm up, our coaching staff discussed second-half adjustments. Strategically, we made one major alteration.

Over the course of the season, we had used a 1-3-1 three-quarter-court press to disrupt our opponents. The traps weren't designed so much to create turnovers, though we did generate some of those, as to interrupt the flow of a team working with a 30-second shot clock. Carolina, though, had beaten our press in the first half and exploited it for some easy baskets.

So then and there, we elected to dispatch the press and rely on our staple: a man-to-man half-court defense.

One point I made to the staff was that it was impossible to overstate the magnitude of this game—and despite what I'd just said to our players about not getting overwhelmed by the moment, the pressure they were feeling was natural. Villanova and North Carolina had been among the nation's best teams throughout 2015–2016. As skilled and talented as we were, the reality was this was still a game contested by young men, aged eighteen to twenty-two, playing on a stage they had dreamed about since they first picked up a basketball. This was unique, and we had to keep that in mind in the second half.

We had done our best to shelter our guys in the days leading up to the Final Four by remaining in our regular season routine and doing our best to stay in our cocoon. Even my wife felt the need to explain that approach. When Patty encountered some of the players' parents at our Houston hotel, she thanked them for their understanding that they hadn't gotten the chance to spend much time with their sons. The parents' response: Don't worry about it; we're all in. Let's win this thing.

As the second half opened, a Brice Johnson jumper pushed the Carolina lead to 41–34. But Jalen Brunson responded with a big three-pointer, kicking off a 19–5 spurt that was, appropriately enough, keyed by our improved defensive work. When Arch dropped in a jumper with 9:53 to play in regulation, we led 53–46.

The Villanova section inside the stadium roared its approval. We seemed to have relocated the flow that helped guide us through the NCAA Tournament.

Carolina cut the deficit to 60–57 on a pair of Kennedy Meeks free throws with 7:02 on the clock. Five straight points from Arch pushed the advantage back to 65–57. We got a stop on the next Tar Heels' possession and picked up two clutch free throws by Phil Booth, who had come off the bench to enjoy a brilliant offensive night.

The lead was 67–57 with 5:29 to play. Back home, a packed house watched the game on screens at the Pavilion. The TBS cameras showed the excitement there to TV audiences across the country. To the Nova Nation, a national title seemed only a few short minutes away.

It doesn't work like that on the floor, however. Carolina was too gifted and well coached to fold. The Tar Heels fought back to within 67–64, before yet another clutch Phil Booth bucket gave us a 69–64 lead with 3:05 to play. Marcus Paige, UNC's standout guard, then missed a jumper, but his teammate Justin Jackson grabbed the offensive rebound. Jackson was fouled by Daniel at the 2:44 mark.

An official time-out was called, and both teams retreated to their benches. I sat on a stool as our team huddled around me.

By this point in a five-month season, I am mostly just reminding our players of things we have absorbed long before. All season in practice, we train to create habits that would serve us well in the most pressurized of moments. Moments don't get much more tense than this one.

The five Wildcats we sent back on the court were Daniel, Arch, Phil, Josh, and Kris. Kris was saddled with four fouls, so we were rotating him in and out of the lineup with Jalen and Mikal Bridges, depending on the situation.

As the guys headed back toward the lane at the opposite end of the floor, I began to wonder if our halftime adjustment to rely solely on a switching man-to-man defense had run its course. It worked well for fifteen minutes, but it seemed to me that the Tar Heels had grown too comfortable attacking it.

Justin Jackson missed the front end of a one-and-one opportunity. Daniel grabbed the rebound.

We moved the basketball into the frontcourt. Our aim was to get Kris and Josh involved in a two-man game. Instead, Phil switched with Kris and it became a two-man game between Josh and Phil. That wasn't what we had planned, but we weren't really in a situation where we could change it. The noise and scale of NRG Stadium made it increasingly difficult for the players to hear our instructions.

With the shot clock under ten seconds, Carolina's Isaiah Hicks was whistled for a foul on Kris. It was the ninth team foul for the Tar Heels in the half, which meant Kris, one of our top free-throw shooters, would head to the line for a one-and-one. His first attempt rolled off the rim, though, and Brice Johnson rebounded it.

Our lead remained at five.

Tremendous defensive work by Kris forced Joel Berry II into an uncomfortable shot on Carolina's next possession. Again, Daniel was there to collect the rebound.

At this point in the game, we were in what we call our "time and score" offensive mode. With the lead late, we want to milk as much of the 30-second clock as we can while still executing crisp offense. If Arch has the ball in transition in a two-on-two situation, for example, he is more likely to ease off the gas and get us into half-court offense than he would be at an earlier point in the game.

As the trailing team, North Carolina was challenging us at every opportunity in an effort to speed up the tempo and force mistakes.

We handled the Tar Heels' pressure well on our next possession. Josh was fouled by Hicks. It was the tenth foul of the half, which put Carolina into the bonus. At the line, Josh sank one of two attempts, and the margin was 70–64 with 1:52 to play.

I have no doubt our missed free throws—first by Kris, then by Josh—raised the anxiety level of the Nova Nation. Within our huddle, though, they were simply "Attitude" moments. Becoming upset with the miss, or yourself, isn't any kind of remedy. Instead, it can snowball on you. By saying "Attitude," we remind one another that the next play, not the previous one, is the play we can impact.

When Josh converted the second free throw, the ensuing dead ball allowed us to insert Mikal in place of Kris. That choice had something to do with Kris' foul situation, but it also had to do with the defensive force that Mikal had become of late. I had also decided to leave Phil on the floor, given his immense offensive contribution and skill as a defender. A year earlier, in another NCAA Tournament game, I hesitated to do that and felt afterward that I had erred.

This time, Phil would be out there.

When play resumed, Mikal made a great block of a Marcus Paige shot, sending the ball out of bounds with fifteen seconds on the shot clock and 1:36 on the game clock.

On the inbounds play, we switched on a Carolina screen. As Brice

Johnson went to make the pass to Paige, Josh reached into the passing lane in an effort to deflect or intercept the ball. He barely missed getting a piece of it. The pass found Paige, who had just enough time to release a fadeaway three-point attempt before Mikal could reach him. He drained it.

We had played nearly flawless defense, switched the screen as we wanted to, and come within inches of Josh making a momentum-changing steal.

But when you're playing against the best in a game like this, that's what you are dealing with. Opponents at this level are going to make huge plays, and it's imperative that your team doesn't get consumed by them.

Roy Williams called for time with 1:33 to go, and the gap shaved to three, at 70–67.

As Arch dribbled into the frontcourt on the right side after the break, two Carolina defenders came to trap him. Arch picked up his dribble, rose into the air, and fired a high pass in the direction of Daniel near the free-throw line. Daniel stands at 6'11", but the pass was well beyond his reach, sailing into the end zone. (Arch gestured to the official that the pass had been tipped, and the replay suggests he might have had a point, but the call stood.)

To me, that was just an indication of how intense the pressure was. Our steadiest and most reliable veteran, a captain, broke two of our cardinal rules. When trapped, he picked up his dribble and left his feet with the basketball. Never before had I seen Arch try to make that play. But it just goes to show: Even the best can be affected by the heat.

After Arch's turnover, North Carolina moved quickly to attack. They took advantage of a defensive switch when Mikal ended up guarding the taller Johnson. Mikal fronted him, but the entry pass was perfect and Johnson banked a short jumper over Arch, closing the gap to one, 70–69.

The Tar Heels had now scored twelve of the last fifteen points.

We took a time-out with exactly one minute left to play.

In the previous thirty seconds, we had produced two good defensive possessions. The Tar Heels had simply made better offensive plays.

The next play we called was designed to isolate Kris and Phil in a two-man game. The concept was to force the taller defender guarding Kris to switch onto Phil, so that Kris would be guarded by the smaller defender, Paige. We could then attack that in one of two ways. Either Phil could use his quickness to elude the taller man and create an opportunity in the lane, or we could wind up with Kris posted near the basket with a strength advantage against a smaller guard.

We got what we hoped for. Phil never hesitated and made a bid to score, pivoting in the lane and drawing a foul on Hicks in the process. (There was some speculation that Phil may have switched his pivot foot and traveled, but after looking at the play on tape, I don't believe that was the case.)

Phil's confidence was palpable. He stepped to the line with thirty-five seconds left and made both free throws: 72–69.

Our intent defensively at this point was to chase the Tar Heels off the three-point line. If they went inside for a quick two-point basket, we would still have the lead and possession. As Paige dribbled quickly into the frontcourt, Arch forced him to his right and away from the three-point line. Paige moved toward the basket and lofted a layup that missed.

Josh and Arch were both under the basket in perfect rebounding position. But in their eagerness to seize the rebound, they may have jumped a bit prematurely. Neither was able to control the basketball. Paige sneaked in, picked the ball up, and dropped in an incredible shot with his back to the baseline. It was 72–71 with twenty-two seconds left.

Again, it was good execution on our part—but a better play by Paige.

We quickly inbounded the ball and pushed it forward, and North Carolina fouled Josh with thirteen seconds left. To calmly step forward and knock in both free throws, as he did here, was incredible. As frequently as we practice free-throw shooting, there is no way to simulate those conditions.

With thirteen seconds to play, North Carolina used its final time-out. We held a 74–71 lead.

Our approach on this defensive possession was the same as it had been on the prior North Carolina possession. We didn't want to give up a three-point basket, but were willing to allow a two. If we fouled in this situation, that was okay as well.

We were well aware of Marcus Paige's aptitude for sinking clutch shots, so it was not a surprise when the Tar Heels entered the front-court and Johnson set a screen in an effort to free Paige. Daniel, guarding Johnson, lunged toward the pass as it made its way to Paige. How he missed it, I'll never know.

Arch switched onto Paige, forcing the Tar Heel guard to contort his body and double-clutch as he launched a three-pointer. It was a smart shot to take and looked even smarter when it rattled through the net and brought the Carolina fans—including Michael Jordan, who was seated next to his pal Ahmad Rashād—to their feet.

Wow.

The game was tied at seventy-four with 4.7 seconds to go.

Tapping the Rock

My mind flashed back to that afternoon's pregame meal, when Father Rob had touched us all with a message that transcended any sporting event—even one as immense as the NCAA national championship game.

He began his homily by citing the words of Saint Paul to the Philippians: "I can do all things through the one who strengthens me. We can do all things through the one who strengthens us."

He then urged all of us to say those words to ourselves, to repeat them, and to use them as we went through the rest of our lives.

He went on to tell this team that he had spent some time searching for examples of faith in sports to illuminate his spiritual theme. He thought of the 1980 United States Olympic hockey team. He said that one of his favorites was the story of *Rocky*. But as he reflected, he decided the best example he could point to wasn't some other team. It was *this* team, *this* group of young men, *this* band of brothers.

But the heart of his point wasn't about winning or basking in glory. It was about staying connected to one another.

"Jesus used a parable about how leaves are strong when they're connected to the vine, but when they break off and get loose, they fly in the wind and lose their strength. So stay connected to the vine. Stay connected to each other, to our core values, and stay connected to what's right. That's your greatest strength. Don't break off the vine and go off on your own."

Now, with 4.7 seconds left on the clock, all I kept thinking was how this team had stuck together and made us all proud.

We had executed properly over the final two minutes. Everyone was in the proper position defensively. And because we were playing the best, we were still staring down adversity.

As I mentioned way back in the introduction to this book, once we were in that huddle, we all knew what play we would run. We work on end-of-game situations constantly in practice. We know what play we are going to run if there are one to three seconds on the clock; if there are four to seven seconds; and if there are eight to twelve seconds. So when the guys looked at the clock after the Paige shot and saw 4.7 seconds to go, they immediately knew how we would attack this possession.

It was almost eerie how this situation resembled what we do in practice. Whenever we simulate a four- to seven-second situation, we set the time much closer to four seconds than to seven, in order to create the most difficult situation we can.

More often than not, the time we set on the practice clock is 4.7 seconds.

We had also trained ourselves to immediately move past what had just happened on the floor. There was no point in bemoaning the shot Paige had drained. Our answer then and always is to say "Attitude" to one another. Even in the din and disbelief after Paige's basket, I could hear the guys repeating that mantra.

As our players made their way back to the floor, we had something else going for us: The score was tied. We were likely to have the final possession of regulation. If we failed to score, the likelihood was that we would play five minutes of overtime. If we were trailing even by a point in this situation it would have been another matter entirely. If not for the clutch free throws by Phil and Josh, that's where we could have found ourselves.

Everyone in the stadium was standing as Arch walked past the

> ## BEYOND BASKETBALL
>
> ### *Stay Connected*
>
> It's when you are under pressure that you most need to lean on others. These are the moments where everything you've worked toward—your skills, your culture, your values—come together, and the group becomes one force, working toward one goal.

midcourt line and motioned to one of the officials to the wet spot on the floor. That's when Daniel borrowed the mop and mopped that floor until it was bone-dry, which became one of the iconic images of the game. At the time, watching Daniel perform such thorough janitorial work in front of 74,340 anxious spectators, I couldn't help but shake my head.

One of the themes we reference often in our program is the story of "The Street Sweeper." It comes from a 1967 speech in Philadelphia by Dr. Martin Luther King Jr.: "If it falls to your lot to be a street sweeper, sweep streets like Michelangelo painted pictures, sweep streets like Beethoven composed music, sweep streets like Leontyne Price sings before the Metropolitan Opera. Sweep streets like Shakespeare wrote poetry. Sweep streets so well that all the hosts of heaven and earth will have to pause and say, 'Here lived a great street sweeper who swept his job well.'"

It's a message that resonates with our players, and that hearkens back to "Everyone's role is different but their status is the same." It's a reminder that no matter how bright the spotlight gets, we are all part of something much larger than ourselves. A player may be among the most skilled and celebrated in the country, but his opportunity to perform arrived through sacrifices made by his parents, family, and teachers.

At this most critical of moments, Daniel saw no shame in mopping the floor. He knew his function on this designed play—setting the screen—was as vital to its success as the shot or the pass.

Standing on the sideline, I was just hoping the play would work.

Kris accepted the basketball from the baseline official. His pass into the backcourt found Arch, who turned up-court and began dribbling. Freed by Daniel's screen on the dry patch of court, Arch raced up the left side of the floor. The Tar Heels' defense stepped up on him as he neared the three-point arc. And then Arch heard Kris calling his name.

Arch and Kris have always had a unique relationship. Both are personable, well-respected guys outside of the basketball program on campus. Both respect that about each other and are playful about it too. In fact, it became something of a running gag. Kris loved to tell Arch that he doesn't like him. Arch would always respond by insisting that they were best friends. It became a constant back-and-forth.

It may sound like a stretch to anyone outside our program, but I firmly believe that all of that stuff that happens off the court feeds directly into moments like this one. The players' familiarity, their joking, their respect and camaraderie cut right through the noise of those tens of thousands of screaming fans.

Arch dribbled to his right and fed that underhanded pass to Kris. Kris elevated into his beautiful shooting form and released the ball. "Bang," I yelled instinctively, as I often have in such moments in an effort to will the ball to land where we all wanted it to land. The ball arced effortlessly toward the basket as the final tenths of a second ticked off the clock and fell through the net as the horn sounded. Confetti immediately dropped from the rafters, and our bench players leaped forward to join the on-court celebration.

In the bedlam, what I heard was the referee's whistle.

I have coached enough games in the era of video replay to appreciate that a game is never over until the officials have studied the video monitor at the scorer's table. I was confident Kris had launched the shot before the horn, but I expected that we would see at least a couple of tenths of a second tacked onto the clock. I anticipated one more defensive possession, which is part of the reason I didn't celebrate immediately.

Within seconds, though, the officials signaled that the basket was good—and the game was over.

Villanova was the 2016 NCAA National Champion.

I shook Roy Williams' hand, knowing full well the roles could have easily been reversed. This had been an epic showdown, a classic that will be recalled whenever great NCAA Tournament endings are rehashed.

After embracing the assistant coaches in front of our bench, I found Patty and our children, and we commenced our own private victory hug. Coach Massimino came onto the court, and that was

In the magic moment after Kris' shot fell, he
was mobbed by Josh (left) and Phil.

special too. Our history, our heritage—including so much of the storied past that Coach Mass and his players had created—had brought
us to this moment.

This victory was as much his as it was ours.

In fact, this victory belonged to everyone who came before us.

There's a line from a poem that is so important to our program that
we have it painted on the wall in our practice facility, there for all to
see, every day, every time any member of our basketball family comes
in or out of the Davis Center.

The line is: Tap the Rock.

It's a line from a poem about a stonecutter. The message is that
everyone recalls the strike that breaks a rock apart, yet no one re-
members the multiple blows that seemed to do no damage. We tell
our guys that each of those first five hundred or one thousand or ten

thousand taps are as important as the one that finally breaks the rock. "Stay focused on the process each day," we tell them, "even if there appear to be no immediate results."

On this day, there were results.

As we gathered in the locker room for a few brief private moments before the press and the whole world flooded in, I told our guys that I wanted them to remember something. "This wasn't just this game," I said. "This was all the days and all the work that you put in before. This was seasons of losing in the second round. This was the players who came before you, building this tradition and foundation. This was just the final tap that broke the rock. That's all this was."

We hugged, and you could feel the elation bubbling in every one of us.

We always hold hands and say a postgame prayer, and this day was no different. Father Rob brought it all right back to his message earlier that day: the importance of staying connected to the vine. He told them how wonderful it was that they had stayed connected during the game—and reminded them it was just as important to stay connected after, as well. "Don't go off on your own now," he said. "Stay humble."

At the end of his prayer, I picked right up where he left off. "Stay humble," I repeated. "And one more thing: Don't let this define you. This can't be the best thing you do in your life. It's just a basketball game. To everybody else it's huge, but you've got to be a good man, a good husband, a good father. Don't forget that."

I looked around at all of those incredible young men, and I smiled.

"This is always going to be a part of you," I said.

And with that, the flood rushed in.

So much of the rest of that evening is a blur to me now. Mostly I was overwhelmed by the joy this moment brought to the Villanova community. The scene at our hotel a few hours later, when we entered a packed ballroom, was one I won't soon forget. The grins on the faces of our friends are etched into my memory forever.

Inside the team-meeting ballroom, where we had spent the better part of our week in Houston, the players mingled with their families. So much of our success was about the parents, guardians, and sib-

On May 31, 2016, our team got to visit the White House, where President Obama congratulated us on our championship. "These Wildcats were about more than just one moment or one shot," he said. "They had unbelievable defense. They had great clutch shooting. A senior class that won more games than any group in Wildcats history. They had a stable of talented players who were as happy hitting the deck for a loose ball as they were cutting down the nets." Mr. President, I couldn't have said it better myself.

lings who had shaped this group of men before they ever stepped foot onto the Villanova campus.

In the wake of the 1985 Championship, Coach Massimino had gone to great lengths to remind everyone in the program that this wasn't just an achievement of the twenty-plus players and coaches on that team. Instead, he pointed to the contributions of individuals over his tenure that had paved the way for this. In his mind, men like Joe Rogers, the Herron brothers, Alex Bradley, Rory Sparrow, and John Pinone were as much a part of that crown as the men who defeated Georgetown.

It was the same way for us.

This was a night made possible by a long list of Villanovans, from our first senior class that featured Brooks Sales and B. J. Johnson, through the 2015 contingent that included Dylan, Darrun, and Jay-Vaughn. Having friends and colleagues like Tom Pecora, Joe Jones, Brett Gunning, Curtis Sumpter, and Kyle Lowry all right there with us in Houston gave us a sense of the vast support network that had lifted us to this night.

As the hour crept toward 3 a.m., I looked over to the portion of the ballroom that we had set up as our own little classroom. It was vacant now, as the celebration had mostly moved elsewhere. It may sound funny, but just seeing that empty space reminded me that this was only one moment in time. There would be a lot of celebrating to come. I would feel the excitement and energy from every student I passed on campus for the remainder of that semester and straight into the new school year the following fall. I would go through another banquet and have to say goodbye to Arch and Daniel and their families at graduation before that. We'd be back into summer training before we knew it.

I couldn't help but laugh to myself, because even after all of this, even after achieving what the whole world thought was the biggest achievement a guy like me and a team like this could ever achieve, my mind was so well trained in the rituals and values of Villanova and of this Wildcat basketball program that all I kept thinking was: *Next game.*

Wildcat Pride

Father Rob's words to our team on that day of days were words we can all learn from. What he told our team when they stood at the precipice of greatness was simply to "keep on being you."

He told them they were succeeding not just because they were physically tough, or mentally tough, but because they were spiritually tough as well.

He ended his homily with these thoughts: "The whole world thinks this is just about basketball. We know our lives are more than what the world tells us is important. We know that it is hard to try and stay on the vine. Staying connected to the vine means sacrifice. Staying connected to the vine means giving up a piece of ourselves. You have washed each other's feet. You know that staying on the vine means trying to avoid the other temptations and distractions in life.

"You have fought as brothers, and we continue to fight every day, with God's grace, to stay on the one true vine, humble enough to be content to be the branches that we are. Stay connected. Stay connected to the one who truly strengthens us. Stay connected to each other.

"Let's stay on the vine. Let's be the branches we are: strong, unbreakable branches. And go bear fruit that will last forever."

Over his eleven years as part of our basketball family, Father Rob's words have touched us routinely. We have, in fact, come to expect them.

On that afternoon, mere hours before we were to play the biggest game of our sporting lives, Father Rob reminded us again that our own lives are much larger than any single sporting event.

This was a season none of us associated with Villanova will ever forget.

We won the national title.

It's an outcome I am proud of.

What I am most proud of, however, is that on every step of their journey, our band of brothers never wavered in their resolve. They owned failure, embraced the hard work necessary for achievement, and became better men along the way.

Through their actions, the 2015–2016 Villanova Wildcats proved to be champions long before Kris Jenkins launched his shot for the ages.

The 2015–2016 Villanova Wildcats

―――――

Ryan Arcidiacono, Phil Booth, Mikal Bridges, Jalen Brunson, Tim Delaney, Donte DiVincenzo, Patrick Farrell, Josh Hart, Kris Jenkins, Henry Lowe, Daniel Ochefu, Eric Paschall, Kevin Rafferty, and Darryl Reynolds. Practice players: Denny Grace, Peyton Heck, Matt Kennedy, and Tom Leibig.

STAFF: Associate Head Coach Baker Dunleavy, Assistant Coaches Ashley Howard and Kyle Neptune, Director of Basketball Operations George Halcovage, Video Coordinator Mike Nardi, Special Assistant to the Head Coach Arleshia Davidson, Head Athletic Trainer Jeff Pierce, Strength Coach John Shackleton, Team Chaplain Father Rob Hagan, O.S.A., Team Performance Consultant Jim Brennan, Graduate Managers Mike Clark, Nick DiPaola, and Ryan Harkins.

Acknowledgments

A FEW YEARS back, one of our more sharp-witted basketball alums made this observation about our end-of-the-year Basketball Banquet: "900 attendees, 800 shout-outs from the podium."

It was a funny line, because it's true. I like to give thanks, and that is especially true when it comes to the 2015–2016 season. To accomplish what we did goes well beyond the work of any one person. It belongs to all of Villanova.

The tone is set by our leader, University President Reverend Peter M. Donohue, O.S.A. Father Peter's vision and compassion are guideposts for our community. Father's team of executives, including University Provost Dr. Pat Maggitti, Executive Vice President Ken Valosky, Senior Vice President Mike O'Neil, and Vice Presidents Reverend John Stack, O.S.A., Ann Diebold, and Debbie Fickler have offered me invaluable guidance and support. Father Peter's predecessor, the late Reverend Edmund J. Dobbin, O.S.A., will always retain a special place in our hearts for bringing me back to Villanova.

Part of what makes Villanova such a caring community is the dedicated professionals and educators like Tony Alfano, Dr. Helen K. Lafferty, Dr. Jeremy Kees, Michael Gaynor, Dean Joyce Russell, Associate Dean Melinda German, Chrissy Quisenberry, Chris Kovolski, Dr. Nancy Mott, Ed Hastings, and Maria Baranski—to name just a few. The late Dan Regan's tenure as Villanova's first Faculty Athletic Representative spanned the era from Joe Arch to Ryan Arch. His impact on generations of Villanovans was enormous. We also owe a debt of thanks to David Tedjeske and the Public Safety staff—including Rick Finfrock, who was with us in Houston—for their efforts in ensuring the celebrations of March and April 2016 were safe.

Whenever a new Athletic Director comes on board—as Mark Jackson did at Villanova in August 2015—there is some trepidation for a head coach. But that anxiety quickly washed away as we got to know Mark and his wife, Tricia. Mark, who came to us from a senior leadership position at USC, brings great energy to every project he tackles. From the beginning, he embraced the university and athletic department's mission in his own unique way. Mark's time with us has been short, but he's already made a wonderful impact.

Mark's senior staff—Lynn Tighe, Dean Kenefick, Mick Keelan, Brian Murray, Katie LeGrand, Lisa Harris, Jacob Whitten, Drew Young, Peter Baran, and Allison Venella—does vital work to benefit our program. Special thanks to Travel Coordinator Jen Burns, Director of Equipment Lionel Brodie, Director of Tickets Bob Nyce, the voice of the Wildcats, Ryan Fannon, and *Inside Villanova Basketball* producer Scott Graham.

Jason Donnelly joined our coaching staff in 2005 and has been a critical component of our success in his former role and his current position in charge of the Villanova Athletic Fund. Two former Villanova players, Steve Pinone and Whitey Rigsby, help keep us connected to the many people who have supported our program financially. We value the friendship and support of Bill Finneran, Bill and Jim Davis, Pat LePore, and Ed Welsh, as well as Villanova's Chairman of the Board of Trustees, Paul Tufano, and our Vice Chair, Joe Topper.

My Special Assistant, Arleshia Davidson, is a gifted educator whose extraordinary work behind the scenes is felt in so many ways throughout our program. Arleshia and Marissa Paffas work closely with Associate Director of Academic Support Jenn Brophy over the course of the long season to be sure our players are on track in the classroom. They should all be proud of the fact that, in addition to the 2016 NCAA national title, the Wildcats were honored with the Big East Team Academic Excellence Award.

Helene Mercanti's official duties list her as my administrative assistant. That description doesn't begin to scratch the surface of her value to our staff. The woman we call "Dream" is an incredible resource for me and has the nearly impossible task of keeping me on schedule. Her wit and wisdom help keep me humble.

Dr. Jim Brennan is another trusted voice. Jim travels with our team and offers me important insight into the mood of those in our program.

When Kris and Daniel were confronted with injuries in 2015–2016, they knew they were in great hands with our team physician, Dr. Mike Duncan, a former Villanova baseball player who knows what it means to be a college athlete. Dr. Bill Emper and Dr. Rob Good are gifted surgeons, and Dr. Frank Furman was always there for us over the years as well. Head Athletic Trainer Jeff Pierce and Strength Coach John Shackleton are the best in the country in their fields.

I have told business executives this before and I will reiterate it here: If you are looking to hire a bright, hardworking college graduate, make sure you consider a former Villanova student manager or office assistant. We did so when we added Mike Clark and Nick DiPaola as graduate managers after each completed undergraduate studies in 2015. Both made important contributions in our championship season, as did graduate assistant Ryan Harkins, who came to us from Marist. The undergraduate office assistants, led in 2015–2016 by Alexander Mortillaro, Kristen Leen, and Cat Quinn, are an important part of our team fabric.

Vince Nicastro hired me as the head coach in 2001, not long after he was promoted to the Athletic Director's post at Villanova. He and his wife, Liz—a Cherry Hill, New Jersey, girl, just like Patty—were supportive friends during his fifteen-year run in that position. Vince's Senior Associate AD, Bob Steitz, put in many long hours working to assist the basketball program.

In the summer of 2016, Vince was hired by Big East commissioner Val Ackerman. Val's team, which includes Stu Jackson and John Paquette, has done terrific work in helping to ensure that the Big East remains positioned as one of college basketball's elite conferences.

USA Basketball has afforded me the amazing coaching opportunity to represent our country on the international stage. The summer weeks spent working alongside Jim Tooley, Jim Boeheim, Mike Krzyzewski, Jerry Colangelo, Gregg Popovich, and Villanova products Sean Ford, Craig Miller, and B. J. Johnson have offered me countless insights into leadership. Whenever we convene for a USA Basketball training camp, I look forward to connecting with Philly's own sportswriting icon Dick "Hoops" Weiss, whose unrivaled passion to chronicle our games takes him everywhere.

A host of special coaches taught me what it means to be a leader, from Mike Holland at Council Rock High School to Charlie Woollum at Bucknell to Mike Neer at Rochester to the late Eddie Burke at Drexel and, of course, Coach Rollie Massimino. Coach Mass won his 800th career game in December 2016 and is still coaching with amazing energy at Kaiser University in Florida at the age of eighty-two years young. Love you, Coach.

A trio of coaching legends are colleagues at Villanova, and I have leaned on the wisdom of Harry Perretta, Andy Talley, and Marcus O'Sullivan often. Mary Anne Gabuzda has served both the men's and women's programs at Villanova with distinction, and her humble way echoes that of her uncle, Father Lazor. George Raveling launched his coaching career under Jack Kraft after graduating from Villanova in 1960, and he always offers wise counsel.

Over my tenure at Villanova I have benefited from the exceptional work of our assistant coaches, including such skilled teachers as Brett Gunning, Joe Jones, Fred Hill, Billy Lange, Ed Pinckney, Patrick Chambers, Doug West, Chris Walker, Keith Urgo, and Raphael Chillious. They helped pave the way for an amazing group of young coaches who were so instrumental in our success in 2015–2016: Baker Dunleavy, Ashley Howard, Kyle Neptune, George Halcovage, and Mike Nardi.

I have been blessed to help guide a range of athletes in my thirty-three years as a college coach. And while it isn't possible to name each of them here, I hope every one of those former players knows how much I appreciate what they gave to our programs and how proud I am of the men they have become.

The patience of our literary agent, David Vigliano, and his associate, Thomas Flannery, with a first-time author is greatly appreciated. We have also benefited from the skilled editing of Brendan Vaughan of Ballantine Books and the storytelling gifts of writer Mark Dagostino. A special thanks to our longtime friend and business adviser, Carl Hirsh, for his guidance on this project and so many others through the years.

Michael Sheridan has been with us for the last sixteen years in his role as Director of Media Relations. His keen memory and writing craftsmanship have been an enormous asset in helping us tell this story. Thanks also to Mike's incredible wife, Kristin. To be able to pursue your professional dreams is a tremendous gift, and it's made possible in our case by the sacrifices of our staff spouses, selfless women and men like Chrissi Dunleavy, Arianna Casanovas, Rachel Donnelly, Rhonda Pierce, Beth Shackleton, Camille Brennan, and Jack Mercanti.

As you have read, Father Rob inspires us every day through his words and the exemplary life of compassion he leads. I am confident that after reading these pages, you have come to appreciate the light he brings to our lives.

The 2015–2016 Wildcats were a dedicated and committed group of young men who delivered our university a memory for the ages. That accomplishment is a product of both their talent and their character. We thank their parents and guardians for allowing us to coach and mentor them.

My parents, Judy and Jerry Wright, supported my childhood dreams and have remained loving and more supportive than ever. My siblings, Donna, Jennifer, and Derek, have been in my corner from the start, and I am grateful for that.

Our children, Taylor, Collin, and Reilly, have always made me proud. I thank them for making it so easy to be a father and a coach. Their character and discipline amaze me every day. I treasure their love, especially on all the tough nights after losses and road trips. My favorite part of our journey was the family hug we got to share on the court in Houston.

A paragraph isn't enough for me to express my thanks to my wife, Patty. She is my heart, soul, and moral compass, and the love of my life. We've done everything together, as a team. Her preference is always to remain in the background, but her strength is my strength. There is never a moment when Patty doesn't help to keep me humble and on the right path.

—JAY WRIGHT, December 2016

ABOUT THE AUTHOR

JAY WRIGHT is the head basketball coach at Villanova University. He grew up in Bucks County, Pennsylvania, and attended Bucknell University, where he played varsity basketball. Prior to becoming head coach at Villanova in 2001, he served seven seasons as head coach at Hofstra University. He is a two-time Naismith National Coach of the Year.

@VUCoachJWright

ABOUT THE TYPE

This book was set in Fairfield, the first typeface from the hand of the distinguished American artist and engraver Rudolph Ruzicka (1883–1978). Ruzicka was born in Bohemia (in the present-day Czech Republic) and came to America in 1894. He set up his own shop, devoted to wood engraving and printing, in New York in 1913 after a varied career working as a wood engraver, in photoengraving and banknote printing plants, and as an art director and freelance artist. He designed and illustrated many books, and was the creator of a considerable list of individual prints—wood engravings, line engravings on copper, and aquatints.